When the Bell Rings

A Firefighter's Journey

Memoir

Robert Gass

Acknowledgments

This book is a testament to the unwavering support and sacrifices of my family. To my wife, Linda, your strength and patience have been my resolute anchor amidst the chaos. To my children, Amy, Julie and Allison, your understanding of my absences and pride in my work have fueled me during the darkest nights. You are not just my family, but my bedrock.

To my brothers and sisters in the FDNY, past and present: Thank you for your service, your courage, and the laughs that echoed through the firehouse even on the toughest days. Your stories, your struggles, and your unwavering dedication have shaped this book and forever mark my own journey in the ranks.

A heartfelt thank you to all firefighters across the globe. You run towards danger when others flee. Your commitment is a beacon of hope in a world that often overlooks the true warriors who walk among us.

Finally, my deepest gratitude to my editor and formatter, Damian. Your expertise and guidance were essential in transforming these raw stories into a meaningful testament to the profession I love.

Note to the Reader

This memoir and collection of stories is based on my personal experiences. While the core events and emotions depicted are true, I have changed certain names and locations to protect the privacy of the individuals involved. Any resemblance to real people, living or dead, is unintentional.

WHERE HEROES HAUNT

The rhythmic rattle of the Long Island Railroad was a lullaby to their familiar routine. Three couples, their laughter like well-worn coins, a touch of silver in their hair, and stories that bound them tighter than the worn seats of the train. Today, it was Manhattan that beckoned: Christmas shopping mixed with the bright lure of a Broadway show, and a dinner reservation somewhere cozy with good wine to cap it off.

He felt the familiar anticipation, a boyish glint in his eyes usually hidden behind his retired accountant persona. But as they pulled into Penn Station, a shadow flickered across his face. There, in the window of a souvenir store was the toy fire truck with the numbers *75* standing out proudly on its side. He fumbled with his coat, eyes glazed over, and muttered a hasty, "something I need to take care of," before promising the others he'd catch them up at the theater. His wife, Linda, frowned, worry knitting a line between her brows, but the practiced choreography of their days together carried them into the crowds.

He didn't head toward the glittering shops. Instead, the subway swallowed him, the rumble of the rails a counterpoint to the pounding in his chest. Tunnels, darkness, the flicker of lights against grimy windows offered no solace. When the train burst into the sunlight, becoming an elevated line, the stations flashed past like lost markers of time – 149th, 167th – each one a ghost whispering in his ear.

183rd Street. It wasn't a decision, more a force stronger than will. He found himself on the platform, descended the stairs like a man walking into his own past. Traffic snarled, buses groaned, and the sidewalks were a surging tide of humanity. Yet, he stood separate, a lone figure frozen in the chaos.

Across the street, weathered brick and boarded-up windows stared back. The old firehouse. Decades had passed, the vibrant red paint replaced by urban decay, but the outline was unmistakable. Engine 75. His company. And with the clarity of a siren, it all surged back.

It began not with flames, but with laughter. The camaraderie forged in the firehouse kitchen echoed in his head; crude jokes, card games, the shared silence of men who'd witnessed the worst the city had to offer. Then there was the clang of the alarm, the jolt of adrenaline that turned ordinary men into warriors, the very air crackling with purpose as they donned their gear.

The roar of the engine, the blur of streets, the focus narrowing to the burning building, the desperate faces trapped in its heart. There were victories – a hand pulling a child from a smoke-choked room, the sweet gasp of revived breath. And there was the relentless weight of the losses – the ones they couldn't reach in time, the empty gaze of a mother who had lost everything.

He felt the phantom weight of the hose, the burn of muscles pushed past exhaustion, the sting of ash in his eyes. The camaraderie flickered, replaced by those who didn't return from the flames, and by the unspoken battles fought with demons brought home from the inferno. Nights haunted by the faces of the lost, and the desperate search for oblivion in the bottom of a bottle.

The sirens startled him back to the here and now. A fire truck, red and gleaming, swept past. Young faces peered out the windows, their eyes bright with the same mix of purpose and fear that had once been his own. It was enough to shake him from the trance.

He moved, crossing the street with an unexpected purpose. Not towards the boarded-up remains of his old firehouse, but to a small coffee shop. Its warmth beckoned, offering a respite from the relentless grip of the past. As he ordered, his gaze settled on the wall, to faded photos of local heroes, some dating back decades. He could almost pick himself out, a younger, wilder version mingled with stern faces and gleaming helmets.

A tremor passed through him. Maybe coming back wasn't about answers, but about acknowledgment. The past wouldn't be outrun, the ghosts wouldn't be silenced. But with the warmth of the coffee in his hands, and the city's relentless energy swirling around him, he felt a sliver of something akin to peace. There would be time to unpack the memories, to honor both the triumphs and the scars.

THE WELCOME SPEECH

They herded us into that room like cattle – 125 fresh faces, still smelling of boot polish and nervous sweat. Academy training was about to begin, and all was well and good, but the second you stepped into a real FDNY training room, you knew they were no longer playing around.

This big-shot chief, one of those guys you thought likely came with more brass on his uniform than brains, stands up front and starts his speech. "Look to your left, look to your right," he barks, voice rough as gravel. "Only one of you three will still be here in 20 years. The rest? Dead, broken, or washed out."

Not exactly a welcome mat, but damn if he wasn't right. This job, it isn't some parade route march. It chews you up, spits you out. Seen guys carried out of burning buildings, bodies black and twisted. Seen others lose their minds, the pressure and the nightmares burrowing too deep. Others too addicted to alcohol to function.

Some guys thrive on it. The adrenaline junkies, the ones with that fire in their eyes. They're the ones who make a career out of this madness. And some, they just weren't built for it. No shame in that, not everyone's wired to run straight into hell.

The thing is, that day, with the chief's words ringing in your ears, you don't know which one you'll be. All you got is that uniform, a helmet and turnout gear, and a whole lot of hope that it'll be enough to keep you whole when the world's trying to tear you apart. 'Most dangerous job in the world' – ain't that the damn truth.

ANIMAL HOUSE: FIREFIGHTER EDITION

They slapped *Engine 75* on the front, but really, a plaque reading *The Animal House* would've been way more accurate. I'm not talking that college movie BS either. They got drunken antics and toga parties, we had soot-stained walls, rats scuttling in the kitchen, and rest that came in ragged jolts between alarms.

See, that visiting chief with his starched uniform and polished shoes wasn't wrong when he sneered, "you guys live like animals." Hell, maybe that was why the name stuck harder than old smoke on turnout gear.

He saw the busted furniture, the walls scarred not by some wild party, but from dragging ourselves back in when another tour turned into a 24-hour marathon. There weren't kegs in the corner, but that smell – a mix of old sweat, diesel fumes, and whatever burnt to a crisp last night – was way more potent than stale beer.

This house was built for horse-drawn carriages and men who had it lucky if they lived past retirement. Now, it strained under the weight of modern equipment and modern problems. It wasn't meant for the endless cycle of exhaustion, near-misses, and that quiet trauma that settles on your bones at the end of a bad run. No wonder when it was quiet with that adrenaline crash we turned feral.

The pranks went beyond sophomoric to downright deranged. Not malicious, just…a need to release the pressure or go insane under the strain. Remember that time with the proby resting when we snuck that smelly fish and hid it in the couch? Revenge for when he accidentally hit the main alarm instead of the intercom, shattering an entire firehouse at 3 AM. It was ruthless, stupid, and when that kid came flying out the door screaming about rotting corpses, even the crankiest old-timer cracked a smile.

There's another name firefighters have. *Smoke eaters*. Tells you the pretty stuff, the danger, the bravery. What it hides is the in-between. The minutes spent waiting, boredom sharp as a rusty nail. The way we gnaw on ourselves, on each other, until sometimes a joke is the only weapon you got left against that bleak voice inside your head.

So yeah, maybe we were animals. Not some slick, heroic kind, but the type built for hard places. Scrappy, desperate to find any joy in the scraps tossed our way. The type that survived in that crumbling zoo they called a firehouse… even if we growled back sometimes. We took back *Animal House* and wore it like a damn badge. You learn fast on the job – to be anything less and you wouldn't last a week.

Inside Out: The FDNY's Strategy for Battling Blazes

Imagine a raging inferno, flames spewing out windows like an angry furnace. Your instinct might be to grab a hose and douse the flames head-on from the outside. But for us, the strategy goes deeper, literally. We employ a technique called *interior attack*, a calculated approach that prioritizes the safety of occupants and minimizes collateral damage.

One reason for this is that a forceful stream from the outside can push flames deeper into the building, creating a super-heated tunnel that endangers firefighters and anyone trapped inside.

Also, imagine a pot of boiling water. Shooting water into a closed environment creates a similar effect – a sudden surge of steam that can scald firefighters and further obscure visibility.

The FDNY's *inside-out* approach tackles these problems head-on.

Using a direct assault, firefighters, equipped with protective gear and powerful hoses, enter the burning structure. Their goal is to find the source of the fire and extinguish it directly.

While the interior team battles the flames, another team focuses on ventilation and rescue. They strategically break windows and open vents, creating a path for smoke, heat, and steam to escape, clearing the way for both firefighters and potential survivors.

The focus is on controlled water application, dousing the fire at its core while minimizing water damage to the rest of the structure.

This strategy isn't without risks. Firefighters entering a burning building face extreme danger. But our training and equipment are designed to mitigate these risks. The *inside-out* approach, while seemingly counter-intuitive, is a testament to our dedication to prioritizing life safety and minimizing property damage.

It's a dance with fire, one where understanding its behavior and strategic application of resources are the keys to saving lives. The FDNY's *inside-out* approach is a masterclass in this delicate art, a testament to the ingenuity and courage of these modern-day firefighters.

THE CHAOS CHOREOGRAPHY

A fire scene isn't chaos. Not to us, anyway. From the outside, those first moments might look like madness: a blur of sirens and flashing lights, figures swarming like ants poked with a stick, but underneath all that is order. Cold, hard order born of countless drills and a knowledge of the city carved into our bones.

Pulling up to a blaze, you're not just a firefighter, you're an encyclopedia. Within seconds, your brain's cataloging the building: Old Law tenement with those flimsy air shafts and rickety fire escapes, or maybe it's a row frame where fire will leap from cockloft to cockloft like a kid playing hopscotch, each type a puzzle with a thousand burning, shifting pieces, demanding a different solution.

You've got your assignment etched into your skull. First-due engine? You're stretching lines, forcing your way in to find the heart of the beast. Ladder company? It's vents and searches, turning those windows into escape routes for the heat and smoke and a chance for the trapped to be rescued. There's urgency in every move, lives ticking down with every second wasted, but it's not about blind panic. Haste makes waste, as they drilled into us at the Academy. Mishandle that hose, misjudge the stability of a floor, and you're not saving anyone, least of all yourself.

The plan, the training – that's your lifeline in the inferno. Yet, the best laid plans can go up in smoke faster than a cheap armchair. Blocked stairway, collapsed roof, the fire having a mind of its own… that's when the other kind of training kicks in. The thinking on your feet, the ability to adapt. If Plan A fails, there's got to be a Plan B, even a Plan C, and you're concocting them on the fly, fueled by adrenaline and that stubborn refusal to give up.

Sometimes, it means going against the grain. That window you were meant to ladder up to is a wall of flame? You find another, bust through a wall if you have to, because the people trapped inside don't care about the rule book. And those times you hit an absolute wall, when the fire's winning? Your radio, if you are lucky enough to have one, isn't just for routine updates, it's a shout against the impossible. You tell the officer what you see, what you need, and hope echoes back down the line with backup or a new tactic to break the deadlock.

From the outside, we might still look like that frenzied swarm. But inside our heads, there's a grim sort of focus. It's pattern recognition at breakneck speed, it's trust in the guy whose boots you've followed through smoke thicker than any fog. Professionalism isn't about looking pretty, it's about knowing your own piece of this battle, this puzzle, and trusting that the guys around you know theirs.

Civilians get to watch chaos unfold. We don't have that luxury. We've got to turn that chaos into a plan, a series of brutal, sweat-soaked moves that maybe – just maybe – will tip the scales back from destruction towards something closer to control. It isn't always successful, and it damn sure isn't glamorous. But under those raincoats, behind the soot and the shouts, we're fighting not just the fire, but for the chance that maybe this time, that ingrained order will win out over the madness.

The Teamwork in the Chaos

The engine screeches to a halt, red lights reflecting in the pools of water already seeping from the well-used hydrant. Johnson, the chauffeur, practically vaults from the cab, his experienced eyes already appraising the situation. Inside the burning building, chaos reigns. Smoke curls in heavy tendrils, choking the air.

Smith is all coiled energy, suction hose slung over his shoulder as he heaves the heavy coupling towards the hydrant with practiced ease. The threads catch with a satisfying thud, and he wrenches it tight.

A blur of motion follows. Byrne, the forcible entry man, shoulders his ax and has the halligan tool out ready for the can man to hold steady, sizing up the battered apartment door with ruthless efficiency. Alongside him, Martinez, the can man, also keeps the extinguisher at the ready, his hook poised to work after they force entry.

Outside, Thompson, the outside vent man, has disappeared through a side doorway. Each agonizing second ticks by as the rest of the team waits for the telltale crash of breaking glass. Meanwhile, the truck chauffeur, sweat pouring down his face, maneuvers the towering ladder truck as close to the building as possible. He knows in just minutes, after his size up and any rescue needed on the front of the building, he'll need to swap that mindset for an ax and join the firefight inside.

On the roof, Reilly, the roof man, pants heavily. He hauls himself up the rusted fire escape of the adjoining building, and every muscle aches. There's the blasted bulkhead door – padlocked. One well-placed swing of the ax changes that. With a screech, he forces it open and peers inside.

Steam surges out through the opening along with smoke and heat, the OV signals success while the engine's nozzle team surges back inside with a roar. Fire and water collide, turning the apartment into a hissing, steam-filled battleground.

This is the rhythm of fire – chaotic yet synchronized. From hydrant to roof, it's a deadly dance where each assigned role is vital. They push against the blaze, relying on that ingrained ability, their tools, and the men (and women!) at their side.

As the engine men advance with the hose into the fire, they try to squat rather than kneel or crawl because, once the nozzle is opened, there is boiling water inundating the floor, and their knees get horribly burned. Sometimes you have to bear the pain as the flesh on your knees melts away.

There's no time for hesitation. Murphy, the nozzle man, knows it's squat or suffer. The floor is already an unseen hazard – not just debris, but the scalding runoff from the first blasts from the water can. Kneeling isn't an option; a second of contact could cause excruciating burns.

He crouches low, knees straining, thighs burning as he and his backup wrestle with the hose, directing the powerful spray of water at the heart of the fire. Every pulse of the line, every inch forward, is a test of grit. He can feel the blistering heat radiating outwards and upwards, threatening blisters, threatening… worse.

But that's the reality: there's no time for self-preservation. They have a job to do. His backup man, legs trembling from the effort of maintaining the awkward squat, inches forward with him. Sweat mixes with soot on their faces. Each man becomes a silhouette against the raging inferno, the very picture of a battle against both fire and the burning agony in their own legs.

Later, when it's over, the adrenaline starts to fade. As the rig rolls back into the firehouse, Murphy winces with each step. It's not just his knee. Blisters are already appearing at the edge of his collar, his neck screaming in protest at the raw, burned skin. The captain takes one look and a chill unrelated to the night air settles around his shoulders. This isn't the usual soot and exhaustion of a job well done.

"Burn unit," he says to the responding EMS crew, voice low. He's seen too many faces contorted just like Murphy's, a mix of pain and stubborn disbelief at being taken out of the fight. Murphy clenches his jaw, but a hiss of pain slips out as the paramedics cut away his pants. This burn isn't just an inconvenience – he's grounded, sidelined by an injury sustained in the line of duty.

And as the ambulance doors shut, he catches a glimpse of his captain in the reflection. Relief and regret war on the older man's face. Relief that a life wasn't lost, but regret at the cost borne by a firefighter under his command.

THE COCKROACH

Man, the firehouse kitchen isn't just old, it's like stepping into some archaeological dig. Walls covered in soot like those fancy cave paintings, except this isn't art, it's diesel grease and who-knows-what-else. Tonight's dinner? Courtesy of Rizzo, the culinary equivalent of a wrecking ball. His specialty: mashed potatoes.

Let me paint a picture: these spuds aren't your grandma's Thanksgiving fluff. They're lumps the size of bowling balls, bobbing in a pot you could bathe a small horse in. Rizzo's attacking them with a masher that looks like it got stolen from a blacksmith. Sweat's pouring down his face, eyes focused, like this is a life-or-death situation.

And then…disaster. Chunk of ceiling decides to join the party, crumbles down like it's got a death wish, and outta the dust cloud lands a roach. Not one of those scrawny city roaches, mind you, but a monster. Mutant thing's probably survived a nuclear blast or two. Lands with a splat right in the middle of the potato goop.

Now, remember, we're firefighters. We see stuff that'd make a butcher faint. But even the toughest of us pauses. Single roach leg twitches. Rizzo? Dude doesn't even blink.

"Free protein," he mumbles, and keeps right on mashing. That roach, it just…disappears. Vanishes into the potato abyss like it never even existed. We're all a bit horrified, a bit impressed, and mostly nauseous.

Suddenly, the bell rings. That shriek snaps us outta the trance. Potatoes get abandoned, splattered all over the stove that looks like it hasn't been cleaned since the Civil War. We're rushing out the door, helmets on, stomachs churning. Pete, the rookie, shoves a spoonful into his mouth as we run.

"Hey," he chokes out, "this tastes a little…nutty."

See, that's the thing about this job. You gotta have a stomach of steel. Not just 'cause of what you see, but because of what you end up eating. Between the adrenaline and the cockroach surprise, sometimes you learn to shut up, grab a spoon, and deal with whatever the hell's on your plate. Because who knows what tomorrow might bring? Could be worse than a little mashed roach. Could be worse.

THE KID

The firehouse teletype wasn't the one that broke the tension. Normally, it would yank them onto their feet, that jolt of adrenaline always waiting beneath the surface. This time, the jolt came instead from a soft knock on the small, metal, rarely used front door.

I had the misfortune of being closest and so I opened it expecting another junkie begging for change, maybe a local looking for help. My breath caught when I met the wide, terrified eyes of the boy in front of me. Couldn't have been more than ten, but there was a desperate maturity in those eyes, a weight far beyond those narrow shoulders. Behind him, a little girl huddled, even smaller, clutching a threadbare doll.

The words tumbled out in a rapid-fire Spanish I only half understood – something about his hermanita, his little sister, about fire, about needing help.

"Muéstranos," the boy urged the girl, pushing his sister towards the gathered men.

"Show us."

She unzipped her worn jacket with trembling fingers. Then, she lifted her shirt. Beneath was not the cut or scrape I expected, but a scene so horrific it burned itself into my retinas forever.

Across her small torso, an angry tapestry of red and blistered flesh stretched over delicate ribs. Some parts were already weeping and crusted, the smell of burned skin cutting through the firehouse's usual mix of sweat and diesel exhaust.

A gasp echoed through the firehouse. Knuckles crossed himself, his usual bravado evaporating under the weight of a terror he'd never imagined.

With urgent commands, they moved. We took care of the girl, the men's touch surprisingly gentle while a torrent of broken Spanish reassurances spilled from their lips. They cleaned around it as best they could, laid her flat upon a sterile white sheet over some cushions, applied cool non-adhesive compresses from the well-stocked first-aid kit, wrapped that freshly laundered sterile white sheet over her – all the while trying not to flinch at the silent tears rolling down the little girl's face.

The ambulance seemed to take forever. When the EMTs finally arrived, their professionalism faltered slightly at the sight, before experience regained control. As they bundled the girl onto the stretcher, the older brother grabbed her hand with a fierceness that broke my heart.

It was during cleanup that the full force hit me. Not just the horror the child had endured, but the chilling fact that she'd suffered it for over twenty-four hours. Where the hell were the family, neighbors or the authorities, the social services that were supposed to protect the innocent?

"Mama," the boy had sobbed, a word that should always mean safety, "she was angry...the oil... she threw it." The police responded and took down all the information muttered from the boy.

A short time later, when we got called out – thankfully, just a rubbish fire – there was a new rawness to our movements, a silent fury as we beat back those flames.

Afterwards, back in the kitchen, there were whispered arguments instead of card games or sports on TV. Some of the men muttered about wanting to find the woman and giving her a piece of their mind, or worse. Knuckles simply sat with his massive head in his hands. In the evening, I retreated to the rooftop to gaze out at the restless city lights. There were no answers there, just an ache under my ribs and a chilling certainty that even on my best days, I would only ever put band-aids on deep wounds.

That ache followed me home, even to my usually rambunctious brood, and there were extra squeezes, a desperate hold on their warm, healthy bodies. My wife watched me, eyes narrowed, then later, when they lay quiet in the darkness, my voice hoarse and unsteady, I told her what had happened. Tears fell silent and unnoticed on our shared pillow. And then, later still, we fell asleep, huddled together, an act of quiet defiance against the world's indifference and cruelty. In those fleeting moments, there was something like strength, like hope, the promise of fighting on, because maybe…just maybe, my tiny band-aids had made a difference for that little girl and her broken heart.

GHETTO CARS

It wasn't an official part of firefighting duty, but every rookie at this Bronx firehouse quickly learned the drill. After getting sworn in, after your basic training at proby school, your next priority was acquiring your *Ghetto Car* if you were assigned to the Animal House. Usually, an ancient clunker bought dirt cheap, these rides served one purpose: getting you to and from the firehouse without ending up stranded with a busted-out window and your stereo ripped from the dashboard.

During the change of tours, a daily and nightly game of vehicular chess unfolded as firefighters strategically maneuvered their Ghetto Cars in and around the front of the firehouse. "Park flush against the wall," grizzled Lieutenant Jackson would advise, "that way they can only nab two tires instead of all four."

Inside the firehouse, it became a point of pride to have the emptiest car possible. Glove compartments were permanently open, like a gesture of defeat to the neighborhood thieves. CD players? Long abandoned. Spare change? Laughable. Some guys got inventive – scattering crumbled crackers strategically to fool would-be burglars into thinking the car held remnants of some tasty snack. It rarely worked.

The local glass importer, a guy named Sal, had a soft spot for the firefighters and knew their struggle. In an unspoken barter system, smashed windows miraculously repaired at discount prices would show up on their cars after nights the firehouse had been particularly busy. He'd wink and, in return, he knew that if Sal's shop ever caught fire, they'd get there maybe just a little bit faster.

Around the grimy kitchen table, it was dark comedy to swap stories of Ghetto Car woes. There was one man, whose ancient Dodge got stripped down one night – he found it propped up on milk crates, naked except for the driver's seat; and another, who went out one morning to find his entire windshield was an artful spiderweb of cracks, courtesy of a late-night brick thrower. The invisible enemy, always waiting to apply one more indignity to the unlucky few, became a hallmark of the Animal House.

One time we'd returned to find him – a scrawny kid, maybe thirteen, with the desperation of a stray dog in his eyes. His hands were fumbling with the lock of Sal's old clunker, a firefighter's car parked just outside our firehouse.

The first instinct was primal. Teach the little bastard a lesson he wouldn't forget. A back-alley beatdown to the soundtrack of sirens, our brand of twisted justice. But then, like a bucket of icy water, we saw ourselves reflected in those wide, fearful eyes. Weren't we just kids once, lost on tougher streets than he could imagine?

Someone, maybe it was Old Man Harrison, his voice rough but surprisingly steady, growled, "call the cops." It hung in the air, heavy and unexpected.

The kid didn't fight, didn't run. Just slumped against Sal's fender, defeat etched onto his face younger than our rookies'. Maybe that was the hardest part. We were supposed to be the heroes, the ones rushing in to save the day. Yet, facing this kid, none of us felt like saviors.

When the police arrived, the cuffs clinking, we turned away. It wasn't victory we tasted, but something bitter and familiar. Another kid swallowed by the city, another potential life tossed onto the bonfire of circumstance. As the cruiser pulled away, we stood in silence, the air thick with all the things we couldn't, wouldn't fix that day.

My VW Ghetto Car

That Volkswagen Bug… man, it wasn't just transport, it was a statement of sorts. Mostly the statement: "I'm a Bronx firefighter, paychecks and common sense aren't my strong suit." Dented, paint peeling like a sunburn, engine sounding like an asthmatic pug…a thing of beauty it was not. But see, those Bronx locals, they understood the genius of ugly. That Bug? Ain't no joyride, parts are worth less than a pack of gum. So, it sat, mostly untouched, while flashier cars vanished overnight.

Thing is, that "safety" was a double-edged sword. Mornings became this ritual of dread. No heat and no air conditioning. Will it start? Will that patched-up window be intact? That glove box, forever flipped open like a beggar's cup, was my sad plea: see? Nothing here, fellas! Just lint and expired coupons!

This wasn't about stolen radios, mind you. It was the principle. That feeling of your normalcy being whittled away. My kids – bless their slightly embarrassed hearts – staged a full revolt. School runs turned into spy dramas, me lurking a block away to collect 'em, like I was some shady character, not just Dad trying to spare everyone the shame of our ride.

Then there's the highway cops. Those fellas must have some kind of radar for old Bugs. Maybe the rattling muffler, the way the whole thing sags like a tired donkey…they pull me over with the enthusiasm of catching Bonnie and Clyde. The routine's always the same: the suspicion, then me flashing that badge. Not "cop privilege," but more like a silent nod of "yeah, I get the paycheck struggle, buddy."

See, in that moment, those fancy cruisers and uniforms don't separate us so much. We're both just working stiffs, that Bug my proof. There's nothing glamorous in it, just stubbornness. Kinda like how the Bronx treats you – one body blow at a time. But damn if that engine won't keep chugging, that window will get patched again.

Ugly, inconvenient, and yet…somehow you cling to it. Maybe it's that feeling of beating the odds, even if the victory ain't pretty. Or maybe it's just 'cause a firefighter and his trusty Bug, both a little battered, make a kind of twisted sense in this city. That, or I'm simply too stubborn (and broke) to admit defeat.

The House That Never Sleeps

The heart of the firehouse thrums on the apparatus floor. Gleaming engines stand at the ready, their chrome and red paint an almost comforting sight against the stark concrete. Each rig – trucks and engines – holds a microcosm of life-saving gear: coils of hose, ladders stacked like fallen giants, axes strapped to compartments, containers of foam concentrate neatly arranged along the upper deck staring down ominously.

The housewatch area is a cramped kingdom at the front of the apparatus floor, and neatly separated from it by a half-wall, its desk groans under the logbook and the hulking teletype – a lifeline to dispatch that chatters incessantly with codes and locations. Here, on those 3-hour tours, a single firefighter holds this post, the nerve center, their focus flitting between phones and alarm panels.

Behind the apparatus floor lies the kitchen, an oasis of chipped mugs and the smell of stale coffee. Faded photos and grimy calendars line the walls, bearing silent witness to years of camaraderie and shared dangers. A chalkboard to illuminate sketches and diagrams for training and drills. Next to the kitchen, in many houses, sits a slightly worn sitting room holding mismatched couches where worn-out firefighters might steal a few moments of quiet after their daily chores, drills, and inspections, the distant clank of gear like a heartbeat.

The second floor offers no such creature comforts. The officers' rooms are mere cubbyholes, more functional than inviting. Beyond lies the sprawling bunkroom. A few beds stand stark against the floor, each holding the promise of an uneasy rest under the constant whisper of anticipation. Here, at night, men rest fitfully, ready to plunge into the chaos below if that alarm rings.

And if those older firehouses still stand, the iconic firepole is both a thrilling shortcut and a grim reminder of how swiftly that call to action can go wrong. One misstep, and it's a hard fall onto the floor where the trucks lie ready. Those older houses had the infamous hose towers where the old cotton hose lengths had to be hauled up and hung down so that they would dry before the next fight.

The layout of the firehouse might seem mundane to the outsider, a utilitarian space dedicated to function over form. But for the firefighters who call it home, it's a meticulously crafted ecosystem. Each element – the gleaming apparatus, the nerve center of the watch desk, the worn couches whispering of past camaraderie – exists in a delicate balance, a testament to the unwavering readiness that stands at the heart of every firehouse. It's a space that hums with a quiet energy, a constant thrumming tension waiting for the next alarm to shatter the calm and propel them back into the heart of the unknown. The firehouse isn't just a building; it's a vessel, ready to launch them, time and time again, into the chaos of the city.

THE HONOR WALL

That wall at the front of the apparatus floor, facing those gleaming trucks, was both a shrine and a battlefield report in one. One side crackled with faded glory, unit citations stacked so tightly, looking like scales on some metallic dragon. Each framed award is a testament to moments the city would barely recall; roof rescues, fires extinguished against all odds, the kind of quiet bravery that only other firefighters truly understood. There was a time when fresh space might have been a sign of glory, but not anymore. The wall was full, victory upon weary victory layered until it blurred into a single wood frame and glass testament.

Then there was the other part nearby. Plaques for our fallen. Thankfully, fewer in number than those citations, but chilling in their contrast. Polished wood and brass with names engraved, cold and empty against the riot of yellowing paper awards. These weren't moments won against roaring flames but battles brutally and tragically lost.

Visitors – those other firefighters from the shiny, well-funded firehouses further out from the city – would study that wall with something caught between disbelief and awe. They saw the citations, evidence of a company pushed to the extreme, and a flicker of respect would cross their eyes. A recognition that we weren't just another house, but one baptized in relentless struggle.

But then…their gaze would creep to those enshrined names. The respect would fade, replaced by something else. Maybe pity, perhaps a flicker of their own anxieties laid bare. It was hard to hold on to the shiny heroism when faced with the brutal cost. Those plaques weren't just memorials, they were ghost stories whispering through the polished brass and diesel fumes of our firehouse.

For us, looking at that wall became a complicated ritual. Pride battled exhaustion, the thrill of a job well done tempered by the stark reminder that next time, the outcome might find its place on the wrong side of that divide. There was a kind of defiance in adding to those citations, stacking triumph against tragedy. It wasn't acceptance of the risk, but a stubborn refusal to let those names be the only thing the world remembered us by.

That wall was a microcosm of the Bronx itself. Unforgiving, where bravery and loss walked side by side. We didn't glorify it, but it became a part of us all the same. Every time we rolled out under that watchful gaze of citations and names, we were no longer mere fire-fighters. We were part of that ongoing story, adding another line to a history written in fire, sweat, and the echoing emptiness of those polished plaques.

THE GIN MILL

La Sirena was an explosion of vibrant decay. It was right next door to the firehouse. Peeling green paint advertised cervezas on special, faded but defiant against the relentless Bronx grime. Even with the firehouse doors closed, the music wormed its way inside, a pulsing salsa beat battling the drone of traffic and the occasional shout echoing down the block. I couldn't decide if I hated it or if the sheer force of the place grudgingly intrigued me.

Some were drawn by cheap booze and dim lighting that hid a multitude of sins. Locals and commuters coming off the elevated subway platform occasionally disappeared inside. On duty guys. That was a no-no.

If you were off duty and went in there, it was like walking into another world. Women wore dresses whose colors made my eyes hurt, men in sharp, sweat-stained suits moved with an easy rhythm beneath the flashing disco ball. Thick smoke from cheap Cuban cigars mingled with the scents of garlic and hot peppers. In the far corner, a dominoes game unfolded with such furious focus that you half-expected a brawl to break out at any moment.

Most guys from the firehouse stayed steadfast, though. "My grandmother would roll in her grave," one guy once confided in me during a rare quiet moment. "Said too much heartbreak and spilled whiskey in those places." Despite myself, I admired his restraint. The chaos of La Sirena had an insidious appeal, a tempting promise of forgetting for a few hours—forgetting the relentless weight of the job, the endless misery we saw, forgetting that all our courage wouldn't change the damn world.

The Jumper

Picture this: a fire so hot you could practically roast marshmallows on your eyelashes. Not those dainty campfires, oh no – this was urban inferno, the kind that turns buildings to charcoal and hope into a swear word. Then, a dreaded sight on the front sidewalk: "Jumper." Ugh. Nothing pretty about that.

Midst the hoses and hollering, I spot Jerry – gangly kid, all Adam's apple and earnest eyes – crouched over the crumpled figure. Not some gawking rubbernecker, mind you, but that grim, focused look they drill into you at the academy. You gotta check, even if that check screams DO NOT WANT.

Suddenly, Jerry's up, a greyhound spooked by thunder. "WE NEED A BLANKET!" Then, poof, he's vanished back toward the rig. Us? We've got other fires, in a manner of speaking. That poor bastard, now shrouded in surplus army green, he's just part of the scenery now.

Ten, fifteen minutes max, and that damn blanket ain't so still no more. Coughing, choking – Jesus, not a wake-up call you expect on a Tuesday.

The chief, bless his mustachioed heart, bulldozes in, EMTs scrambling like confused ants around him. And there, underneath the blanket, some poor schmuck tasting his second shot at life. Picture from a B-movie, isn't it?

Later, there's Jerry, soot-streaked like a chimney sweep, eyes wide as saucers. "I didn't…thought the blanket…he wasn't…" Poor kid, bless his heart, couldn't string together a proper sentence.

From that day on? Every run had that undercurrent of snickering, "Hey, grab some extra blankets while you're at it. You know, the miracle kind."

Don't get me wrong, the teasing was a shield thin as tissue paper. We knew Jerry had guts. That extra few seconds, that damn blanket… sometimes that's all it takes, ain't it? Turns out, even when you're staring down the devil himself, a beat-up old blanket can be a tool of resurrection.

That's the way this whole job rolls: heroic and absurd in equal measure, wrapped up in a single, life-altering blanket on a Brooklyn sidewalk.

THE PRESSURE COOKER

That kitchen of ours? A wolf in sheep's clothing. Sure, those chipped tiles and grimy walls look harmless enough – if your idea of "harmless" is a greasy time capsule from the 70s. But see that stove? That's not for cooking, that's an instrument of torture. Built for feeding factory workers en masse, not a handful of firefighters doing a 24-hour tour in a Bronx heatwave.

See, heat's one thing. You get used to that, wear it like a badge. But that kitchen? It breeds a special brand of misery – the humid kind. Windowless, with a single AC unit wheezing like a dying dog... That first step inside is baptism by sweat. Blast of heat hits you, not gradual-like, but a physical punch. Like, who needs a sauna when you got this, right?

We'd eye each other, testing the waters. Nobody says it, but under the soot, we're sizing each other up. Who'll crack first – drip a bead of sweat too obvious to be ignored, or reach for the dishrag and admit defeat? Thermometer says 85? Yeah, right, that thing probably hasn't seen a proper calibration since Nixon was in office.

Course, you ain't complaining. That's not how it works. But beneath the bravado and unspoken camaraderie…there's a perverse little pleasure, right? Like we're some kind of warped brotherhood, veterans of a kitchen war nobody else could understand.

Sizzle of meat on the grill, pots bubbling like they got personal grudges…it's not so much the cooking as the endurance test. Anyone with a lick of sense would order takeout at this point. But sense? That ain't a strong suit around here. We cook because it's tradition, because sweat and grease stains are badges of honor, proof you can handle whatever the Bronx throws at ya.

The thing is, those moments… they matter more than any fire. They're where you learn your brother will have your back, no matter what. Cramped space, busted equipment, sweat so thick you could hang it on a hook… none of that breaks the real bond. The food? Well, that's just fuel for bragging rights later.

THE POT ROAST

The smell of pot roast was a betrayal. See, we spend our days with the burnt, the broken – the smell of singed soul mixed with cheap carpet. But tonight? Tonight was a taunt, a siren song of meat and gravy that had us drooling like idiots. We weren't Michelin chefs, but dammit, when it came to basic comfort food, we were damn artists.

The alarm cut through it all. Not a polite beep, no, a screech like the devil gargling rusty nails. The pot roast, a glorious testament to slow-cooked hours, sat orphaned, partially sliced, and smoking. A quick curse, then the scramble, the stink of adrenaline, and out we went. Duty before dinner, that's the drill, isn't it?

Mostly – and Lord, don't ask me about the name – was our firehouse mascot. All mangy legs and hopeful eyes, like someone had crossed a Dalmatian with a stray sock. That dog could smell a steak frying three firehouses over.

We get back, stinking of char and cheap antiperspirant, and the pot roast? That symphony of beefy goodness? Vanished. "We've been robbed!" someone wails. Maybe a visitor with a death wish. Accusations flew like pigeons at a dropped french fry.

Then we see Mostly. Curled up, one ear twitching in a dream I'd wager was meat scented. A slick of gravy across his chops, the kind you couldn't fake. The ghost of that roast haunted the air, a specter of salt and succulent sorrow.

Chinese food that night. Bad dumplings and worse aftertaste. Mostly, that gluttonous genius got belly rubs and nightmares. Later, I'd think, maybe we were all a bit like him. This crazy city, always battling, always scrambling for that one good thing – a pot roast, a promotion, a halfway decent night's rest. Mostly, in his thieving glory, had shown us all up. He'd tackled the world, or at least the oversized results of our best recipe, and won. The rest of us were just playing pretend, weren't we?

Ghosts of the
Backstep

The wind wasn't your friend on a speeding engine. It wasn't a playful breeze, but a relentless fist trying to rip the helmet off your head and steal your breath. Rain and cold turned that fist icy, stinging your exposed skin. Yet, there you were, clinging to the back of the roaring beast, a precarious knight on a chrome stallion. We called it "riding the tailboard," a baptism by fire and freezing rain for every new recruit.

Back then, the firehouse felt like an extension of ourselves, rough around the edges but familiar as an old glove. We were a brotherhood forged in the crucible of shared danger, trusting the guy next to you with your life, literally hanging on for dear life. There was a reckless thrill in those rides, a feeling of raw power and camaraderie coursing through you as the city blurred into a streaking canvas of lights.

But times changed, and the city with them. The camaraderie remained, but the streets grew meaner. Bricks and bottles started raining down from darkened windows, a twisted form of welcome from those we were trying to save. One veteran firefighter, Frankie "The Tank" Kowalski, still bore a jagged scar on his cheek from a rogue bottle that found its mark. The backstep became a liability, a sitting target.

The grumblings started first, whispers of change. Then came the new rigs, gleaming and sterile, with enclosed cabs for everyone. Safety, they said. Progress, they said. But some of us, the old guard, felt a pang of loss. The backstep wasn't just a mode of transport, it was a symbol of a bygone era. It spoke of grit, of a time when bravery wore a canvas jacket and a soot-stained helmet.

Sure, the enclosed cabs were safer, but they also felt isolated. You didn't feel the wind whipping past, the city breathing hot and cold on your neck. It was all filtered, distanced, a sterile safety that felt a little too… well, safe.

We grumbled, we reminisced, we adjusted. The camaraderie that had grown on the back of the engine found a new way to thrive within the confines of the new rigs. But on quiet nights, staring at the gleaming metal flanks, some of us couldn't help but harken back to the days of the backstep, a time when danger rode shotgun, and the bond between firefighters was forged not just in fire, but in the raw, unfiltered chaos of the city streets. It was a reminder that some things, like the heart of a firefighter, couldn't be completely sanitized in the name of progress.

Lords of the Wheel

The chauffeur, the man behind the wheel of those fire-breathing behemoths, was an integral yet often overlooked part of the firefighting team. They were a mix – grizzled veterans who'd spent decades battling flames, seeking a less adrenaline-fueled role, and youngsters, hungry to learn the ins and outs of the job. Others were chosen, sent by their captains to chauffeur school against their will, a duty they accepted with varying degrees of enthusiasm.

Chauffeur school wasn't a vacation. Far from the fireground, at the sprawling training center, they spent several weeks immersed in a world of pumps, valves, ladders, and the unforgiving physics of maneuvering a massive rig through city streets. Engine chauffeurs, lovingly referred to as MPOs for Motor Pump Operators, had to master complex control panels. A dizzying array of knobs, switches, and pressure gauges was their symphony, and they were expected to conduct it flawlessly even while the inferno raged.

Truck chauffeurs faced a different beast. They wrestled with rear-mounted aerial ladders, the lumbering grace of tractor trailers, and the delicate dance of mastering the Tower Ladders. And those who piloted the intimidating tiller trucks, the rear-steering position on the massive rigs, were virtuosos of tight corners and near-impossible maneuvers.

All had to conquer the streets. At first, within the safety of the training grounds, they honed their skills. Then came the real test – navigating the chaos of a real city in rush hour, sirens not wailing, no panicked drivers but still a test of their ability to drive the big rigs. Decades ago, it was stick shift transmissions and double-clutching, the growl of the engine a constant companion. Power steering was a luxury for newer regular cars, not the hulking monsters they commanded.

The chauffeur's role carried a unique kind of pressure. Their actions determined if the firefighters arrived on time, if water hit the fire, if trapped civilians could be reached. Their skill, their split-second reactions, could change the course of a fire, a life, a rescue. They were a vital link in the chain, a role that demanded steady hands, a cool head, and a deep understanding of the symbiotic dance between man and machine.

But they also faced restrictions. The need for a trained chauffeur on every tour sometimes curbed their ability to partake in "mutuals," the firefighter's cherished system of schedule flexibility. Their presence was essential, a silent acknowledgment of their importance in a system geared towards action.

Too often, their work faded into the background. It was the men who entered the flames who became the heroes. But we knew – the chauffeur wasn't just a driver. They were the foundation upon which rescues were launched, the unseen hand that guided the firefighters' lifeline, the unsung heroes of every fireground.

THE GROUP SYSTEM

The official schedule at the firehouse was a rigid, bureaucratic beast. Hours tallied with mathematical precision; tours neatly assigned. A system that thrived – the Group System. An agreement with the city, its rules etched in soot-stained hands and cherished among the brotherhood.

Each firefighter, officer included, was assigned a group number from 1 to 25. A magical chart revealed who worked opposite whom, the key to a life-changing privilege known as mutuals or "tour swapping." With a simple request, a formal conversation, you could swap your tour and work a double – 24 hours straight in exchange for a full day off. Bliss.

The benefits were undeniable. It saved on commutes, fuel costs, and the precious commodity of time. Less trips to and from the firehouse meant more time with family, a stolen hour for a hobby, or the luxury of a full night's rest. It was a perk, not a contractual right, and could be revoked at any moment, making it all the more precious.

Snowstorms and weather, however, were the true test of the Group System's resilience. The city, paralyzed by a freezing storm, demanded constant vigilance. Relief might not arrive on time, an unavoidable delay caused by treacherous roads. And that's where the unspoken agreement kicked in. A weary firefighter, who was meant to be heading home, might work a few extra hours, a clandestine extension of their tour to ensure coverage.

The rules stipulated no more than 24 hours straight. But sometimes, practicality outweighed regulations. It was a dance with danger, a calculated risk taken to protect a city under siege. These clandestine extensions were kept in-house, never making it onto official paperwork. The higher-ups didn't need to know, and truthfully, sometimes it was better if they didn't.

The Group System, official or unofficial, was a testament to the unspoken bond between firefighters. A shared understanding that the work transcended the rigidity of official schedules. It was about community, camaraderie, and finding creative ways to balance the demands of the job with the desperate need for a life outside those firehouse walls.

The system wasn't perfect, and the risks sometimes gnawed at your conscience. But you knew, with the certainty of a seasoned firefighter, that the city was safer because of those deals, those extended hours that were never written down. It was the Group System, a firefighter's mutual handshake, which kept the rhythm of the city alive even when the official world was at a standstill.

TELEGRAPH SYSTEM

In the heart of the city, circa 1960s, fire alarms didn't arrive with the digital precision of a 911 call. They arrived in a series of CLANGS, a brazen, archaic code ringing through the firehouse like an insistent pulse.

The nerve center of this antiquated system was the housewatchman's desk. A firefighter, usually with a touch of old-timer grumpiness, was the keeper of the bells. Stooped over a weathered ledger, his eyes scanned rows of numbers: each New York City street corner had its own metallic heartbeat.

When an alarm tripped, silence shattered with the rhythmic clangor: ONE bell, a pregnant pause, then TWO, then THREE. Box 1-2-3. The watchman's weathered finger traced the number in his book, finding the address.

"One-two-three! Mott Street and 158th!" his voice would boom, tinged with a hint of urgency.

Then, the firehouse erupted in chaos. The bells echoed through every corner, a symphony of duty reverberating from bunk room to kitchen to apparatus floor. Men, mid-sentence, mid-bite, even mid-bathroom stop, abandoned whatever they were doing and transformed into firefighters. The counting was instinctive – one, two, three – they already knew the box, the street, the potential fire they were hurtling towards.

That bell system was a bond, a shared language in the brotherhood. On busy nights, the dispatcher would throw all caution to the wind. The bells became a frantic symphony, filling the air with a cacophony of unseen emergencies.

But it was flawed, and everyone knew it. The precious seconds lost as the watchman deciphered the location, the alarm resounding and men fumbling for gear…those seconds could mean lives. And amidst the rumbling of fire trucks and the clangor of those bells, whispers of change began to circulate. The old ways were fading, soon to be replaced by something faster, more efficient, and perhaps a little less… soulful.

But for those who knew it, the bell system was more than an outdated method – it was the sound of an era. A clanging reminder that sometimes, the tools were as weathered as the men who wielded them, and the fight against the flames was as much about tradition as technology.

Some nights, long after my tour ended, I would lie awake, those clanging echoes lingering in my mind. I'd hear the one bell, the two, the three, and know, somewhere in this city, another fire raged, and the cycle of alarm and response played out under the indifferent gaze of the moon.

ERS Boxes

New York City, or many parts of it, in the 1960s and 1970s, was a place perpetually on fire – or, at least, it sounded that way. The clangor of the old bell system rang out day and night, each alarm carrying potential within its metallic heartbeat. But alongside the genuine fires, another epidemic raged: the scourge of false alarms. Malicious pranks, faulty wiring, and a dozen other causes – they all added up to thousands of wasted runs, straining resources and leaving a lingering sense of cynicism in even the most dedicated firefighter's heart.

Then, with glacial efficiency, the city made its move: the era of the voice box was dawning. The old street corner alarm boxes, relics from another century, began to vanish, replaced by sleek metal units. Gone were the pull levers, replaced by a simple red button and a speaker grille.

Change, especially in the stubborn heart of the FDNY, wasn't easy. The old-timers grumbled about "newfangled tech" and claimed that you couldn't smell a fire through a speaker. But the appeal was undeniable – the promise of a direct conversation with the source of the alarm, the potential to filter out pranksters, and cut down on the flood of unnecessary responses.

At first, the voice box system felt strangely polite, even tentative. A citizen would press the button, a dispatcher's disembodied voice would crackle through the speaker, the careful back-and-forth of question and answer replacing the adrenaline surge of unanswered bells.

Sometimes, the change proved its worth instantly. A muffled voice would describe a smell, a flickering light, before admitting in a sheepish whisper, "never mind, it was just my imagination…" A single engine would roll, the quiet victory of a fire prevented far more satisfying than a frantic response to nothing.

Of course, there were the holdouts, the boxes where the line was crackly, the citizen panicked, or the situation too urgent even for a brief exchange. Then, the dispatcher would use their experience and either send one engine or unleash the full force of the response, the familiar clamor of multiple units cutting through the city's din.

Yet, gradually, the change sank in. Response numbers started to drop, not due to fewer fires, but fewer fruitless chases. Those extra minutes saved could mean the difference between a rescue and a recovery.

Some, hardened by years of relentless alarms, found themselves cautiously optimistic. One quiet night in the firehouse, as the chatter faded and only the distant hum of the city remained, they admitted, "well, I'll be… maybe those voice boxes aren't so bad after all."

The others chuckled a low rumble of agreement. It wasn't the end of an era, not by a long shot, but it was progress, a small piece of technology taming the chaos, a sign that maybe, just maybe, they were dragging the venerable FDNY into the 20th century, one voice box at a time.

SOME GOT IT, SOME DON'T

You can feel "it" the second they walk in the room. Not some swagger, not some bullshit bravado, but a quiet kind of certainty. Seen it in a new boss freshly promoted, the way he handled a fire, the look in his eye – knew right then he'd own the firehouse someday. Seen it in a firefighter sizing up a blaze, the calm focus before he charges into hell itself.

"It." You either got it or you don't. No amount of training or academy polish is going to fake it. Firehouse, boardroom, back alley – same deal. Some step up, and it's like a switch flips inside them. They see the whole picture, the upcoming moves ahead of the chaos.

Seen a proby walk into a raging inferno, eyes clear, and take charge like he'd been born in the flames. Heard a fresh-faced deputy chief cut through the radio chatter, voice steady as a surgeon, and suddenly, the whole operation flowed smooth as whiskey. It's more than skill, more than guts even. It's a kind of instinct, a damn-near sixth sense for how to handle whatever mess gets thrown your way.

They're the ones who make the impossible look easy. The ones who step into chaos and bring order, who see the big picture when everyone else is lost in the weeds. Brains, balls, maybe a sprinkle of crazy – yeah, it's got that too. But mostly, it's something else. A kind of instinct, a sense of how the world *should* work, and the grit to make it happen.

Thing is, sometimes it's not about being smart or being the best. Seen plenty of dumb-as-bricks guys with "it" run circles around some college-educated pencil pusher who couldn't lead his way out of a paper bag. It's like those guys who got it were born with a compass in their gut, always pointing towards the right direction, even when everything else is swirling to hell.

Then there's the other kind. The fumblers, the panic prone, the ones who freeze when the shit hits the fan. Seen captains freeze up mid-firefight, eyes darting like cornered rats. Boardroom suits choking on their own fancy words, sweating under the pressure. They fumble, they stumble, and you end up holding their damn hand just to keep things from going completely sideways. It isn't always about being dumb, or inexperienced. Some folks just aren't wired for the storm, no matter how much they want to be. The ones without "it," they'll go through the motions, follow orders, and maybe they'll muddle through. But they'll never lead the charge. Never be the ones you look to when everything goes sideways.

Thing is, "it" isn't something you can teach. It's a piece of the puzzle, the wild card dealt out at birth. The rest of us? We must make do with what we're given, hope we have enough grit to make up the difference, and maybe pray for a little luck when the world gets rough.

THE STREETWALKERS

The old firehouse wasn't just haunted by memories of past blazes. At night, when shadows stretched long across the cracked sidewalk and laughter sharp as broken glass drifted up from the street below, it hummed with a different kind of energy. The bar next door, *La Sirena*, was a beacon for souls as worn-out as the neighborhood itself. We'd watch their parade from the firehouse's dusty windows, a nightly ritual twisted into uncomfortable entertainment.

The girls. Streetwalkers. Hookers. The guys threw around those names with a mix of amazement and a strange fascination. But I saw them differently. Each heavy layer of makeup couldn't hide the flicker of youth, the desperation etched deeper than any eyeliner. They'd prance and posture under the unforgiving streetlights, teetering on heels that could have doubled as weapons, their painted smiles brighter than the neon signs of bodegas. I saw echoes of little sisters and cousins I'd fiercely protected back home. Here, on these streets, they were lambs thrown to a pack of wolves, survival a grim war waged night after night.

Then, one sweltering August night, the sidewalk turned into a stage. A fight – over territory, over a customer, who knew? – erupted in a flash of neon-painted fingernails and curses hurled like poisoned darts. In the chaos, one of the girls, barely more than a kid, went down hard. Someone raised the alarm.

Before I could think, we were out the door, the ambulance not far behind. The usual bravado and crude jokes faded. We patched her up – gashed knee, split lip, and eyes wide with a fear that reached far deeper than the wounds. The ambulance came, a screeching burst of red against the backdrop of urban decay. As they loaded her up, she stared at us – me and the lieutenant with our weathered faces and scarred hands.

"…Thought you guys hated us," she whispered, the words barely audible over the roaring engine. "Thought we were just…trash."

I didn't have an answer. No snappy comeback, no righteous speech. We weren't there to judge, or to preach. We were there to help whoever it was that needed it. But on that grimy sidewalk, under the flickering lights, it felt like more than just a bandage and a kind word. It was a flicker of recognition, a crack in the wall between "us" and "them."

The world, I realized, wasn't just raging fires and clear-cut rescues. It was a tangled mess of grays, of pain and defiance, of desperation and fragile hope surviving against all odds. Maybe being a firefighter wasn't just about the flames, but about learning to see the people lost in the shadows, extending a hand even when it wasn't a clean, simple act of heroism.

Ghosts of the City's Heart

The tenement coughed up thick black smoke, forcing them low as they crept down the hallway. A textbook vacant building fire, set for kicks by bored teens or out of some twisted act of revenge. But abandoned buildings were deathtraps—unpredictable collapses, the unknown factor of squatters or addicts seeking temporary shelter.

In the flickering orange glow cast by the flames in the front room, a silhouette shifted and then solidified into something chillingly familiar.

"Here!" someone's voice called, clear and assertive, and then it choked slightly on the acrid air. "I think…there's someone…"

Human-shaped, half-obscured by a pile of rubble and the relentless smoke, the figure remained motionless. They pushed forward, masks filtering the worst of the smoke, hearts thudding with a dread that had nothing to do with the growing heat. Then, the stench hit them — the unmistakable sweet-rot odor of decay. He wasn't trapped, wasn't struggling… he was a body left untouched.

The flashlight beam in my hand danced erratically against one bare, outstretched arm, where skin sloughed like loose parchment over blackened bone.

I steadied myself. My shock masked a strange wave of nausea that had less to do with the scene and more with the sudden realization —

this was becoming too commonplace. Me, tough and steady under pressure, had to stay focused on the scene in front and not with the stark finality of the city's forgotten.

I kept my voice calm, called the chief over the handie-talkie, routines providing a lifeline even with the chaos. "10-45, we got a DOA here."

We finished our sweep, checking for any other victims or lingering hot spots. Outside, sirens wailed, and other members came to investigate the new complication. It felt like hours passed before they escaped the smoky confines of that room, that place where a person — someone with a story lost forever — had met their lonely end.

Back at the firehouse, the aftermath hit hard. They weren't a bunch of guys prone to long discussions, but the silence resonated louder than any words. When someone did speak, the usual steel in their voice was dulled, edges blunted by something I couldn't quite name.

"He was just there," I thought, gazing into my half-empty mug of lukewarm coffee. "One minute it's another damn empty building, and then…just…"

Later, resting on the thin sheets of my bunk, it wasn't the grotesque image of the man that filled my mind but the sheer madness of it all. It was a moment of stark vulnerability, shattering my illusion of unflappable toughness. That crackling voice echoed louder than any crackling flame. There was no escaping it; in their line of work, they walked a razor's edge between life and its opposite. One misstep, a twist of fate, and it could be any one of them slumped forgotten in some crumbling room.

At home, my wife held me a little tighter, a silent acknowledgment of the unspoken fears I brought through the door after each tour. In her warmth, the chill from that room and the quiet desolation began to soften. There was always another tour, always another call. Perhaps this was simply the toll paid for being in the business of rescue, the hidden invoice tucked somewhere under the heroics and triumphs.

A firefighter wasn't just about pulling bodies from flames. It was about carrying the knowledge of what can get left behind, about holding your fellow crew close when faced with the grim reminder of a city that loved to burn but wasn't so good at caring for its own. I couldn't save people from all kinds of endings, couldn't rewrite the story of that nameless man hunched among the ruins. But in the tender squeeze of my wife's hand, in the faint sound of my children breathing in the next room, I found a different kind of purpose – not about the rescues alone, but about not going numb to what still mattered in a world bent on breaking hearts.

HE NEEDS A STURGEON

That summer, the Brooklyn streets pulsed with a raw kind of energy. Even at mid-morning, the relentless heat shimmered off the pavement, an unspoken menace. Inside the old firehouse, the morning routine hummed – gear checks, equipment maintenance, the constant banter keeping boredom at bay. Then, the eruption. A wave of kids slammed against the door, a tidal wave of fear and adrenaline crashing into the room.

"He's shot!" The words exploded, and instinct took over. Grabbing medical kits, the firefighters plunged into the playground, already painted with chaos. There he lay, a child midst the swings and slides, blood staining the concrete the wrong kind of red. The lieutenant knelt, finger pressed into a gaping head wound, a desperate shield against the gushing flow.

"Get a doctor!" Someone in the crowd screamed. The cries for medical help were tinged with an edge of terror that cut through our training.

From the corner, a voice pierced the panic, high-pitched and insistent, "he don't need no doctor, he needs a sturgeon!"

Even in the throes of trauma, something about the kid's misspoken word jolted laughter from the firefighters frantically working on the poor kid. It wasn't cruel or out of place, but a release valve. A sliver of normalcy, a tiny defiance against the stark horror unfolding in front of them. It was a shared moment, a flicker of absurdity that anchored them in their humanity.

But reality lurked, waiting to slam back with brutal force. The ambulance arrived, shrieking sirens that seemed to tear the sky apart. They took the child, his tiny body dwarfed by the stretcher, his fate as unknown as the bullet that struck him down.

Later, behind the firehouse's closed doors, professionalism was a thin veneer masking the churning emotions. They debriefed, reviewed actions, confirmed every step meticulously. Yet, it was that boy's desperate misspeak that stayed with them. A grim reminder of the innocence caught in a world far too familiar with bloodshed.

That night, going home to their families, their hugs were a little tighter. The laughter around the dinner table came punctuated by silences, eyes gazing inwards. For they were not just firefighters; they were fathers, brothers, sons. And, as much as they steeled themselves, the vulnerability of that boy on the playground echoed in their hearts, a haunting reminder of all that could be lost in a single, bloody instant.

Baptism by Basement

That damn firehouse wasn't just old brick and stubborn soot, it was a chorus of creaks and groans, whispering warnings. Tonight wasn't about sirens or scorching heat, no. Tonight was basement duty, and that was way worse. See, that wheezing sump pump…not just a flood risk, but a gateway to the legend of Sammy and it had to be checked. Enter the proby.

Sammy – and I swear those vets had a twinkle in their eye as they whispered his name – wasn't your average sewer rat. No, sir, this was a mutant monster, forged on toxic sludge and years of spite. A cat-sized terror? Hell, some swore it was closer to a bulldog, dripping teeth and glowing eyes. Point is, no one wanted to confirm those details by actually meeting the damn thing.

Down the proby went, flashlight his pathetic Excalibur against the thick basement gloom. Each drip, each creaking pipe, sounded like some monstrous heartbeat. Half the battle was waiting for the flicker of movement, the glint of Sammy's evil eye mocking him from the shadows.

Then, well, it ain't funny till it happens to you. The door slams shut. Pitch black. He ain't proud of the noises that escaped him. Squeak? Scream? Doesn't matter when the panic's a fist in your gut.

"Help!" Pathetic. Like those cement walls were gonna give a damn.

Answer comes, but not from some rescue team. It's laughter, muffled through the door. Turns out, Sammy wasn't under the pipes, he was above, enjoying a rookie initiation.

Door finally swings open, light searing his eyes. Fury, hotter than any fire, washes over him. Fists fly, prankster goes down, and the whole thing gets swept under the rug of unspoken embarrassment.

Sammy, he vanishes, back into the realm of tall tales and mean jokes. But here's the thing, see: something shifted down there in the dark. Turns out, the real monster you sometimes gotta face ain't some rat on steroids. It's something scarier, that little worm they call cowardice. And sometimes, in the musty dark of an old firehouse, when the rest of the world is sound asleep up above, you find a kind of strength you didn't know you had.

Body in the Park

T he 2 AM alarm shrieked into the night, jarring welcomed rest into startled alertness. "Rubbish fire, Van Cortland Park," dispatch's bored voice crackled across the radio. It was routine, or so they assumed. They grumbled and pulled on gear, routine drowsiness blurring with the predawn gloom.

Across the dark fields of the park, they piloted the engine, headlights carving a tunnel through the mist. Then, the flicker of flames licked into view. But as they closed in, a creeping disquiet settled over them. This wasn't a trash can or pile of debris – the orange light danced too clumsily, flickered with the wrong kind of intensity.

Headlights cut through the smoke, and the sickening tableau revealed itself. A body, sprawled upon the dew-kissed grass, flames licking at its clothes. There was a moment of frozen disbelief before the firefighters surged forward, dousing the fire with desperate efficiency. Then came the choking reek of gasoline, not burning trash. That, and the gruesome details revealed under the harsh white beams: the unnatural twist of a limb, the glint of a knife blade protruding from the chest, and the blackened void where a gunshot had torn through a skull.

Shock was primal, then came the sickening wave of realization. This was no accident. Someone had done this. Gone was the familiar hum of an adrenaline rush – replaced by a cold, hollowed-out feeling. They surveyed the scene in detached silence, each grimly aware that their work had shifted from mere firefighting into bearing witness to something dark and monstrous.

Later, the debriefing was filled with terse reports, not shared emotions. It was easier to focus on the mechanics – evidence secured; chain of command notified. But those images wouldn't fade. That gasoline-soaked body wasn't just a statistic or a job, but a brutal glimpse into the underbelly of their world.

That night, it settled with a hollow thud: drugs, violence…it destroyed not just the victims, but the invisible fabric of a community. We weren't just protecting against flame, but against a far more insidious darkness consuming the city, street by street, life by stolen life.

Some would find a way to bury the horror, focus on the next run. Others would carry that park scene like a jagged scar, a permanent reminder that no amount of training could extinguish the bleakest fires of the human heart.

Our Wrecks, Our Rules

The radio crackled to life, and another familiar call echoed through the firehouse, "ADV, Lincoln and Grant." With a resigned sigh, Mike grabbed his gear. In this neighborhood, it wasn't a question of if there'd be a derelict car fire, but when.

At the scene, the stench of moldy upholstery and burnt rubber filled the air. The sedan, a faded relic stripped of its former identity, was little more than a burning metal shell. It was routine now: first, check for bodies while scanning the nearby rooftops – a flicker of movement or the clink of a discarded bottle often sent a jolt of caution through them.

Then, the battery. If that was still intact, it would come back to the firehouse. One busted headlight later, Mike swung open the hood. Sure enough, there it was – a crusty, acid-leaking car battery, the last scrap of easily removable value clinging to this metal ghost. With a grunt, he disconnected it, hauling it back into the truck.

At the firehouse, their own "salvage yard" awaited. A row of mismatched batteries, scavenged from countless ADVs, lined a dimly lit corner, hooked up to an ancient charger. These weren't for resale, but for survival. Every month, like clockwork, thieves pilfered batteries from their Ghetto Cars parked out front. These scavenged replacements kept them rolling, a bitter necessity in a city fueled by desperation.

After disconnecting the old car battery came the cathartic part –

taking turns with a halligan tool or an ax. Windows shattered with satisfying cracks, sending shards of glass glittering across the asphalt. Headlights crumpled under heavy blows; taillights reduced to plastic fragments. Dents blossomed across fenders, bumpers were twisted into mangled metal art. This wasn't about destruction, but deterrence. Every smashed surface, every mangled panel was a defiant message to the unseen: there was nothing left to take, nothing to sell to the auto body guy; don't bring your stolen cars to our neck of the woods.

It was an unspoken understanding with the street-level car thieves and scavengers. The firefighters would respond quickly to the car fires set by the thieves to cover their crime, but in limiting the spread of flames it left a bounty for the thieves to collect. Parts for the junkyard to buy. Our job, put the fire out and render these vehicles worthless for dismantling, creating an uneasy equilibrium in their gritty domain.

They knew this battle for scraps was just a symptom of a bigger disease plaguing their streets. Still, it was their small way to fight back, their act of defiance in the face of constant theft and desolation. Every battery rescued, every headlight smashed, was a tiny reclamation of both resources and a piece of sanity in their daily work.

Bum Barrels

It became a dark dance, this silent battle playing out in the midst of the crumbling tenements and vacant lots. One night we'd race to a reported "trash fire" with a knowing dread, only to find a smoldering heap of wire in a rusty old metal drum midst the rubble. Blackened insulation curled with acrid fumes, sending wisps of oily smoke towards the cracked windows of nearby occupied buildings.

These weren't faceless thieves – in that harsh flicker of flame, you'd see them. Gaunt figures, eyes red-rimmed from smoke and desperation, hunched over in defeat as they watched the firefighters douse their meager profits. This was the rock-bottom economy of addiction: scavenging copper from vacant buildings, risking a blaze for a handful of cash that would vanish almost as fast as it was gained.

At first, a kind of reluctant pity wormed its way through our stoicism. It wasn't just the risk of bigger fires, but the way these buildings served as festering wounds, stripped hollow for a momentary fix. Yet pity couldn't stay our hands. Confiscation became a routine part of fire suppression.

With practiced motions, we'd hose down the last embers and then haul burnt cables into the rig. There was no satisfaction in this. No badge of honor for denying junkies a fix. Instead, it left a lingering unease. We could snuff out these little blazes, but the cycle would turn, and another vacant building would be next.

At the firehouse, confiscated copper formed tangled sculptures in the yard – mute accusations against the desperation they all saw daily. Word would often filter back of scavengers found collapsed beside an illicit bonfire, lungs blistered and eyes vacant. In those moments, confiscation seemed cruel, just one more defeat in a stack of endless failures.

We weren't social workers, just guys doing a job. We protected others from flames, regardless of how those flames started. Sometimes the job wasn't about victory; it was about damage control for both us and a neighborhood held hostage by desperation. The copper piles served as constant reminders: we battled not just flames, but forces both tragic and deeply human, trapped in an endless, destructive burn.

Death Traps and Decay

News of the fall ripped through the firehouse like a rogue gust of wind slamming a loose door. Vacant building. He fell. Six floors down the gaping maw of an elevator shaft onto a trash-strewn basement floor. Not dead, thanks to the feet-deep trash, which was the miracle whispered with grim relief, but... 'broken' didn't begin to describe it.

The aftermath hung heavier than smoke. Training sessions intensified, safety became a constant sermon. Not in fear, but with a kind of simmering rage the men funneled into vigilance. Each building was a minefield, every step a defiant middle-finger to fate. Yet, under the steely focus, an insidious crack formed. We couldn't voice it, but every echo of our own boots felt like tempting fate.

Wives waited a little longer by the phone, fingers tightening on coffee mugs. Kids clung a little tighter at bedtime, unspoken questions flickering in their eyes. In the silent hours, between fitful rest and false alarms, the darkness echoed with his name. It became a haunting reminder that heroism isn't some noble immunity, but a fragile dance with consequences that could cripple flesh and spirit alike.

Then, after a year or so, the news of his move spread. Out West somewhere. Horses and wide, clean skies. It felt equal parts betrayal and desperate relief. Betrayal, because his escape stung with a raw 'why not me?' sort of ache. Relief, because that desolate horizon offered a kind of distance no city apartment could provide. A separation from sirens, derelict buildings, and the phantom sensation of crumbling ground.

In a way, he became the ghost that haunted the firehouse. His broken body was a physical echo of fear gnawing at them all. Yet his journey whispered a kind of unspoken permission as well: sometimes, survival didn't just mean getting through the next call, but knowing when to walk away from the wreckage. To fight another day, on a different battlefield. Maybe a field so expansive that a man could forget the weight of falling concrete, and the endless, dark shafts of a wounded city.

The Car and the Apron

That firehouse? It doesn't just shake from sirens, on some days it trembles with laughter. And lord, the way it was echoing, you'd think a whole circus had snuck in. Right at the center of it was Joe, "Cement Head" to the guys, on account of both his stubborn noggin and, well, let's just say his smarts weren't what got him through the academy. Bless his heart.

We'd worked a 24-hour shift in a cold snap so mean, even pigeons were wearing tiny parkas. All we dreamt of was hot showers and not answering bells for five blessed minutes. Joe? He had a different demon: his car. More rust than metal, that thing held together by spit and baling wire. Plan was simple: get it idling so the ride home wasn't a death march.

Parked that beauty (*cough*) right outside the apparatus floor doors, and Joe was peering out the window like a doting papa at his newborn. Well, wouldn't you know, that's when Murphy, that rascal, decided to screw things up.

"Yo, Joe! Somethin' about mutuals…" one of the guys calls. Joe whips around, gets snagged into a chat. Now, normally the sight of that heap on wheels wouldn't tempt a fly. But in this split-second of distraction? Fate, that sneaky minx, saw her opening.

When Joe glances back? Empty sidewalk. No car, no clouds of

exhaust, just that gray winter twilight and his own dumbfounded expression. And let me tell you, it wasn't so much the theft, but the fact anyone'd pick Joe's ride that had us rolling.

A quick debate about chasing the fool ensues, more for the absurdity than any real hope. Then, reality sinks in. Poor thief's probably in some alley, frostbitten and cursing his life choices, discovering Joe's heater was just as busted as everything else about the car.

Meanwhile, *The Ballad of Cement Head's Ghetto Sleigh* was born. Told and retold, gaining a new layer of ridiculousness with every pass. Joe, he'd pretend to be annoyed, but you got the feeling he kind of relished it. See, in a firehouse, even bad luck is a brotherhood thing. And besides, who else could boast their car was so undesirable, it became a cryptid of the urban streets?

SCARS BENEATH THE SMOKE

It started small, like a hairline crack in a weathered foundation. A shot of whiskey at the bar after a brutal tour, maybe a six pack for the commute home, to blunt the edges of a nightmarish scene. A few pills passed discreetly from one locker to another, a whispered promise to "take the edge off" before facing another burning building, another possible body trapped inside.

In the brotherhood of the firehouse, these weren't signs of weakness. They were coping mechanisms, a way to stay upright under the unrelenting weight of trauma and desperation. No one wanted to appear soft, especially not when your life, and the lives of others, depended on split-second decision-making and unshakable courage. But some scars ran too deep to be ignored.

There was one man, always reliable, but now with tremors in his hands and a haunted look that no siren could fully shake. And another, once the life of the firehouse, now retreating into quiet, his laughter laced with a brittle edge. Those who noticed tried to step in, but clumsy offers of help just bounced off a silent armor of denial.

The captain, a firehouse legend, understood better than most. He'd seen good men buckle before, consumed by a self-destructive blaze far more damaging than any they fought with water. It became his own private duty – to watch for the telltale signs, the subtle faltering. Then the quiet interventions would start; late-night talks that were less commands and more pleas, the hushed suggestion of "medical leave or Counseling Unit," and the hushed understanding that the department would take care of their own.

They wouldn't call it the "funny farm" here. Maybe that's where it ended up sometimes, but at the start, it was a cabin upstate, a treatment facility hidden by trees, a world away from the screaming sirens and the constant stink of smoke. There, with the support of brothers in arms and the begrudging acceptance that even those who save lives need saving sometimes, a different kind of battle might be won.

It was a victory few spoke of – not celebrated, just mourned as yet another sacrifice. Because even under the brave uniforms, they were flesh and blood. Just men holding back a city's worth of sorrows, sometimes succumbing to the weight, and hopefully, clawing their way back into the light.

Where Shadows Take Form

The warehouse blazed like a monstrous mouth, roaring into the night. Smoke billowed outwards, suffocating, blinding, transforming the familiar street into a nightmarish hellscape. Through the haze, figures moved like gritty specters – the forcible entry team, their ax swinging in metallic arcs against the warped front door; the roof team, silhouetted against the flames as they hauled their gear towards the ladder.

Inside, the fire's pulse was a rhythmic roar. The engine team advanced deeper, hose at the ready, shadows dancing grotesquely upon the inferno-slicked walls. Then, through the choking heat and smoke, a chilling sound cut through: a heavy thud, followed by a choked cry.

The lieutenant, a veteran known for his steady hand and unerring instinct, ordered a man to break from the line and check out the cry. He wasn't abandoning his duty but responding to a deeper one. On hands and knees, he inched away, the smoke a burning, blinding shroud. Then, his flashlight beam revealed an impossible sight: a firefighter, prone on the floor, gear untouched. Unconscious.

Fear ripped through him, hot and sharp. We fought fire, but also the unseen threats, the hidden perils of this consuming chaos. He grabbed the fallen man, dragging him with grunts of exertion back towards the doorway, towards safety. He didn't need words, he felt the questioning glances, a hundred unspoken alarms buzzing through the haze. Back into the night they stumbled, dragging the barely conscious body towards a waiting group of rescuers.

Up on the burning roof, another shout shattered the air. A section of the weakened structure had buckled, sending another firefighter sprawling downwards. It was a scene from a nightmare: a man falling from the sky, engulfed in the fire's terrible glow.

Yet, by a horrifying twist of fate, he crashed to the floor mere feet from the huddled forms of those same engine men advancing the hose line. They hauled him out too, singed and battered but alive. A miracle amongst the carnage.

Later, in the midst of the debris and the reek of extinguished flame, two stories unfolded. A man who'd succumbed to some silent foe within that building, falling through the weakened roof, his struggle lost to the darkness. And another, whose life remained but forever twisted by the brutal kiss of falling flame as a part of the roof finally collapsed.

As I stared at the two men, both casualties of the same hungry beast, the realization was a gut punch. Some left the fiery crucible forever changed, the scars worn invisibly beneath a uniform stained with the grime of their unseen battles. Some left just to breathe at all. That night, as the weary engines rolled back towards the worn brick of the firehouse, victory's taste had turned to ashes in their mouths.

The Gunfight

I t started the way these things usually do – a low rumble of discontent, voices simmering on the tense street corner across from the firehouse. This was their beat too, in a way. We saw more victims of that turf war than anyone with a badge ever cared about.

But tonight, those rumbles exploded. Shouts splintered the twilight, followed by the unholy crackle of gunfire. We weren't cops, but you couldn't turn your back on this; it was practically on our doorstep. Windows shattered, a car backfired with a vicious bang, sending civilians ducking for cover.

Then, we saw them. Three kids, frozen on the cracked sidewalk, too young to understand the sudden descent of their block into madness. One tiny girl with wide, panicked eyes. Two boys, a bit older, but clinging to each other with trembling hands. They were lambs among the wolves, lost in the whirlwind of bullets and blind desperation.

It wasn't calculated, wasn't heroic. Instinct kicked in. A surge of anger at the senselessness, the way innocent lives were caught in the twisted undertow of that street conflict. Before anyone could shout a warning, he was running, dodging shards of glass raining down from shattered windows.

Those kids snapped into focus against the chaos. Fear glued them to the pavement. "C'mon!" His voice was rough, ragged above the gunshots. It might as well have been a whisper; their terror painted them deaf. So, he acted. Scooping the littlest one under his arm, he barked at the boys, the same rough tone he used breaking down stubborn doors. "MOVE!" The fear broke; they stumbled towards him.

Suddenly the firehouse doorway wasn't just an entry, but a sanctuary. In a clumsy scramble, they lurched through, and we slammed the door shut with a force that rattled the whole firehouse.

Silence fell, then, broken only by their small, frightened sobs and our ragged breathing. In those cramped moments, the stink of cordite and smoke clung to us. Later, there'd be questions, maybe a halfhearted reprimand. But looking down at those tear-streaked faces, at the bullet holes pocking the brickwork just outside, all that seemed absurd. In this city, it seemed, firefighting wasn't confined to just burning buildings. We fought against other demons too, for anyone small enough to get lost in the crossfire.

THE PURSE SNATCHER

Returning from a routine drop off, we were weary to the bone. Another night, another few blazes tamed – that gritty routine that numbs you just enough to get the job done. The chief's car rolled home, the world blurring past in a smear of exhaustion. And then, that sharp yell, "hey, look at that!" It wasn't an accident or another plume of smoke, it was something twisted on a dark sidewalk corner, a human drama playing out in miniature.

We looked, adrenaline re-igniting. It was a tug-of-war gone monstrous. A woman, dragged along on her knees, clinging to the straps of her own damn purse. That image cut through the fog like a siren. At the other end of the fight, a figure fueled by desperation, ripping her along the broken concrete. Some low-blow instinct had him using her own damn bag as a leash. Her cries seemed muffled against the rumble of the street, an invisible sound midst the city's cacophony. She'd been on her way to one of those storefront churches down the street.

In a quick desperate move, I leapt out of the still-rolling rig. He went right, I went after him, cutting the purse snatcher's escape route as a reflex. He had the purse, and he was young and fast. But I was a marathoner. My eyes hot with fury, I chased like hell itself was at my heels. The sirens were still just blaring promises on the radio, and for one terrifying second, I felt outnumbered.

When he finally collapsed after a dizzying trek through back alleyways and garbage strewn lots, I grabbed the scuzzy bastard. The guy choked out something about being hungry and needing those crumpled bills for food. I forced him onto his belly and held him down while waiting for help. It was a familiar refrain, another hollow note in the symphony of this broken city's desperation.

Yet, holding that tattered purse as evidence, feeling the echo of the woman's terror-filled wail, it was hard to feel even the smallest pang of pity. There was a kind of perverse hunger we fought too – hunger for a shred of decency, for streets where cries for help didn't get swallowed by the roar of our engines. For a moment, as his pathetic whine faded against the sirens' approach, it was starkly clear we were up against more than just random violence. We were up against the kind of hunger that made a man a monster, and a woman's desperate grip on all she owned into a pathetic life-and-death battle just blocks from our doorstep.

THE HESITANT
LIEUTENANT

The lieutenant was new to this particular dance of destruction. Covering here from a district where abandoned buildings were an anomaly, not a nightly fixture, he radiated a kind of jittered energy that clashed with the weary resignation of his unit. But there's no easing into a hot Manhattan night; it hits you like a blast furnace the moment you roll out of the engine.

This tenement wasn't special – three floors already well-involved, flames flickering like greedy claws through broken windows. Orders for hose lines crackled, gear pulled on with practiced speed. Yet, he seemed stuck. He hesitated. "Unacceptable risk," he mumbled, looking more at the crumbling facade than at his guys.

That look was the final straw. It wasn't about protocol, but a simmering frustration, a defiance born of endless nights like these. They'd watched too many buildings consume entire blocks, leaving nothing but fresh rubble where families once huddled. This lieutenant…he reeked of caution, not cowardice, but that made it worse. It wasn't his life in that blaze, but the potential damage if they stood outside fumbling with textbooks instead of water.

A silent mutiny unfolded. Glances darted between veterans; an unspoken pact made as easy as breathing. "Screw it," someone muttered, and that crack was all it took. Shouldering past their frozen commander, they surged forward. There was a rhythm to this battle, a practiced chaos they embraced. Hoses were charged, streams found their way to the heart of the roaring fire. No glory, no bravado, just the grim work of taming the flames.

It was over sooner than anyone expected. Vacant shells had a way of burning fast and hot, consuming themselves into easily controlled rubble. Smoke still snaked skywards as they emerged, battered and blackened.

There was the lieutenant, looking more lost than ever. That wasn't insubordination burning in their eyes, just a pitying disdain. One murmured excuse to regroup was offered, not with respect, but a bitter necessity. Later, back at the firehouse, the word got around. No formal rebuke needed – this kind of hesitation carried its own punishment. He vanished after that, quietly absorbed back into some cushy district. Maybe that was for the best – some fires burned too quickly to be extinguished by textbook safety, others, too deep to fight until you'd walked through the flames yourself. He knew then, deep down, that he hadn't been fit for this battlefield, this ballet of smoke and sweat and men bound not by rule books, but a weary oath sworn to the crumbling shells of their district. He could take his caution elsewhere. This city burned by its own rules, and it took a special kind of madness to charge into the flames on purpose. He clearly wasn't one of them.

Don't Feed the Firefighters

E ngine 75, our old brick fortress in the heart of the Bronx, wasn't just a firehouse. Sometimes, it felt more like a battle zone. Not with fires – those we could fight head-on – but rather a slow-motion war with our building itself. We'd outgrown it decades ago, and the strain showed. Gear crammed wherever an inch of space opened, leaky roof turning any hard rain into a chaotic indoor obstacle course.

But the floors…that's where things got downright apocalyptic. We'd plead with the brass every budget cycle, every inspection. Those trucks aren't light, not the modern monsters designed to carry more tools than an ER team has. Add 500 gallons of water to the tank of just one, and that old concrete's holding its breath until it decides to quit. Floor cracked like broken pavement, a sinkhole waiting to claim one of our rigs whole.

Finally, after what felt like a lifetime of near misses and crossed fingers, they sent workers. Only, those boys were working a whole different angle of crazy…

First, they split the damn apparatus floor in half. Like slicing a cake gone moldy, the idea being we could still roll, but only with one truck. The other rig had the honor of living outdoors, nestled within this monster chain link cage they slapped together like a chicken coop for

Godzilla. They say those fences were for security – like anyone in their right mind would be dumb enough to break into a 20-foot-high chain-link fortress with a firefighter sitting right nearby. It looked more like a zoo exhibit than a firehouse.

We became the joke of the whole damn borough. *Bronx Zoo expansion site*, they called us. Kids hung on the fence, snapping pictures while we scrambled through the gates to reach the truck. "Don't feed the animals," some clown wrote on a cardboard sign one day. Laughs were cheap and easy while we sweated.

Of course, the stress didn't quit just because you stepped outta the cage. Those alarms weren't waiting for our construction site circus to pack up. There were a couple of close calls when we took wrong turns in the chaos, and the tension hung thicker than summer smoke after a four-alarmer.

Then there was the city engineer. Young, cocky thing fresh from whatever fancy college they breed 'em. Watching one day like we were some reality show instead of men working around death traps. Didn't take more than a loose shoe and a patch of slippery grime. Kid tripped, tumbled straight down with a yelp that cut through even the construction noise. He vanished into the deep end, that basement we were lucky to avoid most days. We all froze…then scrambled. Took half an hour to pull him out. Alive, barely hurt, but after that ambulance peeled away we never saw him again.

They finished the floor eventually, though it was another year of hell. Can't say I was sad to see the back end of that cage when they rolled up the fencing. Now? I got other headaches, different battles. But when I'm stressed, when someone up top gets all hot and bothered about some statistics, a corner of my mind drifts back to the Great Caging. We survived it, got used to being ridiculous for a while. It's a reminder, I guess – there's worse things than some public embarrassment when you're fighting the good fight.

THE OLD LADIES

The tenement groaned under the assault of the fire, crackling and spitting like a furious beast. This wasn't some vacant shell – people lived here. The order echoed over the radio: "Two elderly women trapped, top floor rear." We would try a rear fire escape access if possible. With that, we shifted from extinguishment to rescue.

Each step of that ancient fire escape shuddered under our weight, sending rust rattling into the night. But there was no time for finesse, only adrenaline-fueled desperation matching the blaze within. Reaching the top, a shout from the roof pierced the roar of flames. One of our guys, silhouetted in the sun's glow, waved frantically. "Got 'em, but stairs are blocked! Heat's coming from the open bulkhead door – followed us up when we hauled 'em up to the roof!"

Our boots hit the roof, and my stomach hit my knees. No longer just onlookers, we were part of this chaotic scene. Two figures huddled behind Pete, barely more than shriveled forms swallowed by bulky nightgowns. In their ancient eyes, I saw mirrored images of the inferno churning behind me. The bulkhead door belched flame now, then, suddenly, it wasn't just smoke pouring out, but burning roof tar itself, ignited by the unholy heat. Panic flickered, mirroring the blaze engulfing our only escape route.

Forward was blocked too. Flames were already painting the edge of the front roof line, cutting off access to the ladder truck. One choice remained: the flimsy looking fire escape leading down to the backyard. But that drop…a good fifty feet down to the concrete below.

Fear wasn't an option now. Commands were curt, a staccato beat against the mounting roar. "Gooseneck ladder. Civilians first. Guide them, one by one." Somehow, those fragile legs found the rungs, each agonized step a victory against the creeping fire at our backs.

Luck was with us that day as the fire never burst from any of the rear windows. I was the last one down, heart pounding a furious rhythm that nearly drowned out the crackling of the burning roof flames. Every muscle burned with the sheer effort of controlled descent. My heavy gloves left streaks of soot on the grimy metal as I went. One foot after the other, fighting the urge to just jump and hope for the best. Below, the safety of the backyard beckoned, but my focus was upwards. One last step, boots finally scraping against rough concrete, and the fire above roared with renewed hunger, having devoured the escape route in the time it took us to get down.

With a final gasp, now on solid ground, a wave of relief crashed over me before it was eclipsed by a jolt of horror. There, on my fire coat, smoke slithered from singed material, testament to how close we'd come, how little room we had for mistakes.

Later, watching the water streams finally vanquish the blaze, all I could remember was the feel of brittle bones under my hands, guiding old women down a ladder under the shadow of a roaring inferno. Each rung and each step, each agonizing second, was a victory forged in the terrifying knowledge that for any misstep, those lives, and even our own, hung in a dangerous, fiery balance.

THE VERBAL ALARM

The firehouse, never a hushed sanctuary in the still of the night, exploded into chaos. A thunderous pounding shattered the silence, jolting the house watchman out of a restless daydream. Someone outside was screaming, their words barely audible over the relentless banging on the massive firehouse door.

He leaped to his feet, heart pounding, and hit the house alarm as he sprinted towards the doors. A blast of acrid smoke billowed in as he raised the door, flooding the house with a haze that pricked his eyes. Beyond the cloud, the streetlights flickered with an eerie orange glow, and shapes moved – panicked figures stumbling blindly through the darkness.

Adrenaline snaked through the firehouse. The firefighters, ripped from fitful rest and barely awake, scrambled into their gear with practiced speed, adrenaline burning off the remnants of fatigue. Each man felt a flicker of apprehension, the gnawing sense of the unknown that went with every call into the night. But years of duty and an unspoken trust forged in a hundred shared blazes propelled them forward.

As the engine roared out of the firehouse, their captain, a grizzled veteran with the weight of his profession etched into his face, leaned forward, scanning the smoke-choked streets. The blaze had swallowed something large. With each turn of the firetruck's wheels, the smell of destruction grew worse – burning wood, plastic, the indefinable metallic tang of things disintegrating in flames.

The men shared silent glances as they sped closer. Experienced men, they didn't speak of the potential horrors awaiting: mangled bodies, trapped families, lives teetering on the brink. Not because they were hardened, but because their focus had to be razor-sharp on the work ahead. It was a kind of mental compartmentalization vital to working in the realm of raging infernos.

And beneath it all, there was a flicker of raw, existential terror. Every fire was a reminder of their own mortality. One small miscalculation, one unseen structural weakness, and it could be the last flames they would face. Yet they kept racing towards the heart of the danger because that was their oath, their life, and someone out there in the choking darkness desperately needed them.

Toga Party

After weeks of close calls and too many nights with the adrenaline buzzing long past dawn, the firehouse crackled with restless energy. Something had to give, or they'd start bouncing off the walls… or worse, start snapping at each other.

Then, as if sensing the unspoken desperation, someone let out a mischievous bellow, "TOGA PARTY TONIGHT!"

It was a spark to dry leaves. Within seconds, the bunk room exploded with laughter and groans. The rookie looked nervously at the captain, but the weathered firefighter only rolled his eyes with a hint of a smirk. These boys needed to blow off some steam, and a toga party was about as harmless (and ridiculous) a way as any.

Sheets were yanked from beds, transforming into makeshift Roman robes with dubious levels of authenticity. Pillowcases became laurel wreaths, shoelaces morphed into makeshift sandals. Suddenly, a hulking firefighter draped in a pint-sized bedsheet with a colander on his head was Caesar and the old, lumpy sofa a Roman chariot.

Someone cranked up the dusty firehouse radio, finding a station lost in a time warp, all crooning vocals and doo-wop beats. The rhythm spilled out of the kitchen, echoing down the apparatus floor as firefighters shimmied and twirled in their ludicrous outfits. Even the usually stoic captain unbent, reluctantly allowing someone to twist a dishtowel into a crown upon his head.

They limboed to Chubby Checker, using a salvaged broom as the pole. They held chariot races (read: pushing office chairs at breakneck speeds down the wet concrete). Between improvised gladiator battles and tries at interpretive dance, laughter bounced off the usually quiet firehouse walls.

Then the call came. In an absurd flash, togas were hastily hitched up, bulky firefighting gear was thrown on, and the sheet-clad gladiators became firefighters once more. Sirens wailed, and they thundered out into the night, a strange mix of duty and amusement lingering in the air.

As the engine roared back several hours later, battered and soot-covered, someone stumbled onto the radio dial, and it was like time hadn't moved at all. Elvis crooned from the old radio, and with a shared grin, the exhausted crew picked up right where they left off. After all, every once in a while, even Caesar needed a break.

WHEN COMRADES CLASH

Dinner wasn't usually a boisterous affair at the firehouse. Raucous banter never replaced the tension of the job, the long kitchen table a place where rivalries dissolved over plates of steaming pasta and stories both grim and hilarious. This night, though, the air hummed with something different.

The troublemaker, with his barely-contained temper and two years on the job, was needling the new guy, the proby. Just a kid, really, still wet behind the ears and trying desperately to keep up with the pace and ingrained banter of the firehouse. He was 22 years old and admitted that he had never eaten pasta with tomato sauce before. Go figure. The topic seemed harmless enough: the makeshift water fountain rigged up in the corner with some tubing and a huge jug. Mike had forgotten to empty the drip tray – just one more proby task among a hundred.

"Come on, kid," Tommy drawled, "even a monkey could remember that much. Maybe they give out trophies for forgetting at proby school these days?"

A flush spread up the proby's neck, but he bit back the retort that hung on his tongue. The older guys were always 'testing' him, but it got harder to stomach with each jibe. The captain, slumped at the head of the table, just shook his head. He saw where this was heading.

Then, something snapped in the new kid. Without warning, his words curdled into something worse, a sharp insult about the trouble-maker's family that no one heard clearly but which cut too deep.

Before anyone could react, he reached across the table, and his fist connected solidly with the new guy's jaw. The table tilted as he fell back, a trickle of blood blossoming at the corner of his mouth.

Stunned silence turned into a roar of chaos. Food went flying as men surged to their feet, some holding back the seething proby, others trying to restrain the troublemaker, who, in his blind rage, seemed ready to do real damage. The chairs scraped back harshly, the room filled with yells and curses.

It was the captain, a veteran of a thousand heated squabbles, who brought the melee to a halt. His bellow cracked across the chaos, and men who could face down infernos reluctantly backed down. One, chest still heaving, glared at the other, who stared back with defiance. It was an ugly tableau.

"What the hell is wrong with you two?" The captain's voice was deceptively calm, but its underlying growl chilled the room. This wasn't just a breach of discipline, it was a breaking of the brotherhood. "My office. Both of you. NOW."

They spent the rest of that tour scrubbing walls and floors, punish-ment doled out swiftly and silently. Later, in the quiet of the bunk room, whispers rippled: this wasn't just a dust-up; this was a crack in their foundation. It would take more than a couple hours of elbow grease to repair it.

The Wayward Chauffeur

The firehouse thrummed with a mix of frustration and simmering anger. Getting beaten to a job, especially twice in a single tour, was both embarrassing and potentially dangerous. Lives could hang in the moments lost fumbling for directions. And tonight, tempers were already strained thanks to the relief chauffeur, a grizzled Vietnam vet, who seemed more at home on a battlefield than navigating the twisting city streets.

First, they'd gotten turned around responding to a rubbish fire, smelling smoke long before a ladder truck, sirens wailing, sped past them. Then, on a more serious structure alarm, they'd gotten lost in a maze of one-way streets, watching hopelessly as another engine beat them by precious minutes.

After the second mishap, back in the cramped kitchen, tension boiled over.

"Come on, man, get it together!" somebody yelled. Another, usually the most easygoing of the guys, finally lashed out. "My grandmother could read a map better than this!"

The chauffeur bristled, years of combat instincts flaring. "Maybe some respect for your elders, rookie? Did they teach you anything down at the academy beside polishing that helmet."

One insult triggered another, voices overlapping in a rising cacophony. It was someone else, a brawny firefighter with a notoriously short fuse, who delivered the final blow. "Come on, put up or shut up. Let's settle this outside like men."

What followed was brutal and swift. They tumbled out the firehouse doors and onto the cracked sidewalk. He, younger and bulkier, swung first, but Frank, the chauffeur, countered with the honed reflexes of a soldier. Then, there was a flash of pain, a muffled shout, and the short fuse was on the ground, clutching his eye.

The chauffeur stalked back inside, not a triumphant victor, but a man grimly satisfied a point had been made. An unsettling hush fell over the firehouse. Then, like a pot boiling over, the captain exploded into the kitchen. He didn't need details to know what had transpired.

His enraged bellow cracked through the quiet. "What in the hell…?" The rest was lost in a curse as his gaze fell on the guy, grimacing. He grabbed a half-empty mug of stale coffee and hurled it against the wall, the ceramic shattering as muddy spray scattered across the apparatus floor.

"Now clean up your damn mess!" His voice echoed harshly, eyes darting to each man. It was less about the lost coffee and more about the lost discipline. Tonight, a fundamental rule had been broken – firefighter against firefighter – and the captain wasn't about to let that slide. They spent the rest of the night scrubbing and polishing, their silence even louder than the captain's earlier rage.

THE CITY'S FORGOTTEN

Twenty calls before noon, and that didn't count the walk-up who thought a leaky faucet qualified as a major flood. City streets baked in the relentless July sun, and they dripped sweat instead of water, grimy uniforms sticking to tired bodies. Each clang of the alarm felt like a blow, each scorching sidewalk they pounded drained out another piece of whatever optimism they had left.

That's how they were on the return loop when the shout came. Kid couldn't have been more than seven, all wide, terrified eyes and waving arms. "A man in the park! He's…" The shout trailed off, the gravity a lead weight hitting them right alongside their exhaustion.

The playground's a splash of tired color midst the gray. Jungle gyms painted peeling blue, rusted swings, one lone basketball bouncing through the usually busy court. A handful of kids stare from afar, suddenly somber in the bright light. And there, on the ground, along the back fence…he lies. Still and impossibly small, dressed in that ragged overcoat like some bizarre joke about seasons. Death's stillness hung in the air.

They know. Even before that brief pulse check, they know. The smell, that sour-sick odor of neglect, is as telling as any monitor read-out. The city symphony blares through radios, oblivious. A siren echoes far down the street, but for this man, their race was against a far grimmer clock.

Anger was the first flare of emotion. Red-hot and visceral. "Nobody saw him?"

Someone turns on the kids. Usually, it's banter, maybe teasing them about being brave firefighters someday. Now, my voice scrapes low in the summer heat. "You see him this morning? Anyone check?"

They shrug, silent. One girl with tear tracks tracing through the playground dirt finally whispers, "thought he was resting. Lotsa fellas rest there." They worked quietly to shield the scene, to respect the body of someone forgotten by the world. In that moment, their uniforms felt inadequate, a painful reminder of how much they couldn't fix.

Resting is what you call it here. Resting off a bender, resting away a fever, resting until someone had the kindness to drag your broken form home…or the indignity of calling an ambulance for another unclaimed lost soul.

"You see something wrong?" one guy rasps out, staring hard at the kids, trying to make it a lesson for life, or one for their own aching consciences. "You say somethin'. Yeah?"

But what good are lessons to kids in a city this unforgiving? They learn fast – to turn away, to let things lie, to see only what doesn't directly disrupt their small slice of life in the harshness of all the concrete they call home.

He had a name, the man. Someone's brother, maybe, or son. Or perhaps, the worst outcome of all, he was a nobody to anyone.

Back at the firehouse, meals turn to ash in their mouths. It's the not knowing that cuts deepest. Was he homeless? Or someone with a family somewhere, a wife, maybe kids of his own, who simply stumbled and never got up? And did some mother go from worrying and pacing to the icy shock of a knock on the door that night? Questions with no answers, because in this city, sometimes there isn't anyone left to ask.

A deep sense of unease settled. Could they train a city full of children to look beyond the basketball game and see the people – the ones at the margins, the ones falling through the gaps? That question sat, stubborn and accusatory, long after the man was taken away.

THE DIVORCE

The strain wasn't just in the firehouse, it bled into homes, whispered arguments behind closed doors, and strained smiles before kids were tucked into bed. For the firefighters' spouses, every ring of the phone might be a harbinger of disaster. Every news report of a fire was a frantic search for familiar faces among the flashing lights.

She knew the rhythm of this life as well as her husband did. In the early years, there was a thrill mingled with the worry – his stories of rescues and close calls kept her on the edge of her seat. But as time and children ground them down, the balance between excitement and terror tipped sharply.

She'd lie awake with each noise, picturing him swallowed by a burning building, every muffled boom making her heart jump into her throat. His odd hours meant snatched conversations over cold dinners, kids vying for attention alongside the ever-present TV. And always, there was the unspoken fear that one day, it would be the worst kind of knock on their own door.

The house felt empty even when he was home. He was either bone-tired and unreachable, or jittery with adrenaline, an unseen fire flick-ering in his eyes. Their conversations grew stilted; she was afraid to voice her worry, and he had no words to describe the horrors he held within.

Then there were the missed moments. The school plays he never caught, the birthdays celebrated late and halfheartedly, the arguments sparked by exhaustion on both sides. They were drifting, two ships tethered by thin filaments of fading love and the stubborn hope that somehow, things would change.

The fights started innocently enough – a snippy remark after a restless night, a forgotten anniversary that cut deeper than anyone intended. Each clash chipped away at their love, the tension from the firehouse bleeding into their sanctuary. Eventually, the only heat between them was fueled by anger and despair.

Sometimes, divorce notices arrived along with promotions and commendations, the irony almost as bitter as the tears shed in lonely kitchens. The weight of the badge carried over into their personal lives, crushing intimacy. What chance did love have against a foe this brutal, this insatiable?

Not every firefighters' marriage crumbled, of course, not by a long shot. Some found strength in the shared understanding, a kind of unspoken covenant against the chaos. But for many, the job wasn't just a career, but a slowly eroding force. Like some invisible chemical, it ate away at the foundation of their relationships until there was just too much damage to repair.

His house had always been a boisterous whirlwind. Kids of all ages tumbled and played, and even a shouting match was usually followed by a spontaneous singalong. That energy hadn't faded, but somewhere along the line, it curdled into something less cheerful. Now, with 11 children ranging from wailing infant to defiant teenager, the old house seemed filled with the constant echo of chaos.

He was a firefighter through and through. The job gave him purpose, an undeniable rush. But at home, he was adrift. The weight of all those mouths to feed, all those eyes constantly needing his attention, overwhelmed him. And at the bottom of an increasingly empty bottle, he found his escape.

It started as a beer to unwind after a particularly tough tour. Then two, then three. Eventually, he was sneaking sips on slow days at the firehouse, stashing half-full bottles in his locker with a grim sort of determination.

His wife loved him fiercely. There was still a flash of the young girl behind the tired eyes, the one who'd fallen for his easy smile and unwavering sense of responsibility. But now, that responsibility seemed to crush him. They tried. They went to counseling, but the silent chasm grew – him on one side, his demons on the other, and Maggie struggling desperately to keep some kind of order for their sprawling brood.

Then came the inevitable: the arguments, slurred and ugly, late nights where he didn't come home at all, and the morning afters filled with hollow promises. Each crack deepened the fault lines of their lives. There was no single breaking point, but rather a slow, agonizing crumbling. Eventually, she simply…couldn't do it anymore.

Their parting was quiet, an almost apologetic acceptance of defeat. He moved into a tiny apartment above a pub, a fittingly solitary existence for a fallen hero. She soldiered on, the kids becoming her battleground, her purpose. There were tears and hushed explanations, then life continued with a hollow, gaping space where he should have been.

They had the typical visitation, every other weekend when he was off duty, where he tried to cram years of fatherhood into two chaotic days. But something was fundamentally broken. Without her to steer them, the visits descended into a mix of sugar-fueled mania and simmering resentments. He couldn't be the dad they all deserved, and they couldn't love the ghost of the man he used to be.

They grew up. It's what kids do, with or without a parent. But there were graduations marked by awkward handshakes, weddings where empty chairs stood as an accusation. As he stumbled through a haze of alcohol, he carried not just the trauma of the job, but a different sort of wound – the slow-motion tragedy of 11 kids slowly, but inevitably, growing up without a father.

THE FIRE INSIDE

The scent hung in the air, not the sharp sting of fire-charred wood, but an even more insidious threat. Alcohol – sometimes blatant, other times masked by a hasty splash of mouthwash. Every officer knew the smell, a sign of a battle fought on two fronts: against the raging blazes, and the slow burn of inner demons.

For some, it was a way to dull the horrors witnessed on the job, to blot out the recurring image of charred bodies, the screams etched into memory. For others, it was the siren call of escapism, a way to numb the relentless adrenaline rushes, the fractured rest, the gnawing knowledge that any call could be their last.

The captain was as vigilant against this unseen enemy as he was against structural collapses. A grizzled veteran with too many funerals etched into his memory, he'd seen how easily lives could unravel even off-duty. A warning – sometimes stern, sometimes with a heavy hand on a slumped shoulder – at the first whiff of trouble. This wasn't about punishment; it was about a desperate attempt at preservation.

His warnings fell on mixed ground. Some men heeded them, seeking solace in healthier ways, even turning to those in-house counseling sessions the fire department was grudgingly starting to recognize as a need. Others simply got better at hiding the problem, pushing their limits until that inevitable slip-up.

Then there was this one guy. Young, a natural firefighter, and utterly out of control. It started with beers to celebrate close calls and spiraled into shots swallowed at dive bars well past the point when most firefighters were catching a few uneasy hours of rest. Rumors swirled before any officer took notice – stories of reckless calls, and erratic behavior. Yet there was Peterson the brave, saving lives one tour, drowning them the next day.

It wasn't the fire that claimed him, but the invisible war waged within. His death sparked a somber reckoning in the firehouse. The captain doubled down on vigilance, forcing even the reluctant ones to see that a hidden bottle was no badge of toughness, but a ticking time-bomb. His words, usually curt and practical, grew heavy. "Don't let his last call be to pick up your body."

Some would never listen. For too many, the lure of a drink after a grueling tour would always eclipse the threat of self-destruction. The line between self-medicating and succumbing to oblivion was shockingly thin. It was a constant struggle – keeping the booze out of the firehouse wasn't just about maintaining order, but a desperate race against a different kind of blaze, one that consumed a firefighter from the inside out.

THE LOFT JUMP

U p on the roof, we moved with the grim choreography of a thousand firefights. Chop of axes against tar, hiss of the Partner Saw…all with the relentless pulse of adrenaline in our ears. Below, concealed by thick smoke, the beast gnawed its way through old floors and who-knows what those old loft workshops housed.

We were its counterpoint, carving escape routes for the heat and smoke with each brutal swing. It was a calculated fight, not reckless bravery. Get the damned roof open, let the heat and poison vent skywards, give the guys pushing back the flames on the floors below a fighting chance.

Then, that sickening lurch. Not an earthquake, but something bone-deep in the building itself. Cracks snaked outwards, widening with horrifying rapidity. Over the handie-talkie radio, the message crackled with an urgency that iced our blood:

"Mayday! Collapse! Get out, repeat, evacuate! "The roof team looked at each other in frozen horror. The fire escape was on the far side of the roof, already beginning to twist and bend in the intense heat. Beyond that, the ladder truck stood as their only other line to safety — now impossibly far across a sea of angry flames.

"Cap," someone gasped, the terror choking his words. "What do we do?"

He glanced at the adjoining building to the right, the one connected to theirs by a treacherous gap. Its flat roof lay ten feet below, with only a chain-link fence on the far side acting as a meager safety net.

"We jump," Ramirez barked, his gaze unflinching. "That's the only way."

One by one, with prayers mumbled between gritted teeth, they leapt. Two firefighters crashed hard on the neighboring roof, cries of pain confirming shattered ankles. The captain was last. He took a running start and vaulted over the abyss. The impact jarred his entire body, and then a wave of scorching pain seared through him as his torso slammed into the rusty chain-link. A gasp tore from his lungs. He clung precariously to the metal, legs inches away from dangling over the yawning drop. With a grunt of superhuman effort, he rolled his body over, just ahead of the collapsing loft that would have become a roaring tomb for everything left inside.

Someone called on the radio, voice choked. No heroics, just the flat statement of fact. Two busted ankles on the jump. Guys wincing but standing on battered limbs. This wasn't about clean getaways; it was the brutal calculus of a job where any escape route could kill you or save you to suffer another day.

The Lieutenant's Choice

The smell of smoke clung to their bunker gear long after the flames were extinguished. They had just pulled a family from a burning row house, and though all survived, the images wouldn't easily recede – charred furniture, desperate tears, a child's scorched, beloved teddy bear lying abandoned on the sidewalk. Every man bore the silent burden of what they had seen, the adrenaline masking the cracks starting to form.

Their lieutenant was a temporary fill-in, covering for their unit's regular officer for a handful of tours. He'd had a reputation as an off the rails individualist, the type who never read the Rules and Regulations. Then as they trudged back to the firehouse that grim day, something in him shifted.

He didn't say much as they went through the post-fire rituals, the cleaning of gear, the filling out of endless reports. His gaze flickered across the faces of his men, noticing the haunted tightness around their eyes, the hollow silence that lingered after the job's usual rush faded.

Then, with a curt nod, he broke routine. "Anyone feel like… decompression? Bar's next door."

It was a blatant breach of procedure. Drinking alcohol was an absolute no-no, not just because of obvious liability issues, but it created a breeding ground for deeper problems. The firefighters glanced at each other in uneasy surprise. Yet, in that shared look, an unspoken under-standing passed between them. Even the most disciplined among them could see the potential cracks in their armor widen.

They stumbled into the dimly lit bar, a stark contrast to the blazing house they had just left. Beers went from hesitant sips to long, thirsty gulps. Conversations started slow, about everything and nothing, before cautiously circling closer to the fire, the images replaying behind their eyes.

There were no heroic confessions, no bragging. Just the raw weight of shared experience, spoken and unspoken. As the drinks flowed, something eased. It wasn't a resolution, it wasn't healthy in the long run, but in that moment, with a lieutenant bending the rules for them, there was a kind of grim acknowledgment of the horrors they held at bay.

The captain was furious when he found out. Yet, beneath the predictable rant, he saw a silent plea in the lieutenant's eyes. Instead of disciplinary action, the captain quietly called the manpower desk. A simple statement – "This man can't cover at our unit again" – left no room for argument. The lieutenant was discreetly reassigned, and no official reprimand went into his file. The captain never even needed to explain. Sometimes, compassion meant bending rules to prevent some-thing far worse from breaking. And the lieutenant, maybe for the first time, seemed to realize it wasn't the ignoring of regulations that made a good officer, but a deeper level of understanding that existed some-where in that hazy space between a stiff drink and the lingering ghosts of another fire.

THE PHOTOGRAPHER

The rig rattled through the Bronx, engine growling under the sticky weight of a July night. Sweat pooled beneath my shirt, mirroring the damp sheen on the streets outside.

Pierre, the photographer, hunched in the back. One hand death-gripped a battered camera, the other bouncing nervously on his knee. Not our typical passenger, that was for sure.

"First time doing this, huh? Ride-along, in the Bronx?" someone asked him.

"Yes," he offered a smile, sweat already dappling his forehead. "But I hear, is very…authentic."

Right on cue, we got the call. Reports of a rubbish fire, some big tenement where they pack folks in like sardines but twice as smelly. Dispatch barely finished speaking before I slammed on the siren, voice whooping over the loudspeaker. The city blurred and shifted as we pushed the truck hard.

We screeched to a halt. The crowd in the building's courtyard wasn't so much a riot as a party gone sideways. Hundreds of bodies spilling into the space, salsa blasting from some busted-up radio, kids chasing each other. But there was an edge under the laughter, the way everyone's eyes tracked us. Pierre was out the door before I could say anything, camera already raised.

"Hey!" I scrambled after him, my chauffeur close on my heels. "Pierre, maybe wait…"

His first camera flash burst, stark and unyielding against the orange glow of streetlights.

Just like that, it turned. I've seen it dozens of times – that animal instinct flash when a crowd feels cornered. Yelling, a thrown beer bottle that smashed harmlessly at a wall. A surge forward. And in that sudden sea of angry faces – knives. Glints of cheap metal in the night, nothing fancy, but damn sure dangerous.

My training kicked in – voice booming, hands raised, trying to deescalate. That's the real job more than anything – talking someone down is worth ten times tackling them. It wasn't just the crowd, either. One hand was clamped on Pierre's shoulder, urging him back.

"Listen, man," I hissed once things were simmering and not boiling over, "this isn't a postcard. You can't treat this like some kind of safari, huh?"

His face paled under the accusation. "I am professional! Showing life as it is…"

"This isn't 'life as it is' for them," I snapped back. "They see some guy with a camera, they see you taking without asking, like they're just…an exhibit."

We finally calmed them down, smoothed things over with the building's unofficial super, someone these folks would actually listen to. Pierre stood by, chastened.

"Look," I said, softer now. "These people, they haven't had life easy. Struggle and hustle every damn day. They aren't objects in a photo. Get that? If you want to tell their story, you gotta earn the right. With respect, not just a fancy camera."

By the time we were back in the truck heading toward the next call, he just nodded. Maybe he heard me, maybe he didn't, but in his eyes, I saw something flickering anyway…maybe the start of understanding.

THE TIRED CHAUFFEUR

The clang of firehouse boots on worn concrete floor was the soundtrack of my life. Twenty-seven years of it, from green rookie to Chief. Not that you couldn't count those hours in sweat and scars, too. It'd wear down most folks, but something inside me always got refueled when that damned voice alarm screeched.

Except…there's the kind of bone-deep tired, where rest does damn-all. One weekend when I was a captain was like that – three tenements gone up like matchsticks, a chemical spill down by the highway, more car wrecks than I could count. Just me and the team, pushing as hard as we could until "response" wasn't a choice, it was reflex.

Even the endless mugs of firehouse coffee wouldn't cut through the fog in my head. Paperwork blurred, guys asking questions I kept needing repeated – it was embarrassing. Still, you push on, right?

That's when he showed up in the doorway of my cramped office. Kid looked worse than some of the survivors we hauled out this week. Usually bright eyes dull, jaw set in that stubborn line I recognized even as a rookie myself. He was good behind the wheel, steady nerves you could count on.

"Cap," he cleared his throat, and that's when I really started to get worried, "Cap, no way I can drive anymore." The words echoed in the quiet like a hammer falling. He kept going, though. Didn't wait for an answer. "Arms feel like lead," he admitted. "Tried grabbing a catnap between calls, hands wouldn't stop shaking. Messed up nearly backing into a hydrant. Can't risk that, not me."

Now, there's that pride young firefighters got, and I am not one to crush it. But even pride's got limits. And I saw more than exhaustion in his face. Saw the fear that maybe he wasn't cut out for this. That's a whole other nightmare to wrestle with.

I stood, forcing my aching joints to obey. "Damn right, you can't risk it. And no one with an ounce of sense will think any less of you for being smart, kid." I saw him relax just a fraction, even under the crushing weight of that near-confession. "I got another chauffeur. Take yourself downstairs, get some real rest. Hell, get them arms rested."

"But Cap…" he started to protest, that ingrained dedication kicking back in.

I cut him off. "That wasn't a suggestion, son. An order. You can drive when you're fit to drive, not a moment sooner. Understand?"

The nod was almost too slow, but he squared his shoulders and turned to go. Then, just before he pushed through the door, he paused. "Thanks, Cap," he mumbled, voice thick. "For, y'know, under-standing."

"Not all battles are fought with hoses and axes," I said quietly. His back was to me, but I'd bet my pension he was smiling just a bit. You didn't last in this place if you didn't learn a thing or two about strength beyond muscle.

Paperwork

The rank comes with some privileges: less hauling equipment in a burning building, more strategizing the fight. What they don't mention in the brochures is that with it comes a different kind of weight.

The exhausted hum of the firehouse never truly goes away. Even in those small, snatched hours I call rest – that never really feels like rest – there's always a sense of dread coiled tight. The next bell. The next scream over the dispatch radio. That split-second choice that could tip the scale between heroism and heartbreaking loss.

Sure, the guys got it hard. Running into fiery buildings, pulling folks from wrecked cars…it eats away at a man in ways a medal will never fix. Yet, the officers – we catch hell from both sides. There's the heat from downtown. Bosses who've barely seen a real fire in their lives, barking up the chain of command on response times and incident reports that look neat on a boardroom spreadsheet.

They never factor in the endless variables. The traffic snag that delays deployment by precious minutes. The old lady refusing to abandon her burning building without her damn cat. The sheer, raw exhaustion that gnaws at my men by hour twelve of a twenty-four-hour tour. We're supposed to be superheroes, not mortals with limits. The higher-ups don't want to hear excuses, only results.

Then, there are the men I command. Their tired eyes, a trust placed squarely in my decisions. My heart twists seeing them stretch past breaking point, the weight of that command pressing into my spine. We all share those harrowing moments: flames devouring homes, the metallic smell of blood mixing with smoke. But their burden drops when they get back to the firehouse. Mine keeps growing.

Midnight oil burning in the office as I finish paperwork – there's always paperwork. Reports, justifications, endless forms about equipment we desperately need…forms I sign while replaying scenes of the latest emergency. I'm an officer, but also a clerk, a medic, a damn counselor because when your crew runs on adrenaline and instinct there's often trauma left unspoken. Each line typed out in this cramped room might mean another man is a touch safer next time. I owe them that.

A shadow lingers at my doorway. One of the lieutenants, eyes heavy with concern. It's not the first time I've been found hunched over the keyboard at an ungodly hour.

"You need rest, Cap." Not a shout, more like a quiet plea.

"This report isn't going to write itself," I grumble back, trying for a smirk that probably looks more like a grimace.

Rest. They always tell me to rest. That easy fix for a man running on grit and bitter coffee. But the mental ticker tape won't stop scrolling. Each near-miss, each decision to take a risk or play it safe – they cycle through my mind, gaining power in the stillness. If, because of this endless stack of paper, tomorrow they get home in one piece…if it makes someone, somewhere just a little safer…then what are a few lost hours of rest anyway?

THE CAR CRASH

The call crackled over the radio, deceptively routine, just another car accident. But on this occasion there was an icy edge in the dispatcher's voice. Stolen car? High-speed pursuit? The energy coursing through the rig was different this time – grim anticipation hanging heavy alongside the usual adrenaline surge.

The scene greeted them in a chaotic mess: overturned metal screeching against asphalt, crumpled like an abandoned soda can. The stench of gasoline and burnt rubber was choking. The chief, a veteran hardened by decades of seeing the worst, felt a surge of dread unlike any before. Five kids – that's what the dispatcher had relayed. Joyriding. Just kids.

The extraction was brutal. Steel groaned as jaws of life twisted through the wreckage, prying open space where mangled bodies were entangled. Each piece of the car seemed to hold a piece of a life that ended way too soon. The rookie firefighter, with heart and determination far outstripping his experience, held steady for the first two – their stillness eerily contradicting the violent chaos of the scene.

Then came the third body. It was something about the mangled leg, the tilt of the head, the too-small sneakers. He backed away.

This job...with each horrific scene, it devoured a piece of your soul. They didn't teach you that in the academy. No manual outlined the right way to swallow back the bile, to blink away the image of a kid's broken body. All the slogans about duty and bravery felt hollow against that brutal landscape of wasted lives.

Later, back at the firehouse, the debrief was coldly practical. Equipment replaced, reports meticulously filed. There was no comforting pat on the shoulder, no space to process the horror. In this line of work, that was considered weakness. It was understood you just sucked it up. Get tough or get out. But those unspoken rules made the weight even heavier.

That night, under the pretense of exhaustion, he forced himself to rest. The faces of the dead teens in the car haunted his dreams. But beneath that was another gnawing fear: what if tomorrow was too similar? Could he find the strength to carry this burden again and again, without support, knowing each gruesome scene eroded another piece of his spirit?

WORLD'S BUSIEST

The magazine, a wonderful glossy testament to all that gritty exhaustion we call daily life. *World's Busiest Firehouse*, the headline screamed. Inside, they laid bare the numbers the city brass was always so damn afraid of; the relentless alarm bells, the stacked calls back-to-back, the sheer density of people and problems crammed into those few blocks of the Bronx.

Pride? There was a flicker of that, sure. Vindication maybe, for those times when some suit at HQ called us lazy, overstaffed, and under-worked. But mostly, it felt like lighting a flare across a battle-field just as night starts to fall.

First, they trickled in, then it turned into a flood. Fire buffs. You got your different levels of those folks. Some are harmless, wide-eyed kids eager for a story and an autograph. Then there's the obsessive kind, gearheads geeking out on our truck specs, or those who memorize alarm box locations and practically beat us to the scene for a front-row show at the next fire.

Suddenly, every Joe with a scanner thought he deserved a ticket on the ride-along express. It'd be one thing if it slowed down after the article faded from memory. But then, we got that damned T-shirt. Some bright spark from the house got those printed up – *World's Busiest* –

like it was a souvenir you snatched from Disney and not testament to an endless grind.

Wham. Firehouse tourism just exploded. Busloads would literally pull up outside, snapping endless pictures like we were just more urban blight to gawk at. The sidewalk got permanently clogged with wannabe junior firefighters peppering us with questions. Every other day brought someone pleading for a look inside, a peek at "where the action is."

I get the fascination. They want that thrill, the glimpse behind the scenes. Curiosity's got no respect for rhythm and routine.

Being featured in *Firehouse Magazine* was a double-edged sword. Sure, it wasn't always easy being the *World's Busiest* firehouse. The constant action meant less downtime, and filling out incident reports after another long shift could feel endless. But there was also a sense of pride in that title. *Firehouse Magazine* recognized the dedication of our guys, showcasing our work on a national stage. It brought awareness to the challenges we faced — challenges that firefighters across the country could relate to. While a few moments of peace would've been a welcome change, the recognition from *Firehouse Magazine* also fueled a sense of camaraderie with our fellow firefighters everywhere.

Going Down the Chimney

The Mayday crackled through the radio, sharp enough to cut through the shouts of fleeing occupants. It wasn't just a plea for help. It was a name, a face, one of our own – gone. Everything shifted at that moment. The building became a beast, the thick black smoke not just an obstacle, but a shroud.

The chief's words sliced into me. "You gotta get down there."

That enclosed basement staircase morphed before my eyes. Every concrete step, a descent into a roaring kiln. But it wasn't just fear for me – it was a bone-deep terror for whoever was lost down there.

My order to the guys felt automatic, "follow me ", yet it vibrated with an urgency I had never tapped into before. It was primal. Masks on, tight around my face, no more breaths of fresh air. Each gasp through the regulator sounded like a countdown tick against the missing firefighter's life.

Down we went, a blind line of men crawling against the inferno. We followed the hose – our lifeline – its presence a weak reassurance against the hell below. The first taste of heat was like a hot poker against exposed skin. Then it seeped deeper, under turnout gear, prickling and blistering as we moved further in. Smoke swirled, not just filling lungs, but the world itself. I couldn't see my own hand in front of my face, let alone a fallen comrade.

We reached the nozzle, the end of the line, the apartment door warped and screaming from the heat behind it. "Keep it closed – don't let it lock!" My own voice sounded tinny inside my mask. Then those burning hands, searing against the knob, pain lancing up my arm as I searched. It wasn't my strength, but that damned fear, that desperate knowledge that seconds made the difference. We must have crawled right over that guy in the hallway, missing him in the thick smoke, but someone found him, thank God.

Fire blasted back as the door edged open. I shoved it further, yelled for another man on the nozzle. It took forever, a warped eternity of flames and coughing fits until water overwhelmed the burning. Just then our air ran out. But we had to go on and finish what we started.

In the sputtering half-light, we move deeper. Finished the job with a last burst of water.

When they got him out, he was barely breathing, that precious air gone too long. I'd never truly dwelt on that word on the radio until that moment – how close those men who share my patch come to death in a baptism of fire like this.

He was taken to the hyperbaric chamber, healing smoke ravaged lungs. This victory came dear.

The fear…you don't get over that. I'd be a damn fool not to feel it lurking deep under my skin. But it isn't a weakness. That heat on my burned ears, it lingers too, a fierce reminder. What stays is an image of that guy, opening his eyes after so close a call. They didn't find words there, just a shared look – gratitude and something that's even deeper than friendship forged in ordinary ways. Maybe the courage isn't about snuffing out fear, but the choice to crawl towards it anyway because there's someone depending on you.

THE FIREPROOF HI-RISE

That alarm hits like a physical blow, rattling your bones. But there's this switch that flips within you – muscle memory kicking in. Not calm, but…focused. Like every call before, it's a battle in a box, the variables stacking up: forty-five stories. Standpipe, and not sprinklered. Fireproof, yeah, but that just means the building won't go, people still will. Calls coming in from as far away as Manhattan. Gonna be a good one.

We move in time to the chaos, rhythm honed from sweat and practice. Hands already working the gear, not thinking, just doing. That damn standpipe bag's an anvil with its wrenches and couplings, every step up to the entrance another blow, but you don't dare linger.

Then it's the damn elevator – that box of terror and trust. Every groan of the cables ratcheting up tension. Cramming in – engine men, roll-ups, forcible entry team, officers – shoulder to shoulder, eyes flickering between the floor numbers…33, 34…and the faces of your guys. Use the fireman's key to take control of the elevator – if it works. No words, just that tight set of a jaw, that same tired flame in the eyes.

Stop below the fire, always two floors below. Safety margin against it stopping at the fire floor. It hits harder there in the stillness before the storm: the faint echo of yells, the scent of charred metal riding the breeze through open shafts. Then it's boots hitting the floor, adrenaline shoving down the ache in your back.

Hook-up at the standpipe on the floor below is routine – hose couplings biting into fingers, wrench clatter like gunfire. Voices boom over the radio, but they're background. Water surges as water is called for. Bleed the line. The line comes alive, and suddenly, everything's on fast-forward.

Out onto the fire floor. Every cough brings ash-flecked spit if your mask is hanging loose. Sweat turns cold as you inch towards that heat. Find the right door, and there it is – the beast itself, that smoke-billowing hallway transforming into a hellish cavern. Crawl…the only way now, flames searing the ceiling, licking overhead. It's all touch, the sting of searing tiles on a skinned knee nothing against the fear crawling down your spine. Test the nozzle – relief flooding when that water's there.

Pop the door and it's like staring into a furnace. In. In. No looking back now – there's life in there, maybe. Search team snakes in the flickering half-light, checking dark corners where fear turns to flesh and bone. Extension…always looking for that flicker behind a wall, that hidden ember waiting to break loose. Each shout over the radio is a heartbeat, sometimes of pure triumph, sometimes…not. And through it all, that hose in your hands, your anchor in the chaos, spitting back heat like a cornered animal.

And the aftermath…that's when the weight slams down. Not when the flames turn to soggy remnants and the cheers fade. It's that heavy quiet on the way down, bodies spent more than exhilarated. It's the look you avoid in the mirrored walls of the elevator because, by now, who stares back is part machine, the humanity hidden under char and the lingering stink of extinguished desperation. The aftermath is those unanswered calls that stick in your craw, the ones buried by an unforgiving clock, and the knowing that tomorrow, that alarm will crackle into life all over again.

TUFFY BRADY

Brady didn't just walk into a room, he filled it. A giant even among us firefighters, with shoulders so broad it looked like he carried the damn buildings on his back. No fancy tool could match that raw power in his frame. Tenement door gone stubborn? Brady just put his head down, feet braced, butt against the door, and that whole wall shuddered with each heave. The crack of ancient hinges and door locks gave way like a gunshot, wood no match for that force of nature.

We used to joke he was some kind of Norse god in disguise, that there was fire instead of blood in his veins. Not entirely wrong, as it turned out. It started subtly – that sharp smell of beer cutting through the morning coffee stink at roll call. Just one can, but in that quiet before everything explodes into noise and action…those little signs shout louder than sirens.

Maybe we all saw but turned a blind eye. Not that it was easy to tell him anything back then. Guy never talked of where that strength came from, what kind of burdens he shouldered under the turnout gear. But burdens…everyone carried those. Every run into another burning tenement building, every life yanked back from the brink…or not…it weighed heavier than even Brady's solid form.

Then it stopped being just one six-pack in the morning. Then it was rumors – a bar fight gone ugly, screaming matches outside his building. Even those granite shoulders started slumping. It gnawed at all of us – that slow-motion crash and burn of a good man eaten from the inside. Nobody wants to pull rank on someone like Brady, even the lieutenant danced around the issue. The Brotherhood and all that, yeah. And there's just some darkness a fellow firefighter knows not to tread alone. But that fire we fight in the streets…he'd chosen a different devil to battle at a point.

One morning, there was just this emptiness where he should have been standing. No explanations, rehab was the whispered word afterwards. One of those upstate clinics tucked away where the city could pretend this was a problem that went away instead of festering under our boots. It never fully does, though.

You'd like to think someone like Brady wins in the end. That strength resurfaces, tempered by those flames into something stronger than before. Maybe he did, maybe he rebuilt somewhere quiet, the scars hidden as deep as the stories he'd never tell. The ghetto…it takes its toll in different ways. That fight never leaves you, changes you. That image stays with me – Brady's broad back, pushing against those stubborn tenement doors. We could break in…but some cracks take more than force, and some demons hide deep down where even a hero might not always reach.

Utility Hole Covers

It wasn't just fires and crumbling buildings we fought every tour. No, in the Bronx, even the damn streets had it out for us. Utility hole covers weren't just innocent bits of urban scenery. They were ticking time bombs waiting for the right moment to send you flying.

Beneath that cracked pavement wasn't just a peaceful maze of sewers and forgotten wires. Down there, some big electrical lines were smoldering. Insulation chewed at by time, gnawed by salt, hungry for one precious gasp of extra oxygen. You'd never even know about them, those unseen coke ovens waiting beneath our boots, till… BOOM.

A blast like a cannon shot, echoing down the block like thunder. Concrete, asphalt, and grit raining down around us, followed by that cursed metallic ping – a cast-iron utility hole cover gone airborne. Those things? They weighed dozens of pounds, but some unseen force could launch them fifty feet in the air. The lucky ones were just deafened for a few hours, feeling that ringing blast wave deep in their guts. The others…well, you didn't think too close on those.

They seemed to never strike twice in the same place, those things, but sometimes a string of them would blow, the noise like a musician following a cheat sheet. The explosion itself released the pressure, and finding the spot of another simmering burnout took time. That didn't mean we could relax. You had to walk like you were stalking a beast: senses constantly honed, eyes sharp for that flicker of smoke, nostrils catching the whiff of burning plastic before it grew stronger.

"Stay off the covers!" It became a barked ritual, repeated by every weary lieutenant. "We have to check all the basements of these buildings for any extension." Not like you could ever completely avoid them, those metal circles dotted along the cracked streets like an insane hopscotch course. Even parking the rig was a gamble – some dormant patch ready to rumble the moment it felt the weight.

It wasn't only the big fires that gave me nightmares. It was that constant tension, the need to treat every step like you were playing roulette with the devil under the city. That split-second flinch every time a car backfired, every time your boots clanged on solid metal. There's a reason we scanned the street just as diligently as the windows for any hint of trouble.

We were like scavengers of a hidden warzone, picking our path through a battlefield we couldn't map. It was draining, exhausting in a way even pulling survivors from a blazing building couldn't match. Fighting an enemy that could strike anywhere, anytime…you don't ever fully win against odds like that. You just learn to dodge it, stay alert, stay alive for one more tour. And pray those unseen flames stay smothered another day.

THE BAKERY LOCKUP

That alarm wasn't just a siren wailing. It was a drumbeat against the thin membrane between sanity and the sheer absurdity of our world. "Fire at a bakery" – it sounded innocent, almost familiar in the way our calls had a twisted normalcy of their own. We rolled with the punches, expecting some oven fire gone wild, an electrical fault…not this.

Smoke didn't lie. Thick and roiling, it poured from every single crack in the old Italian bakery, turning the streets into a choking twilight. But something was off. We'd busted doors and roll-down gates in similar joints before – smoke slamming against them from the inside as heat roared in pursuit. No pounding this time, just a muffled cacophony. Shouts…or was it an old machine of some sort finally deciding to blow?

One glance told me this wasn't just some kitchen fire escalating. Gates. Thick metal rolled shut over every door and window, each secured with padlocks as chunky as your fist. They transformed the place into a damn bunker. My first reaction wasn't heroism, it was pure disgust. Someone was afraid of losing pastries overnight…and that kind of security screams 'innocent lives at stake'.

"Get the saw!" There are moments when that metallic shriek can make a man sing, even if it's a mournful tune. Blades spinning blurred

red under the streetlamp glare. Sparks sketching their fiery path into nothingness. Each lock went flying, and everyone felt like a shackle breaking off our own minds. That desperate yelling wasn't getting quieter, only shifting tone as it became clear there was open air to fill. There was fear in there alright, but a different flavor than you smelled off a trapped victim.

Then, the doors finally flung open – just barely before my boot helped that process. What poured out of that bakery wasn't just men or smoke, it was…desperation made flesh.

No proud Italian figures clutching ancestral dough recipes here. It was six skinny guys, all Spanish, faces smeared not with flour, but soot and terror. Dressed in white aprons, they looked like bakers gone wild, right? Except, when those aprons came off, and we took in the hollowed eyes and trembling limbs, they looked less like kneading dough than punching timecards at a sweatshop under the threat of fire.

This wasn't the first time those flames had been more about punishment than accident. You hear about it, rumors swirling around like greasy gossip – workers locked in by ruthless owners, every cent squeezed out, even if it meant gambling with lives. We put out fires, not wage crusades – a bitter pill to swallow on nights like this. But those unspoken tales became grim badges. Every siren scream, a question we knew no answer could ever really fix. What price bread? What price flour?

In the Bronx, a life could cost less than a burnt loaf. We patched up the cuts from broken glass, settled panicked nerves down from smoke inhalation. The cops called those bakery owners to the scene. Law had a long line in this city, and a short attention span. As sure as little apples the workers scattered into the streets, and whatever meager life awaited was better than burning alive for some miser's pennies.

The scent of char didn't leave our coats for days. We scrubbed down, engines gleaming fresh-washed even against the grimy brick storefronts. Still, I smelled it under everything. A reminder that those unseen fires – fueled by greed, despair, the simple brutality of living on the edge – they were the slowest burn of all.

WHEN DEATH KNEADS THE DOUGH

The bakery alarm had rung out at 3 AM, a harsh note slicing through the rare kind of silence the Bronx only managed for a few hours a night. At that hour, most fires felt almost expected. A kitchen flame out of control, a smoldering electrical fault, food on the stove from a drunk returning home from the local bar…But as I rolled onto the scene, something just felt…off. No licking flames, no panicked chaos. The bakery storefront looked dark, almost peaceful, under the dull glow of streetlights.

Inside, it was cops, not smoke, who greeted us. They'd already cordoned off a makeshift section – two officers leaning over one of those industrial metal mixing bowls with an intensity that had nothing to do with baking. No cadaver in sight, and a nagging unease started crawling its way up my spine.

"Where's the stiff?" My question to the nearest cop echoed hollow in the cavernous kitchen. There was the boss, or owner – looking rattled, not singed. My firefighter brain flicked uselessly through emergency scenarios…gas leak? Electrocution?

The answer was one of those gut-punch moments that you can't train for. "You walked right past him." No dramatic pointing, just a weary statement of fact. I turned…back towards the mixer. Still just that lone figure, slumped awkwardly over the rim, one arm inside the gaping metal bowl. No blood, no fire. Nothing but the sickening hum of the machines in that room and a stillness that made my bones vibrate.

Then, with dawning horror, came the details. The angle of his neck, the dough-covered hand still clenched tight. No struggle, no splash of gore. Just…a man consumed by machinery, caught in that slow-motion trap and pulled in. He'd been alive one moment, reaching for a snag in that batch or scraping down the pieces of raw flour from the sides of the bowl, the last residue maybe, and the next…it was the dough doing the kneading. There's something uniquely horrifying about an object built for creation swallowing something so whole, so quietly.

We shut the power to the machine. I still think about those blades in my nightmares, even though we cleared them in seconds. But it was always those few stolen moments my mind returned – the instant his life ended, that terrible shift from baker to ingredient. My eyes played tricks. That lump under the dough – did it twist just slightly?

Bread's one of those staples. Humble, comforting. After that it all seemed grotesque. Took weeks before I could look at a fresh loaf without picturing that bowl, those blades, the way death can hide in the most ordinary of tasks. I'd seen plenty of violence on the streets, but this…this was something different. Not loud and fiery, but insidious, the way those mixers kept humming after. Like the machinery itself didn't know, or care, what it had just done.

They say "only in New York," like any city can claim tragedy this absurd. But the truth is, the Bronx wasn't a bakery that night. It was a battlefield, with a battlefield's kind of casual brutality. I ate bagels for a long while after that, couldn't stomach sliced bread. Some battles you win, against burning buildings, even bad odds. That morning, even with sirens silenced, and the body taken away, there was only that crushing loss. There are some shadows even a firefighter can't outrun forever.

THE WINDOW FALLOUT

The rumble of the train on the elevated subway line outside wasn't just a backdrop at Engine 75. It was our heartbeat, a gritty drumbeat to the endless days. But that vibration became something sinister: a death rattle for our ancient fortress. Every time a train roared by you didn't just feel it in your bones. You felt it in the crumbling masonry, the ancient wooden window frames that held stubborn glass against the world.

We weren't just facing fires. We were fighting age, decay, and the termites the old place practically bred in its bones. And those termites…city vermin with six legs don't play by the rules we expect from rats. They weren't beady-eyed scavengers scuttling for scraps, but a slow-motion army. Each time a train shook the walls, you'd hear it… a faint crackling, like laughter from under the floorboards. They were gnawing away, not just at the wood, but the very foundations of our refuge.

That big double-hung window in the front office wasn't meant for those modern El monsters. Original to the firehouse, built back when horses pulled the wagons out. And while a hundred years seemed impressive, those years hadn't been kind. Every rattle chipped away at crumbling sashes, weakened frames chewed through by generations of silent invaders. We'd point 'em out to the higher-ups, giant termites grown so fat they could almost be mistaken for rodents. It felt like talking to ghosts…budget shortfalls and all that bureaucratic moaning. It's always tomorrow, tomorrow…until suddenly, it wasn't.

One day, in the midst of the usual rush of pedestrians outside, that 'tomorrow' arrived with a vengeance. They say you always remember where you were when that big moment hits. For me, it was the kitchen…scent of burned coffee in the air, guys trying to act casual around that sweating stove. Then, over the train and street noise, came a sound like a gunshot, and a collective flinch that had nothing to do with our usual line of work.

Silence. That split-second of utter terror where everyone holds their breath. Then the crashing thud, screams from outside, and a rush to the front with that gnawing fear in my gut. There it was, that entire damn window, frame and all, lying midst shattered glass on the sidewalk. Miracle of miracles, nobody hurt. Just dust, some splinters, and that gaping hole looking out – no barrier now between us and the chaos.

They brought new front windows over…eventually. Ripped out from some other aging firehouse getting ready for the wrecking ball. It felt surreal, that secondhand safety netting against the world. You half-expected those replacement frames to come with termites preinstalled, an unwanted bit of firehouse tradition. We never really dealt with the termites. Not properly. Like so many things around the firehouse, you patch, you endure, you pray that next 'tomorrow' isn't the one where everything finally collapses.

Maybe those bugs were a metaphor for a bigger thing. Not the fires – those we could knock down, drag people out of. It was that ever-present gnawing under the surface…that creeping neglect. They didn't need a match or an electrical fault to burn the place down, just indifference, and time. I loved that old firehouse, scars and all. But with every window replaced, every tremor felt beneath my boots, there was a whisper at the back of my mind – how long, really, until the whole structure fails?

MEDAL DAY

Those City Hall medal ceremonies were supposed to be the pinnacle of everything we stood for…firefighting, heroism, all that shiny stuff. Yet, if I'm honest, I remember those rides in the school bus we hired to get us there a lot more clearly than the stuffy formality of it all.

It started early. Not the ceremony, which was 10 AM sharp, when even the toughest guy from the Bronx had to play dress-up in that starchy wool uniform. We weren't used to fancy clothes, but at least it was an excuse to break them in with a couple of discreet beers to cut through the nerves. And that was before boarding that rented yellow monstrosity – like a prop from some warped comedy sketch. Every year, it rattled through the Bronx, loaded with heroes sporting slightly bleary smiles and loosened ties. There were never any empty seats.

With every mile, it transformed. You had your front-of-the-bus guys, mostly officers, swapping stories polished as old silver. The back held the real heart of the units, where boisterous cheers replaced quiet contemplation, and beer cans started magically multiplying between seats.

That machismo…you couldn't bottle it, but damn if it didn't flow freely along those worn aisles. There's a wildness in men after they've faced death and walked away, even for a little while. Not aggression, more like an unleashed energy that civilization can't fully contain. That energy turned every mile marker into another challenge, another tale told louder than the roar of the engine. Medals mattered at some level, yeah, but it was that raw camaraderie in the belly of a school bus that fueled the true heart of our firefighting brotherhood.

Then came the antics; usually on the ride back. It'd start small, an extra raucous song maybe. One year someone decided the roof held superior views, that hatch rattling open over the highway while hearts stopped below. For those ten minutes, we weren't firefighters, not medalists, just a ragged crew daring the world to keep up with our madness. That guy? He clung to the rim like a conquering madman, wind whipping his face, while below we held our breath and counted the exits we hoped we wouldn't have to use. The bus didn't stop. Because stopping on that highway would mean confronting the fact that some guys carry bravery a bit farther than is entirely smart.

We got him down, eventually. Cheers drowned out any scolding, and somehow, those beers tasted even sweeter than on the ride down. At City Hall, we all put on our serious faces, stood at attention, and let those medals get pinned on. Mayor had his speeches, families watched with that mix of pride and fear that was uniquely ours. Then it was back on that bus, a few of us a little wobblier on our feet, but with every roll of the wheels back towards the Bronx, we shed those official honors for the messy truth underneath.

They'd make speeches about courage, how those medals repre-sented an elite crew. The guys on that bus knew otherwise. It was something wilder that couldn't be explained in polite company. Part battle cry, part laughter in the face of everything we battled in those streets. They called it recklessness. For us, it was just…life unleashed, roaring along that highway towards our corner of the Bronx. We didn't win all the fights, sometimes we won despite barely clinging to sanity. That bus ride – we never got a single medal for those, yet sometimes they felt like the greatest victory of all.

Subway Fires

Regular fires were monsters – subway fires were a whole different level of hell. First off, there's that trapped feeling. Above ground, at least you have options; get to a roof, chop through whatever's burning. Down there? Those narrow tunnels and jammed train cars made you feel like an ant running through a maze on fire. The walls weren't just barriers, but an echo chamber for any kind of noise.

That third rail…with those wooden covers it should've been the safest of our worries. Except that ancient timber would go up like kindling if an electric arc danced its way over or it might crumble if you stepped on it and then – boom, your foot hit the third rail. And there was always the nagging doubt – did some higher-up actually cut the power like they were meant to? The MTA guys swore they did, but with their system? Best trust that adrenaline over blind confidence.

Speaking of blind…that's how you fought in those tunnels. Smoke even turned flashlights into pathetic yellow smudges. It clung, slithered, choked off what little air wasn't being devoured by the fire itself. Our standard air tanks gave a pitiful ten minutes if used right. Most of us would be coughing the first five just getting to the heart of the chaos. But hey, better than the old days when some guys gave up on masks altogether – figured choking death came either fast or slow in that heat, might as well see what your eyes could pick out while your throat burnt away.

That desperation was as much our enemy as the flames. You ever tried cutting your way to a fire under the plywood floor of a subway car? No training manual existed for that. Sometimes, the only chance to put the fire out was going full medieval on those million-dollar monsters. Saw roaring, metal screeching as we made our own path to the fire, our own path by cutting the plywood floor...not a damn thought for what those suits at HQ would have to say later. It's hard to worry about property damage when you're gasping breaths between choked cries. That was the nightmare fuel that pushed you through, though.

Then, of course, paperwork. Reports that seemed to take longer to finish than the actual extinguishment. Each cut we made, every panicked face dragged back to a soot-covered platform came with a trail of scribbling and shouted justifications into radios. Those burns barely had time to start stinging before someone up higher demanded details – why this train, why that spot, how much will it cost, why so many men went sick with smoke inhalation. It was just as exhausting, in its own way, as hauling all the gear and the hose line back into the faint glow of safety above ground.

Subway fires left a whole other kind of ache. You never got just that fire smell out of your gear, that underground damp odor mixed with sweat, something like fear. Maybe because when we peeled up a section of those charred floors, it revealed that there's only a thin shell of civilization between our world and something far less forgiving. More lines were opened as rush hour approached. All we saw were shadows dancing against those walls, reminders of just how easily it could've been a funeral parade and not just another commute.

NEW YEAR'S EVE

New Year's Eve and my assignment wasn't battling blazes or pulling some poor partier out of a wreck. Instead of that familiar soot-and-sweat scent clinging to my uniform, I was surrounded by a strange perfume of grease paint and stale velvet. I'd gone from Captain in a firehouse to shadow inspector under Broadway's blinding lights.

See, promotions come at a price. "Covering" meant no regular firehouse, just a nomadic existence plugging gaps all over the city. It was a year or two of being a stranger in your own world, of getting the lay of the land one temporary assignment at a time. Most nights were spent in the Bronx somewhere. But fate has a weird sense of humor even in the FDNY, because tonight…tonight was different.

They'd assigned me to a glittering Broadway stage, a show all about Merlin and his mystical tricks. I felt about as far from the Bronx as you could get. Spotlights replaced sirens, and the air throbbed with a nervous energy that was pure theater, not an impending blaze.

My official guide wasn't some stern building super. Instead, a frazzled stage manager thrust some forms at me to sign before hustling me deeper into the labyrinth beneath, behind and along the sides of the stage. That waiver I signed felt more surreal than a dozen burning tenements – I'd gone from watching for flames, to keeping the secrets of illusions. And there were lots, from floating candles to caged tigers.

It was a night of bizarre contrasts. Standing on creaking floorboards, surrounded by dusty ropes and weights, smelling that mix of sweat and old canvas…yet, midst it all, these flashes of brilliance. A glittering sword appearing from thin air, a dove fluttering out from a supposedly empty box and Merlin rising from the floor, levitating for all to see. I watched it all, less like an inspector seeking flaws, and more like a kid let loose in a magic shop. How could those musicians function in that tiny pit and why so many mattresses under that trap door to the basement?

Met the stars, too. The movie kind, and the tired-eyed magician who sweated buckets to pull off that impossible shine. They saw me for what I was – a guy in an ill-fitting uniform among their flamboyant costumes – yet there was a flicker of respect. One even offered to show me how a simple sleight of hand worked after the show. It turned out fire and magic weren't so different – both demanded precision, hiding the grueling work behind a spectacle that left you breathless.

When the curtain rose and the roar of the crowd swept over the footlights, I went with that stage manager for the entire show and watched all the illusions go down. My job was far less glamorous than theirs for sure. Checking to make sure the flash powder and pyrotechnics were used correctly felt absurd after watching levitations. Yet, as that audience laughed and gasped, I patrolled the perimeter, watching for signs of real danger.

It was a New Year's Eve unlike any other. No family, no fireworks over the Bronx. But even as I missed the comforting chaos of home, there was a different warmth here. Not just the packed house, but a quiet satisfaction. Those illusions I'd witnessed were crafted with care, not carelessness, and my presence was a tiny part of making that magic safe. It wasn't the kind of heroism that makes headlines, but later, as that clock ticked towards midnight, I raised an unseen glass midst the ropes and shadows. Here's to protecting the show, to keeping dreams alive in a city that could sometimes feel like a battlefield. Maybe there's magic in that, too, and on this night, that was enough.

Between the Skyline
and the Bedrock

The bragging right was a quiet one, not shouted over burnt coffee in a firehouse, but a truth echoing in my boots when they hit pavement. They say only birds see New York like this, all sprawling concrete and reaching spires. Me, I'd seen it from the extremes most folks barely imagined. A thousand feet up, and then a thousand feet down. Same city, two different worlds that held my breath hostage at different points.

Let's talk about that roof first. The World Trade Center wasn't a welcoming place then, just raw steel against an unforgiving sky. I was 'covering', filling in the blanks in my officer training, when that assignment landed. It felt like climbing into an unfinished sketch, the wind biting where guardrails should have been. No admiring the view through neat windows, just the vastness of the city laid bare and me clinging to a piece of machinery on that roof with white knuckles.

The fear wasn't just about falling. It was seeing just how fragile our mark on the world could be from up there. Cars shrunk down to scurrying beetles, the familiar grid of streets suddenly flimsy. I wasn't a spiritual guy, but something shifted in my gut, that deep respect for the forces I usually fought head-on, not witnessed from up high. The wind howled like a warning, and down below, life seemed to be moving at an impossible speed.

Then came the tunnels. Going down was scarier, not in a plummeting kind of way, but that slow-motion descent into the unknown. The construction elevator clung to a cable so thin it felt more like a spider's thread than a lifeline. Each jerk and clang echoed louder than any engine roar, bouncing off damp rock walls closing in as we descended.

That first cavern, three hundred feet down, was like dropping into the belly of the city. It was the distribution chamber. They said it could hold St. Patrick's Cathedral, and it felt that way. Echoes skittered off the unfinished walls, men flitting like ants around scaffolding and the exposed veins of the place – pipes, cables, that dripping that felt unnervingly organic. I was used to fire, to chaos that could be fought, but this…this was the city laid bare, its workings exposed in a way that set my teeth on edge.

Going deeper still…that was madness. A mini railroad chugging along down there, a thousand feet under the bustling streets. The sandhogs were like some other breed of human, at home in the dimness, heat and dampness. Their shouts over the drilling and hammering weren't fear, it was…ownership, maybe. They were creating this, carving out the veins the city would rely on without ever seeing their work. It was humbling in a gritty, bone-deep kind of way.

Up top, the wind had felt like it would strip me bare. Down there, it was the weight of the city pressing in, the knowledge of a million oblivious feet above your head. Two different kinds of pressure, two different terrors, and somewhere in between was me. Not bragging at home when they asked about it…that perspective isn't earned with a punch card. But you carry it, nonetheless. In the sweat that soaked my uniform after a scary rooftop inspection, in the grit that clung even days after climbing back out into the light from the tunnels, I held proof of a secret New York. It wasn't pretty, and it damn sure wasn't in the tourist brochures. But it was mine, earned one terrifying foot at a time.

DEAD AT THE LIGHT

It started as an annoyance. A single car horn, impatient and blaring. Then another joined in, and another, the dissonant chorus growing just outside the firehouse doors. In the mid-afternoon lull, the cacophony was jarring, enough to break the rhythm of a training drill and half-watched TV shows.

"Someone finally snapped at the traffic," someone joked, rolling his eyes. But when the horns kept going, an uneasy prickle spread among the firefighters. This wasn't just impatience, there was an unhinged desperation clinging to the blasts.

The captain, a man of few words and a lifetime of instincts, was the first one through the door. Stepping into the street, he surveyed the scene: a luxury car idling at the red light flickering overhead. Traffic snarled behind it, drivers waving fists and leaning on their horns in relentless fury.

But something was off. The car's windows were tinted dark, no movement visible inside. He approached, caution and apprehension warring within him and then, as he peered through the window, his blood ran cold.

The driver wasn't annoyed, or delayed, or asleep. Slumped against the steering wheel, eyes staring lifelessly through the glass, there was an unmistakable stillness to the figure. A hole drilled through the tinted window and blood streaking the upholstery were grotesque confirmations – this was no medical emergency.

Silence descended, smothering the chaos of blaring horns. The image of the corpse pierced through the firefighters' usual veneer of bravado. Even in a city pulsing with violence, death always hit hardest when it was so jarringly out of place. Right there, at their doorstep, while life had continued just feet away.

They went about the grim protocols with efficiency. Securing the scene, contacting dispatch, their practiced motions shielding them from the full impact of the chilling tableau. Yet, that unsettling feeling didn't fade. Later, gathered in the kitchen, the usual banter seemed subdued.

The echoes of honking horns became a strange metronome, marking the moment when they were jarringly reminded of the fragile line between ordinary and oblivion. Even surrounded by the camaraderie of the firehouse, an unspoken chill lingered. Each man saw not only the dead driver, but a dark reflection of their own daily vulnerability – one bad day, one random turn of fate, and everything could end at a traffic light.

Ship Fire

That ship mess wasn't just a fire, it was a tomb. No windows, narrow passageways, and no easy exit route in case things went south, just metal walls painted battleship gray, sealing us in as surely as if we'd been bricked up alive. We were doing a relocation that day, far from our usual stomping grounds. But a fire's a fire, whether in a tenement or a naval cargo ship docked in Manhattan. Orders were orders, and in we went.

Four decks down felt like a descent into another world. Ten minutes of air on your back. The usual ship smell of oily air and unidentifiable funk was overlaid with that acrid scent of something far more dangerous than old rope and grease. That storeroom…it'd transformed into a furnace. Flames gnawed at cardboard boxes holding plastic components for some naval piece of fluff, the air shimmering above the orange glow with a heat that defied logic within that enclosed space.

It's funny, you train for the burn, but not its insidious cousins. First comes the sweat, your body rebelling against the heat even as you douse the flames. Then the mask alarms go off and you remove your face-piece, coughing, not just smoke stinging your lungs, but that dry, rasping feeling – like you're choking even with a mask on.

Our air ran out. Those tanks aren't made for fighting an endless supply of fire in a steel box. My head started pounding like someone was hammering away inside my skull. Vision blurs, and those embers seemed to dance with a mocking shimmer. The guys started going down, collapsing with a thud that seemed louder than the fire's roar. It's a domino effect out of the textbooks – when the first guy drops, a primal panic kicks in that even the best training can't always fully conquer.

Carbon monoxide…the invisible killer. Every fire throws it out, but in that cramped metal belly, it wasn't just a danger, it was winning. We'd been fighting flames, but the real enemy was stealing oxygen itself, turning the very air against us. It's an insidious thing, that poison. There's no choking gasp, just a subtle slide into something like drunkenness, limbs heavy, head throbbing. That two-day headache afterwards? That was me being lucky.

I won't lie, the fear still sits deep, even years later. Not of the flames – those we could handle. It's the memory of how fast things shifted from a routine call to barely clawing our way back to daylight. No windows down there to smash out for a gasp of fresh air, no familiar streets above if you get disoriented. Every time I smell burning plastic, that panic flickers – what if the air itself turns traitor, that invisible breath becoming a noose?

We patched them up and, that day, hammered that fire into submission with sheer stubbornness. But even on the pier, gulping down lungfuls of exhaust-heavy air, that ship haunted me. Sometimes the most dangerous enemy isn't what you can see, but what fills the spaces between the flames. They don't give out medals for surviving bad air, but I carry those unseen scars just the same.

The Author and the Smoke

That call stuck with me, not for any blaze or daring rescue, but for the walls put up before we even got past the front door. This wasn't your typical tenement. Swanky Brownstone, a shiny brass knocker the size of a dinner plate, and a polished woman eyeing us through the cracked door like we were selling stolen goods. I was in Brooklyn Heights for a day, mixing with the social elites.

"Domestic" was her only explanation, along with a whole lot of "it's none of your business" and a voice pitched for arguing with lawyers, not soot-stained firefighters. She wasn't some frightened victim either, but a gatekeeper, holding the line with a steely gaze that promised trouble the minute her manicured hand slipped off the doorknob. We heard shouting from inside, muffled behind those solid walls. Perhaps a fight, maybe just an overheated argument – but with that smoke snaking from the top floor window, my gut was screaming something was very wrong. We were setting the sails, but the boat wasn't moving.

This was no longer so much about saving property. There are rules, procedures, ways you kick and shout until a judge rubber-stamps permission to do what needs doing. But inside that swanky townhouse, time felt like it was running on a different track, and that smoke was a clock ticking down on its own.

Backup arrived, the cops adding their uniforms to our grimy turnout gear, yet still all we got was that maddening back and forth. Get a warrant. No, there's clearly an emergency. The minutes stretched, and through the window, that smoke still pushed. You could almost smell the fear behind the soap-clean facade, and the muffled shouts turned a little more desperate.

Finally, a break. Some half-hashed deal – one firefighter only, no tools, just eyeballs to check where the smoke was coming from. I volunteered – maybe I looked less threatening than the others, who knew? – and slipped inside, leaving my guys at the door. The inside…it was like that Brownstone was in two different realities. Downstairs, all polished wood and gleaming floors. Upstairs, the same but even richer looking. I knew I was dealing with some big city boys here.

And there it was – the "fire" in all its ridiculous domestic absurdity. A clothes dryer, venting steam that the winter air turned into a convincing smoke signal. But it wasn't that part of it that set my teeth on edge. It was the people. The well-dressed guy arguing with the arriving cops, a flush of anger hiding something deeper…shame, maybe. And beyond him, two figures shrinking further into the shadows: a Black woman with fear in her eyes, and a young girl holding tight to her hand.

Why the secrecy, the desperate act? Theories spun in my head, none of them comfortable. But there, in that moment, wasn't the place to solve those riddles. If there were secrets to unravel the cops would handle that. For me, case closed, emergency over, we retreated back to the street, the Brownstone door slamming shut on whatever drama simmered inside.

The aftermath, that's what still bothers me. We train for flames, for rescues, but not for those invisible walls folks put up. The danger isn't always the thing burning, but the secrets it might be hiding. We're meant to be first responders, but when a person in need becomes a chess piece in some other twisted game, sometimes all we can do is retreat and wonder what blaze might smolder undetected until next time. As for that famous author? His name still makes bookstore clerks smile, but I think about him, that closed door, the smell of steam, and wonder what stories will never get told.

FOURTH OF JULY

Fourth of July around here? Isn't about grilling or flags, it's about proving you got bigger cajónes than the guy across the street. Take Broadway – just asphalt, really, but over the years, it's turned into this invisible DMZ. Folks to the east, different folks to the west, and come Independence Day? Forget Betsy Ross, it's all-out war.

These guys ain't picking up sparklers at the supermarket. Nah, it's those backwoods stands over the state line – the kind with names like "Uncle Boom's Discount Pyrotechnics" where questionable fuses and bulk purchases go hand in hand. Night falls, and it isn't some orchestra tuning up, it's a bombardment. Screaming rockets, whistling bottle rockets…makes our usual firefights seem like a church picnic.

You got the stench of gunpowder, the manic grin on some kid's face as he sends a mortar lobbing across the street, sparks showering like confetti…and there's us firefighters, ringside seats to the insanity. Too big to stop, see, so we drag out some beat-up lawn chairs, keep the radios on low, and settle in. Kinda awful, kinda awesome, in that way only the city can be.

See, these fireworks, they aren't about pretty patterns. They're middle fingers arcing across the street, fiery shouts of "this is MY turf." Surprisingly correct for how many beers are likely involved, mind you. Each explosion lights up windows, brings cheers, counterattacks…ain't freedom they're celebrating, it's pride.

We watch, and let me tell you, there's something in that chaos. Like, sure, there's the usual – the kid with the singed eyebrow, the trash can fire…but mostly, it's that reminder: this city, it isn't just tired buildings and burnt-out dreams. Underneath it all, there's this firecracker energy, this refusal to just lie down and take it.

Those lines on the map, those flags…they aren't the real fight. It's about jobs, respect, a future beyond sirens and dodging bottle rockets. Things we spend all year trying to manage, control…and then July 4th rolls around, and boom! Reminder that some fires burn inside long after the smoke clears.

So, we watch, we mop up after. Tiring, kind of poetic, and messed up in a way that makes sense here in our corner of the city. Because yeah, it's America's birthday, but it's also just another Tuesday, in its own explosive way.

Roof Air Mail

The crackle of flames wasn't the only soundtrack to a Bronx blaze. There was the thud of rocks hitting truck roofs, the sharp ping of bottles shattering on the pavement, the chorus of jeers and insults hurled from above. Fighting fires turned into dodging a hail of urban shrapnel.

Rubbish fires, car fires…those weren't just accidents on the streets below. They were the spark, the excuse for some unseen enemy to rain down their own twisted kind of fireworks. You learned to look up, not just at the flames, but at those shadowed rooftops. Windows like empty eyes, transformed into sniper nests by bored kids looking for a thrill.

It's a strange sort of calculus you develop on the job. Assessing the burn, sure, but also factoring in escape routes, the curve of the street that might leave you exposed. You assign one guy, the unlucky rooftop watcher, his eyes not on the fire itself, but peering warily upwards for any flicker of movement against the skyline.

It was kids, mostly. Not hardened gangbangers, just youngsters with too much energy and not enough outlets. But age doesn't matter when something heavy enough to dent a helmet is arcing down towards you. The rush of adrenaline wasn't heroic anymore, just a primal need to survive when the job you signed up for turned into an ambush.

Those calls to the cops felt halfhearted. More habit than hope. We all knew the drill – the overworked precinct stretched thin, the arrival of sirens temporarily scattering the rooftop snipers, only for them to regroup soon after. Catching some kid red-handed was rare, rarer still was any punishment that might make them think twice next time a fire truck rolled in.

That powerlessness lingered even after the flames were out. The anger too. It wasn't the blaze that felt like the real enemy, but that constant vulnerability, the way a simple call could turn you into a target. We put our lives on the line, but not like this – not some cheap game for delinquents with nothing better to do. That sense of betrayal, of being hunted on the streets you were meant to protect, festered under the soot.

Still, when you work in the Bronx, there's a stubborn streak as vital as any hose. We didn't retreat, didn't shy away from those Bronx danger zones. We just adapted: helmet pulled down a little tighter, the rooftop watcher's voice a little more urgent on the radio. The job morphed into a kind of morbid battle, our hoses and axes against not just flames, but the malice that rained down with them.

The victories were small. Putting a particularly stubborn fire out before any major injury, that felt like defiance. Some mornings, you could almost convince yourself it was getting better, maybe word was spreading that attacking firefighters was a line even boredom shouldn't cross. Then the next alarm would ring, the smoke would rise, and you'd brace yourself once more, scanning the horizon to see what waited above the flames.

THE RIOT

The riot didn't arrive with a bang. It was a wildfire simmering beneath the surface, sparked by rage and fueled by the city's long-festering wounds. News of the shooting snaked its way through the streets like a fuse, and by the time we got the call, upper Manhattan wasn't just on fire, it was at war.

The aftermath of that 5th alarm we had just left still clung to us — smoke in our hair, the lingering ache of battling a blaze that devoured a whole row of stores. Just as that final '10-8' crackled over the radio, something shifted. No peace, no lull in that relentless cycle. Instead, a new call spat out the address like venom — a police precinct under siege, cars ablaze, and us smack dab in the heart of the chaos.

Taping those windows, it wasn't about keeping out debris. It was sealing ourselves into a metal cage as the reality outside warped into a waking nightmare. We went in convoy formation, a flimsy shield against the storm. Cops front, the fire engines, and lastly the chief, defenseless against the rioters.

The closer we got, the worse it became. Flames licked the night sky, no longer neat blazes confined to dumpsters, but entire buildings ablaze. Rubbish in vacant lots swirled in glowing tornadoes, hurled at us like weapons as we passed. Stones thumped onto the taped-up windows, every clang like a fist pounding on our coffin lids.

"Keep up, keep up!" I was shouting now at my driver, not the crowd, but at my driver. It wasn't about speed, it was about not breaking that chain, not becoming isolated in a whirlwind of fire and fury. This was madness unleashed, any sense of order shattered. The roar of the mob drowned out sirens, and smoke turned streetlights into blurred, demonic eyes staring us down. We were no longer saviors, but trespassers into a battlefield we had no hand in making.

There's fear, and then there's this…the knowledge that the city itself has become the enemy. Not an inferno to be tamed, but a living, seething creature with you trapped in its belly. Each Molotov cocktail that arced through the smoke wasn't about property – it was defiance, a raw scream that echoed inside our own protective shell. Every thud against the truck, every crack of glass, whispered that next time it might be our blood instead of gasoline that fueled the flames.

We made it to that burning precinct; we did our job. But that night, there was no satisfaction in the dying embers, no sense of victory when dawn finally washed the soot-filled air clear. It was a Pyrrhic victory at best, won at a cost we weren't ready to tally. We carried back more than exhaustion and the stink of ash. It was a fear that lingered, a chilling reminder that the fires we were trained to fight paled in comparison to the ones that rage in hearts and streets.

I can still picture that drive back, the buildings charred but defiantly upright, burnt-out cars, and streets littered with the evidence of rage. It wasn't the end, just a single night in a long, slow burn. That fear? A piece of it will always be with me…not as a scar, but as fuel – a reminder that there are some fires even the bravest firefighters can only navigate through, not truly put out.

THE SPANISH MIX

In the Bronx, it wasn't just about Spanish-speakers. It was a tangled web of accents and attitudes, where the same language masked deep divides. Textbooks might lump them together, but we learned the real distinctions on the streets, in the way blood pooled and fists flew.

Back then, we didn't have many Mexicans or Central Americans, not like now. Our slice of the world was heavy with Dominicans – mostly bigger guys, not the tallest bunch, but with a pride that ran taller than any skyscraper. You'd catch it in the way they held their heads, a flicker in the eyes, even when they were outnumbered. Maybe it was that island fire, or just the scars of coming up hard on a crowded stretch of the Caribbean. They'd tangle, sometimes with us, but usually not for long. A brawl, then a handshake over a beer if you earned their respect.

Now, the Cubans…those were a different breed entirely. Boat lift era, most of them, eyes holding a thousand demons they'd hauled over on that rough passage. There was an edginess to them, a hair-trigger tension that was never far from exploding. You didn't pick fights with those guys, not unless you absolutely had no other choice. They'd had enough scrapping for a lifetime and weren't afraid to share it around.

It played out in the streets, a brutal kind of anthropology we learned on the fly. More than once we'd stumble across a group of Mexicans or Central Americans lying battered after a night out. Booze and some stolen cash were all it took to make them targets. Those muggings weren't about careful planning, just raw opportunism – they were in the wrong place, with accents that marked them as outsiders. It was a bitter thing to see, how those cultural divides played out in bloody beat downs.

There's no heroism in that kind of education. No bravery in patching those guys up in the back of the ambulance, just a bone-deep weariness. It wasn't that we loved one group over the other, but we understood those unwritten rules. The Cubans caroused hard, but it was mostly among themselves. The Dominicans defended what was theirs with a ferocity that bordered on scary. We learned to read the signs, the twitch of a hand, the set of a jaw. It was self-preservation, yes, but also bore witness to the way a city tears itself apart along lines that guidebooks never teach you.

Sometimes, in those quiet moments when the sirens fell silent, I'd look out from our beat-up firehouse and wonder about those invisible borders we navigated daily. They shared a language, a vague sense of being 'other' in this American landscape, but under that umbrella raged completely different storms. We didn't get taught this in the academy, but every bandage peeled back, every fire hose aimed at a brawl-turned-inferno was a lesson. The Bronx wasn't just a melting pot, it was a battlefield. And some nights, staring at those flickering street-lights, I'd think we were fighting battles beyond our understanding… and losing as often as we won.

THE NIGHTCLUB

That call didn't come booming across the firehouse, it crept in like a whisper through the dispatch. Overcrowding at a club. Address in the heart of a tough neighborhood. 2 AM. And that final note, barely audible in the radio's monotone crackle: no cops available.

We rolled up not with sirens, just that low rumble of engines idling. This wasn't your typical safety check. The second we walked inside that club, it hit – that feeling of being a stranger in your own city.

Wall-to-wall people. Bodies pressed together so tightly that sweat painted the air itself. Not a single familiar word, just that throb of Spanish music blasting in a language we didn't speak. It was a different kind of heat to a fire, a pulse that felt ready to explode beneath the flickering disco lights.

In or line of work, you learn to size up a situation fast. This wasn't just a party gone wild. It was a powder keg – too many people, not enough space, and a building code violation turned tinderbox waiting for a spark. We searched for the manager, the flicker of recognition in his eyes, the only foothold in a sea of wary faces.

Broken English was the bridge, cracked and fragile like an old fire escape. No cops, we explained. This is a danger. We don't want to shut you down, but…those words hung heavy in the air, the unspoken threat of force if things went wrong.

That moment, it could have tipped either way. We're used to being in charge, barking orders with the authority of those shiny badges behind them. But in that overcrowded club, those badges felt more like liabilities. This wasn't a fire to be fought, it was a riot waiting to ignite if we stepped wrong.

Pride's a funny thing. You need enough to wear that uniform, but not too much when the situation calls for swallowing it whole. We made the deal. No threats, no pushing, just the music stopped and the plea for calm, offered first in stumbling Spanish from the manager, then echoed in English from us. It was a gamble, a trust placed in the hands of strangers that could easily turn against us.

I still remember the silence when that music cut off. It wasn't fear, exactly, more a ripple of confusion that ran through the crowd like a chill. Then, slowly, it started. The thinning out, not a stampede, but an ebb tide of bodies reluctantly releasing their hold on the night. Whispers and sidelong glances, but no one spoiling for a fight. Not that night.

We stood there, watching them file out until the club that had felt close to bursting was reduced to empty chairs and echoing silence. It wasn't a major fire averted, no medals pinned on for that one. But the relief was just as sharp. We'd walked a tightrope in that place, our usual rulebook left behind at the firehouse door.

Maybe the city works like that sometimes – not by force, but by strange, unspoken truces. It's humbling to realize just how thin the threads are that hold back chaos. A flicker of trust from strangers, the simple act of turning off the music, and a potential riot defused. We headed back to the trucks, the pulse of the city feeling a little less foreign, knowing that somewhere out there, a powder keg didn't ignite. It wasn't in any report, that small victory, but I carried it with me all the same.

SAFE DRIVING AWARD

Driving that rig wasn't about navigation, it was combat. The streets of the Bronx were a battlefield – crammed with cars, swarming with pedestrians, and those damn steel elevated train pillars holding everything together like rusty rivets. We were a hulking beast, a symphony of sirens and flashing lights, trying to force a path through impossible gaps with precious seconds ticking down.

Accidents…they were the ghost haunting every turn, the whispered fear every time you climbed into the cab. There's not much between you and the world in those rigs. A thin wall of metal, a windshield offering an illusion of safety – it didn't take much to realize just how fragile those divides were.

Forget seat belts. That was a luxury for later eras. The riding compartments? A cramped metal box straddling the engine, a couple of hard jump seats facing each other, with barely enough room to sit. The roar of the engine, the radio crackling with panicked updates…it was a recipe for adrenaline-soaked chaos, where a sudden swerve could send you flying if you weren't braced just right.

Those tower ladders – monsters of machinery, essential in our world of towering vacant buildings – were their own special kind of terror. Top-heavy, prone to tilting ominously even on gentle curves. You had to trust the driver, pray their reflexes were sharper than their nerves, because if those outside wheels lifted off the ground…well, that's the kind of mess that makes the news.

The month we had five accidents, that was something else. It was like we had a target painted on the side of the rig. We were T-boned more times than a steakhouse. It wasn't carelessness, but desperation. The sheer volume of calls wearing us thin, every run feeling like we were gambling with fate. Downtown didn't get it. All they saw were statistics and crumpled metal. Demands for reports, threats rang in our ears as we surveyed the wreckage, hoping nobody was seriously hurt midst the twisted steel.

Then our captain, bless his wily heart, played their game against them. He got the stats – not just our accidents, but citywide averages of accidents per response. And guess what? Turns out, even with our battered rig, we were below that magic threshold. More runs, more risk, but somehow, a lower accident rate. It was insane logic, the kind that only worked in that upside-down world of firefighting bureaucracy.

Next thing you know, he's applying for a damn safe driving award. I could almost see those suits downtown choking on their coffee when the application landed. Engine 75, kings of the Bronx, asking for a pat on the back after nearly demolishing half the spare rigs. The twist was, we actually were awarded the thing.

It's funny, in a dark kind of way. That award didn't mean we drove better, just that we survived more often than the odds should've allowed. We patched up the rigs, gritted our teeth, and every time the alarm screamed, rolled the dice again. The Bronx, it didn't reward safe, it rewarded getting there, whatever the damn cost. That piece of paper hanging in our firehouse? It wasn't a testament to skill, but a reminder: for all our bravado, we weren't in charge. We were dodging the blows, clawing our way through another tour, and praying to whatever gods might be listening that our luck wouldn't run out on the next turn.

TRAINING DRILLING CROSS TRAINING

After lunch hour, training at Engine 75 was less education, more a daily duel with exhaustion. The guys just back from a dozen calls, soot-streaked and yawning, were about as receptive to lectures as a cat is to a bath. The bosses mandated those sessions, but motivation…that was something we had to manufacture ourselves.

It depended on the topic. New tools? A flicker of interest in those weary eyes. Anything that promised to make the job a sliver easier was worth paying attention to. But rules and regulations? Fuhgeddaboudit. Those sessions dissolved into slumped shoulders and thinly veiled snoring from the back row.

Weekends were for multi-unit drills. Out in some empty lot, engines and ladder trucks descended like a small invading army. Some captains treated these like a chore to skip – "Drills? We do it for real every day!" But in our patch, we were meticulous. That wasn't about playing soldier, it was about survival.

The engine guys and the ladder guys, we weren't separate species. A sudden workforce shortage, an unexpected detail…meant any fire-fighter might be doing a job they'd only practiced on faded chalkboards in the firehouse. So, we drilled on stretching hose lines, on ladder raises, on tactics that blurred those neat lines between the units.

Some fellas moaned, even got their union reps in a huff about being forced out of their comfort zone.

Then came the inevitable – the call where the truck was delayed, the fire raging, and those engine boys suddenly found themselves thrust into action that should've been second nature to a ladder company. That's when the griping stopped. It was sweat equity – those begrudging training hours paying off in less injuries and lives saved.

The Bronx wasn't a place that let you specialize in only one aspect of the job. A tenement blaze didn't care if you were holding the nozzle or setting the aerial in place. We had our routines, sure, but routine goes flying out the window the minute that alarm screams in your ear. Training – even the boring, mandatory kind – wasn't about perfection, but adaptability.

You see it in their faces, that moment a regular Joe firefighter must step into unfamiliar boots. Maybe a flicker of panic, but underneath it, muscle memory kicking in. They knew enough to be dangerous, to bridge the gap until backup arrived. Because we practiced those routines, because someone forced them to learn things beyond their usual jobs, chaos reigned a little bit less.

Those drills, they didn't just hone tactics. They built trust. The engine crew, knowing the ladder guys had their backs, and vice versa. That knowledge flowed in our veins just as surely as the adrenaline surging through them. Some might not have seen the value in a few hours spent maneuvering trucks around an empty lot, but out on the streets, where those lines between life and death were drawn in flames, that "wasted" time could be the difference between coming home a hero, or not coming home at all.

THE MEDICALS

Those "surprise" medicals... See, that's code for getting hauled downtown for checkups, and the unspoken question of "did someone spike our coffee with something stronger than usual?" But, hey, trip outta the Bronx, maybe snag some decent cannoli...you learn to find those slivers of light, right?

But then there's Joe. Joe "Meathead," and not just 'cause the guy could bench press a Buick. Now, I am not one to judge a man's undergarment choices, but let's just say subtlety isn't high on his list.

We're rolling, diesel roaring, then Joe starts to squirm. Look on his face, like he's trying to will a fire out of existence through sheer force. Turns out, in his rush to get suited for medical nonsense, he forgot something crucial. We're talking no underwear. Just Joe, in regulation gear, fighting an invisible battle of chafing that no hose could fix. When the doc says "drop your shorts," Joe would have no shorts to drop.

Here's the thing: we're supposed to be professionals. But that sight – Joe announcing he forgot his boxers, radio crackling with confusion, officer cursing – you couldn't make this stuff up!

Of course, we screeched back to the firehouse. Folks on the street must've thought the Bronx had finally gone full-tilt crazy. Dignity's in short supply up here, but that image...it was something else.

Little Italy, we hit it later, lunch after the medicals, the story already a legend whispered across the firehouse network. And Joe? He's got himself a new nickname. "Remember that underwear thing?" – battle cry, good-natured taunt, reminder of the absurdity we live with. Medicals, lunch, that faded into the background.

See, the Bronx, she ain't kind, but she's got a wicked sense of humor. It's those moments, the stupid and the brave, which get woven into the tapestry of this place. Joe took the ribbing, grumbled about it. But secretly, I think there was a flicker of pride, too. 'Cause in this city, a story that makes you cringe is proof you've lived to tell it. And, hey, who's going to question a guy who could probably fight a fire bare-handed? It's all part of the glorious mess, isn't it?

Red Lights and Racing Hearts

Commuting to the firehouse was less a journey and more another tour in itself, with its own set of dangers lurking outside those battered firehouse doors. You weren't just battling traffic, but the knowledge that every delay put one more exhausted firefighter between you and a much-earned rest. The guy waiting on you to relieve him wasn't just a faceless stranger, he was the specter of responsibility chasing you through the streets.

Snowstorms…those were something else entirely. A delicate dance of desperation. Leaving early to beat the worst of it meant not stranding the outgoing guy in a city shutting down around him, his commute becoming impossible. Staying home meant risking missing your tour, maybe forcing that same man to face another unwanted, grueling one. It was unwritten, this juggling act of self-preservation and unspoken loyalty, but it happened more often than the brass in their cozy downtown offices ever realized.

Morning rush hour was its own gauntlet. Those predawn Bronx streets were eerily empty at 5 AM, casting long shadows that made every corner, every shadowed doorway, a potential threat. You were a firefighter, sure, but first and foremost, a target – a man alone, likely on a predictable schedule, before the rest of the city awoke. Red lights became suggestions, not rules. Not a place to linger. You learned to sense trouble brewing, a shift in the air, before a figure materialized from the darkness.

That's the thing about the Bronx – it wasn't just the fires that could get you. One of the guys…he'd been careless, figured it couldn't happen to him. Red light, a mugger approaching, and panic blurring his judgment. A gunshot echoed through those empty streets, a stark reminder that those battles never stopped, even when you clocked out. He survived, the bullet a graze more than a kill shot, but the fear, that lingered.

The commute, it grounds you down in a quieter way than the blazes you fought. It was isolation in a crowded city, a stark reminder of an unspoken truth. You were a firefighter, a public servant, but out on the streets, alone under that flickering dawn sky, you were also a survivor first. That drive became a warzone, not just against time, but against the knowledge that a wrong turn, a moment of inattention, could be the end before your tour even officially began.

The news reports never captured those moments. The muggings that turned into a blurry face at dawn, the snow-choked roads trapping tired heroes miles from their families. They told stories of burning buildings, civilians saved, but the journey to do the saving? That was our private hell, a battle for every inch of pavement.

We wore the grime and weariness of the city on our faces, even before the soot of a fire could leave its mark. The Bronx didn't just hold firefighters, it held commuters who had dodged the unseen bullets on the daily grind. Our wars didn't have neatly defined front lines, and some days, just getting to work felt like the bravest act of all.

CAR BREAKDOWN

My old car, bless its rusty heart, ain't what you'd call… trustworthy. More like a stubborn donkey – three good days, then a tantrum. Well, wouldn't you know it, mile from the firehouse she goes kaput. Not a bang, mind you, more a disappointed sigh, like a smoker denied their last cigarette. No cell phones in those days, no AAA, just me and those bulky turnout gear in my arms.

So, there I was, a firefighter in limbo, parading down the street like a reject from the Thanksgiving parade. People, they spot the uniform, but something's off. They give me that sideways squint, the "cop, not cop?" assessment. Finally settle on "best to just nod and act like those bulky pants are normal."

Every block, it's the same: the quiet, then the wary eyes. See, the city, she isn't fully awake yet. No screeching tires, no yelling matches. That silence is worse than a fire somehow. Makes you wonder who's sizing you up and if you'll be a target before even making it through the door.

Sweat-soaked by the time I stumbled into the firehouse. Lucky for me, some fellas from the night shift are still lingering, reliving their heroics over burnt coffee. I see their faces…like someone replaced their mugs with fishbowls. Turns out a firefighter showing up on foot is cause for entertainment.

There isn't any sympathy, just laughter and "bet that walk sucked, bud!" Then, miracle of miracles, they're under the hood of my beast, grunting and swearing. Thirty minutes later, the damn thing's purring, kind of. See, that's the thing about this job, it's brotherhood born of shared absurdity.

Sure, I made the tour, engine knocking in protest. But that walk, the awkwardness, getting rescued by grease-stained heroes…that's the Bronx baptism, right there. See, we aren't just firefighters, we're survivors, of the blazing kind and the stalled car on a deserted street kind. That city, she throws a lot at ya, but if you can laugh, can make it in with your pants on (even if you had to walk the last mile), then maybe, just maybe, you've got a shot at belonging.

THE FORTY THIEVES

There isn't any glory in the "Forty Thieves." No sirens, no firetrucks, just a van that rattles like an empty toolbox and a name that tells you what the real firefighters think. Cleanup crew, damage control…the ugly aftermath they leave to salvage. Stuck there for a tour, maybe it was, punishment for something I said to somebody at the assignment desk I never figured out.

Thing is, it isn't like a regular crew. Bunch of kids, mostly, city toughs and those "summer job" types, overseen by one of us officers – the unlucky ones, stuck with babysitting instead of blazes. That van wasn't home, more like a leaky boat with no compass.

This one scene, it sticks with me…flooded apartment, the usual mess of waterlogged dreams and folks clinging to whatever we could haul out. Back at the makeshift firehouse, I walk into the kitchen expecting the usual sad coffee, maybe a box of stale donuts. But no… there's one of the kids, youngest, maybe 18, holding a raw chicken leg. Bare hands. And he's dipping it, casual as can be, into a pot of boiling oil on this beat-up stove.

"What the hell you doin'?" My voice cracks like a whip, even though I'm not meaning it that way.

He looks up, startled, but more confused than scared. "Cookin' dinner, you want some?"

Now, that offer, so matter of fact…it hits like a punch. It isn't just the fact that he's breaking every food safety rule there is. It's that disconnect, that echo of something so far removed from my world. Is this some home cooking he learned, some cultural thing I'm too ignorant to get? Or is it just…survival? A kid so used to hustling, he doesn't see the line between this duty and fending for himself? Hell, maybe both.

I pass on the chicken, of course. Something 'bout it feeling wrong, not the health risk kind of wrong, but…desperate. There are no group meals for the cleanup crew. They clean up other folks' messes, but their own hunger? That stays hidden, like the mold under the carpet they rip out.

Tried talking to him later, that hard-ass officer thing gone, just two guys who barely knew each other. He shrugs, kid bravado replaced by something tired. Turns out, like I guessed – isn't some family recipe, just a kid used to making do, even if it means frying chicken where others dry their boots.

Don't know what happened to him. Maybe that unit toughened him up, maybe it just made him another bitter Bronx story. But that image lingers – him, the chicken leg, the grease smell mingling with damp plaster. The Bronx, she's more than fires. She's got these quiet battles, and sometimes, a half-cooked meal is the dividing line, clear as any fire.

Disappearing Roofman

My heart pounded a rhythm against my ribs, each gasp of air burning as I clambered to the top of the ladder. Seventy-five feet up, the city was a blur, sirens a distant scream. Up here, it was nothing but fire, sky, and instinct.

Tom was already hunched over the Partner Saw, engine starting, spewing smoke that mingled with the choking plumes billowing from the roof. With a yell, I tossed my tools across the tar, the clang masked by the inferno's greedy roar. It was time to cut away the roof, let this beast vent its anger upwards instead of pushing the fire further horizontally across the building.

Then, Tom began to sink as I watched, stunned. A surreal horror movie shot not in one sharp drop, but with excruciating slowness. The roof rippled under him like rotten fabric giving way and the saw clattered from his hands as he flailed for purchase on a surface dissolving into nothingness.

"TOM!" My shout was swallowed by the fire's roar. Only his head and arms were visible now, like he was being dragged downwards by some monstrous, fiery hand.

I lurched forward, too slow, too useless. Then he vanished. Just a rush of red-orange flame where he had been, and then…emptiness. No thud, no cry, just an impossible absence.

My mind stuttered. There was protocol and tactics and a hundred drills hammered into my brain. None of it prepared me for this – my partner swallowed by the flames beneath my boots, consumed by the burning beast we battled.

Then, through the swirling madness, the story. Hours later, doing the grim paperwork and endless replays in my head, a detail appeared. Through the blinding smoke, Tom had seen light when he dropped into the fire in the apartment below, not in the gaping roof hole, but somewhere in front of him. One narrow shaft of light – a single window with a fire escape. Not something he knew, but it was there. Tom didn't explain himself, couldn't; just that blind lunge for one pinprick of hope in the midst of the searing hell. It was the only window in the entire apartment that had a fire escape, and he blindly jumped through it. Fate? Divine intervention?

His shoes were gone, his pants a charred ruin, flesh and fabric melded in the unholy heat. But that damned window…the only one in the entire apartment with any hope of escape. . Some called it divine intervention, others just blind luck. I called it sickening irony. This man, expert in roof operations, fell beneath, and fate offered him an escape in another direction.

It's that twist of fate that ate at me. He survived, scarred to the bone but breathing. His return never came, he became a ghost haunting the Bronx – a man forever broken by the monster we faced each day. We fought with axes and skill, but it was chance, some cruel roll of cosmic dice, which decided he lived while others lay under crisp white sheets. It chipped away at our courage, made every roof seem like a trapdoor, every flame a waiting mouth to swallow one of us whole.

Situational Awareness

I always told my guys, "know where you are at all times. The fire building? The floor? The room? Don't get turned around. When you're calling for help, it means life or death; knowing where you are. You want to stay alive? Follow me."

Situational awareness was more than that, though. It begins on arrival. For instance, the front facade of an Old Law tenement…it's not just bricks and mortar, it's the first chapter in a textbook written in smoke and flame. One glance, and you're already decoding the chaos that awaits inside.

No fire escapes gracing the front? Odds are you're facing railroad flats. That means two apartments per floor, a long, narrow warren of rooms, windows at the back, probably a rickety fire escape clinging to the rear with a gooseneck ladder up to the roof. That shapes your plan instantly. The engine attacking from inside and out, you, forcing your way through the front, sending the outside ladder team to vent and search through those rear windows. Those apartments were deathtraps, and that escape at the back was often the only lifeline.

But if you see fire escapes plastered on the front…that's a different beast. Could be two apartments per floor, front and back, with that same rear escape setup too. Or, and here's where things get tricky, those escapes might be balconies spanning the back of two separate buildings, offering a precarious bridge from inferno to potential escape but no way for you to climb up to the fire floor. No roof access for you that way either. That adds a whole new dimension – getting to the roof through the adjoining building.

And the floor, oh, the floor matters. Each rise adds difficulty. Those top stories…that's brutal. Maybe the aerial can reach the roof, maybe you can move to and from neighboring rooftops if they're close enough and nearly the same height. Old Law tenements had those shafts, air currents that turned an apartment fire into a chimney. One window blowing out, and it can send flames licking up like a rocket, reaching the windows above and maybe the building next door before you can blink. Those shafts weren't only for light and air, they were highways for the fire to spread. Brownstone? Fire in the basement apartment? Get a line up the stoop and into the first floor to protect those stairs to the upper floors.

We studied tactics at the drills, sure. But the real lessons were etched in the city itself. Each crooked fire escape, every crumbling cornice or parapet – they told a story about the battleground we'd be facing the minute that alarm rang. That's professionalism, the right way. It's reading a building on the fly, translating fading paint and soot-stained windows into action. It's knowing the patterns those flames will follow, anticipating the collapse before the floorboards give way.

Outsiders see a burning building, we see a puzzle box with lives trapped within. It isn't about theory, but grim experience. Situational awareness. Every scar on those tenement walls whispered of blazes past, lessons learned in sweat and ash. We carried the ghosts of those battles with us. So, every time we rolled up, that first glance wasn't just assessment, it was the weight of history settling on our shoulders. A silent promise to fight smarter, harder, to maybe – just maybe – outwit the flames this time around.

THE ARMORY MOVIE

The Armory. That over-sized brick structure squatting in our Bronx domain, a monument to military drab. Checking its guts for violations was akin to exploring the digestive tract of a constipated bureaucrat – thrilling, it was not. But hey, the government pays, and duty, or at least boredom, calls.

This morning was different. Army green was MIA. Instead, a circus on wheels – a caravan of Hollywood parasites – choked the lot. This wasn't order and discipline, it was organized vomiting. Think less Omaha Beach, more Burning Man with catering.

Inside? The armory had been gutted, transformed into a fever dream on speed. Blinding lights, cameras like praying mantises, more skinny people sipping designer water than you'd find in a juice bar convention. Turns out those army boys had been replaced by an even more terrifying force: a film crew.

At the epicenter of this clusterf*ck was their holy idol. Not a missile silo, but a cardboard and plywood monument, bathed in the kind of artificial light that gives you instant melanoma. Movie magic, they call it. We call it a taxpayer-funded delusion.

Some big-shot actor was slumming it in the Bronx. Our little slice of urban decay was the unlikely backdrop for his next Oscar grab. My usual inspection tour became an involuntary stroll through La La Land.

Overpriced coffee, nervous laughter echoing off the concrete, a stressed-out crew scurrying like cockroaches at a picnic – it was strangely familiar. Firefighters, film crews…same game, different dumpster fire.

The smell was part set workshop, part cheap cologne, part existential despair. Turns out staging disaster is just as chaotic as dealing with the real deal. For a few absurd hours, I was an outsider on the inside of their bizarre little world.

Back on the street, the sirens seemed almost soothing. Sure, maybe some junkie had set his mattress ablaze in an alley, but at least it wasn't lit by some hipster lighting tech with a triple macchiato twitch.

We'd survived an alternate reality, one where the Bronx was a prop and fake drama was king. Now, a burning building didn't seem so daunting. If they could build a fake Times Square in a weapons bunker, dammit, we could handle a three-alarm blaze. Maybe, just maybe, with enough cynicism and strong coffee, we could make it through another day.

The Peeping Toms

Trading the Bronx for a Manhattan firehouse should've been a relief. Less chaos, fewer crackheads setting buildings ablaze…what could go wrong? Well, let's just say these guys were masters of filling idle hours with creative pursuits – think less 'astronomy enthusiast' and more 'perverted Peeping Toms'. Turns out, their rooftop telescope wasn't for stargazing, but for…well, let's just say their interest in the 'celestial bodies' was a bit earthlier.

My initiation into their little voyeur club came with a stage whisper: "Cap, problem." Bad news is always served with that verbal appetizer. Visions of collapsing buildings and toxic spills danced in my head…but no. It was dynamite. Some amateur Timothy McVeigh across the alley, apparently keeping his explosives on display like it was a flea market find.

"How the hell do you know that?" Well, those rooftop astrologers had been busy. I'm all for a healthy dose of curiosity, but geez, there's a line between a little neighborly interest and full-on Rear Window creepiness. Being the new guy meant my concerns about this blatant invasion of privacy landed with a dull thud.

So, there I was, phoning in the world's most embarrassing bomb threat. The farce unfolded like a rejected SNL sketch: cops swarming, panicked evacuations, every bad movie trope in full, sweaty display.

Finally, SWAT bursts in, primed for a showdown with domestic terrorism…

…and there, on the dresser, was the culprit. A cheesy dollar-store alarm clock. Ticking away, the picture of innocence. Relief? Nah. Mostly, I felt like I'd been dunked in a vat of secondhand shame. Never worked that firehouse again, and I'm betting my face graced at least one bullseye in their backroom.

The crew swore they were being "thorough." But that day, boredom didn't just breed laziness, it ignited full-scale idiocy. Sometimes, the firehouse isn't where the danger lurks. Sometimes, it's fueled by a misguided telescope and too much time to kill.

I've faced infernos, the mangled aftermath of accidents. But that fake dynamite? That's got me cringing still. It's a humbling reminder: the enemy isn't always the blazing kind. Sometimes, it's the punchline of a joke on your back, the burn worse than any flame.

The Thin Line
We Walk

That unmistakable tang of gasoline leaking onto the street…it wasn't just a smell; it was a ticking time bomb. A single spark, a careless cigarette, and the whole block could go up in flames. Car accidents, busted fuel lines – those calls rolled in with frustrating regularity. And sometimes, especially those ringing in the dead of night, they revealed a darker side to our job: the bad habits borne from exhaustion and exasperation.

See, the thing about a slow gasoline tank leak is, it's like a dripping faucet – annoying, even dangerous, but stubbornly persistent. We'd show up, lights flashing, and hose down the street. The fumes would dissipate, the worried caller would be satisfied, and we'd roll back to the firehouse…only to get the same damn call an hour or two later, the scent of gasoline creeping back like a stubborn ghost.

Some units, the ones with less patience or maybe just a twisted sense of problem-solving, took matters into their own hands. Out would come the halligan tool – that pry bar firefighters swear by. But this time not for forcing open doors. They'd crouch by the leaking car, booster hose ready, a flicker of grim determination in their eyes, and deliver a swift, brutal blow with the pointy end – straight into the underbelly of the gas tank.

I'd hear the stories, whispered with a mix of awe and unease. The sudden gush of gasoline, the wash-down of the street, the problem solved with ruthless efficiency, and the end to those infernal callbacks. It was pragmatic, in a twisted way. But I couldn't shake the image of it: that spark of metal, the gasoline pooling underneath, waiting for that one fatal moment...

The risks were staggering. A fire, an explosion that could engulf not just the car but those foolish enough to stand too close. And yet, in those predawn hours, with rest deprivation blurring the line between right and expedient, it must have seemed like a justifiable solution. A shortcut in a world that didn't often offer them.

Maybe it was my hard-won idealism, maybe just common sense, but I couldn't stomach it. We were firefighters, not saboteurs. Our job was to contain danger, not create it. Every time I caught that whiff of gasoline, I'd grit my teeth, picturing those guys with their crude solution. It was a reminder that in our line of work, the battles weren't just against the flames, but against the shortcuts born of desperation and the darker impulses that could creep in during the quiet hours.

We had tanks full of water, tools honed for rescue...yet the temptation was to use them for something far more dangerous. It was a chilling thought, that hidden battle of doing what was easy versus what was right. And as I went about the methodical, less glamorous task of containing those leaks with a plug, some water and a few swear words, I swore to myself that I'd never cross that line, no matter how many damn times the phone rang with that same familiar complaint.

ROOF RESCUES

Roof rescues weren't just tactics we learned, they were a lurking nightmare etched into the back of our minds. Those ladders reaching into the sky promised heroic action, but the reality buzzed with a different kind of tension. You train for the worst, hope for the best, and deep down, there's always that whisper: what if today, it's me dangling over the edge?

Truckies with their gleaming harnesses, snap hooks winking in the sunlight…it looked reassuring, but every clink of metal was a reminder of the void below. We'd go through the motions – those 'safe' single slide rescues and self-rescues, and, even riskier, lowering a firefighter down with a rope wrapped around them, trusting those knots and the man holding the line on the roof. Both were dangerous, especially when the adrenaline's pumping and that unforgiving drop is just a slipped boot away. But it wasn't just about the physical act, it was the weight of responsibility – the knowledge that someone's life was literally hanging by a thread you were responsible for.

Training was tricky. Our firehouse roof was our makeshift cliff-side – cracked, littered with debris, barely resembling the desperation of a real-world rescue. But it was all we had. That first step over the parapet edge…you can't replicate that fear thudding in your chest. Every movement had to be precise, muscle memory kicking in to fight the panic. The rope's rough texture against your palms wasn't a tool, it was a lifeline, and you clung to it like your soul depended on it.

Now, rappelling…that had its own grim thrill. The controlled descent, the rush of wind against your face, a flicker of reckless liberation before reality sunk in. It was easy to forget how brutally physics could betray you with a mis-tied knot, a fraying rope. They didn't train us for elegance, but desperate, brutal efficiency. Get down, get that trapped civilian out, and pray the whole way you wouldn't become a casualty yourself.

Those exercises had a hollowness against the backdrop of the Bronx. We weren't conquering pristine mountains, just navigating crumbling parapets and smoke-stained chimneys. The heroism was muted, grittier. No crowds cheered at the bottom of those descents, just a weary nod from the guys, the shared knowledge of the danger we cheated, at least for now.

We got good at those rescues. Maybe too good. Familiarity bred a dangerous comfort, made us forget how precariously even the best training balanced us on the razor's edge between savior and victim. Each time I buckled on that harness, I pictured not just the fire below, but the long plunge. It was a healthy terror, a grim sort of respect for those unforgiving heights and the thin line separating bravery from a fatal mistake. Those rooftop drills weren't just about skills, they were a constant confrontation with our limits, a reminder that some battles could cost more than anyone was willing to pay.

DUMBWAITERS

A fire in a dumbwaiter shaft wasn't just contained within those grimy walls, it was a ticking time bomb, a wildfire waiting to burst free. Those shafts were hidden arteries within a tenement's frame, a perfect vertical path for flames to devour, hungry and unseen. We learned to dread the telltale signs: acrid smoke seeping through cracks where none should be, a faint crackling sound traveling through the shaft like some malevolent whisper.

Each floor was a new battlefield in the making. We'd be fighting a fire in one apartment, thinking we had it contained, when suddenly, a fresh eruption in the room above – the flames had found their secret highway. It was a relentless game of cat and mouse, the fire outpacing us, gobbling up floor after floor as we scrambled to keep up. You took the first line up as high as you could and forced your way into an apartment to meet the beast.

The roofman had an unenviable task. That door over the shaft, hiding the top of it, became the war's epicenter. Get it open too late, and the pent-up heat and fire would explode outward horizontally, turning the interior itself into a blazing inferno and possibly finding its way into those adjacent buildings. Timing was everything – vent fast but get lines in place to combat that burst of flame.

The radio crackled with urgent updates, each unit reporting a new flare-up. "Fourth floor, east side!", "Breaking into the sixth now!" Water had to flow into that shaft, a desperate attempt to drown the blaze as it climbed relentlessly upwards. Coordination was key, yet the chaos of multiple floors ignited at once made every shout, every command, feel like a race against the inevitable.

Those dumbwaiter fires devoured buildings with terrifying speed. The Bronx had seen too many of them, leaving behind charred skeletons and the lingering stench of defeat. You needed manpower, and lots of it, not just to fight the flames floor by floor but to safeguard lines of escape, to evacuate terrified residents who might be trapped just ahead of the fire's advance.

Those fires were more than just flames and smoke. They exposed the fragility of the structures we battled to protect. A discarded cigarette, a faulty wire, and those flimsy walls and hidden shafts turned a home into a tinderbox. We fought with hoses and axes in a war that seemed rigged against us from the start.

In the aftermath, standing midst the sodden building, the exhaustion hit harder than usual. These weren't glorious battles, but grim slogs against a hidden enemy that exploited every weakness. We saved lives, sometimes, and sometimes we just watched the flames win, the echoes of panicked shouts still ringing in our ears. They were a harsh reminder that some fires wouldn't be extinguished with water alone, some vulnerabilities burned far deeper than the wooden bones of those old buildings.

THE FLOOR ABOVE

Being on the floor above the fire, that was the special kind of hell even the bravest of us learned to dread. Below you, the heart of the beast raged, sending waves of suffocating heat swirling upwards. Your knees would sear against the hot floorboards, your ears burn like they'd been licked by flame. Those precious 10 minutes of air in your tank suddenly felt pitifully short.

Getting there was a gamble. Go too early, with flames shooting out of the fire apartment into the interior stairs before the guys on the fire floor had water flowing, and a sudden mishap could cut off your escape, leaving you trapped above a roaring inferno. We'd seen it happen, losing water, the transformation of a normal room into a blazing pyre in a horrifying heartbeat. The fire gods were fickle, and the timing had to be precise, or you were paying the price. Some guys went up the stairs to the floor above no matter.

In the choking darkness, visibility was a cruel joke. Swirling smoke thicker than any fog, the flashlight's beam cutting a pathetic path through the murk. Every creak, every groan of the building, your over-heated imagination made it sound like impending doom. And then, glimpses of the enemy – tendrils of flame licking through cracks in the floor, fingers of flame racing overhead on the ceiling in a symphony of pops and sizzles.

The search demanded impossible choices. Crawling low, groping your way through the maze of rooms, it felt like every move was too slow, every second wasted one less chance of finding someone alive. The heat built with every inch gained, the weight of responsibility crashing down alongside the limited air in your tank.

In those moments, courage wasn't some abstract notion. It was the prickling heat on your neck, the phantom taste of ash in the back of your throat, and the stubborn refusal to retreat until you'd scoured every possible corner. It was the crackle on the radio, if you had one, updates on the fire's progress below, a constant countdown against your dwindling air supply. It was the knowledge that above that roaring beast, you were all that stood between the flames and any potential survivors.

The retreat, when it came, wasn't defeat, but a calculated withdrawal. Down ladders, stairs, or out windows, the fresh air would hit like a shock, momentarily erasing the oppressive heat and claustrophobia. But the memory of it lingered. The way your sweat boiled under your turnout gear, the rasp of your labored breaths, the grim realization that some floors were traps, where no amount of bravery could change the outcome.

The floor above the fire was a battleground few outside our brotherhood understood. We didn't just fight the blaze itself, but the invisible enemy of heat, the relentless tick of the clock against our air supply, and the knowledge that every move could be our last. It tested a different kind of courage than charging into the heart of the inferno. It was a slow burn, a grueling war of attrition fought in darkness, fueled by duty and the desperate hope that maybe, just maybe, this time we could cheat the fire gods and emerge dragging someone back from the brink.

The Fireboats
Disappear

That fiscal crisis in the 70s, it wasn't just numbers on a spreadsheet for us. It was a gut punch that rippled through the ranks, twisting loyalties and shattering dreams. I remember one guy in particular, a dedicated soul who'd spent years studying for his Coast Guard licenses, sweating over navigation charts and books. His goal was singular: becoming a pilot on the fireboats. It was a tough path, demanding, but those boats held a mythic appeal – fighting blazes on the water, that constant dance with the unpredictable tides and currents.

Those harbor fireboats, they were lifesavers. Back then, the waterways were a different beast – crammed with ships, tugs and barges, those old creosote soaked wooden piers that flared up like tinderboxes with a single carelessly tossed cigarette. But piers and boats…they don't pay taxes, don't make a fuss in the papers when they get neglected. When the budgets tightened, it was easy pickings. Fireboats shuttered – some entirely, others left running with skeleton crews. The Coast Guard would handle the rest, they figured, those pencil-pushers in their ivory towers.

For the guys who dedicated their lives to that specialized service, it was a disaster. Not just the sting of being sidelined, but a deeper betrayal. They weren't just firefighters, they were mariners, their skills hard-won through endless hours of practice and study. Families uprooted; futures capsized along with the budget cuts. I wondered what became of that guy with the salt spray in his eyes and a seagull's cry in his voice. Did he stay on, the fire in his belly dimmed by bureaucracy? Or did he walk away, leaving a piece of himself behind on those docks?

You see, politicians play games with numbers, with abstract notions of cost versus benefit. But there's a human toll they don't factor into those spreadsheets. It's the workers who get caught in the crossfire; their dedication trampled by the tides of fiscal panic. It's the families back home, bracing for the next curve ball that might leave them adrift.

Those who stayed, the few, learned a bitter lesson that week. We were part of a machine, subject to its whims, and even the most fervent passion couldn't shield us from the blunt force of a budget cut. Every day we rolled out on those rigs, we carried the weight of those fallen fireboats, the echoes of lost dreams a grim soundtrack to our work.

The city still burned; the rescues still had to be made. But in those quiet moments between the blare of sirens, a new kind of cynicism would creep in. Our loyalty wasn't unbreakable, not when it could be so easily sacrificed. Those wounds took longer to heal than any battle-field injury. It was a reminder that some of the fiercest battles we fought were against the forces that could extinguish the spirit of the job itself, one heartbroken firefighter at a time.

High and Low Relief

Firefighting…it's the art of imposing order onto unrelenting chaos. It's about discipline and drills, but also about being ready for that flaming apartment fire on a day when everything, absolutely everything, goes sideways. And then, just when you think you've seen it all, the Bronx throws you a punchline like that whole Lieutenant High and Lieutenant Low switcheroo, when Lieutenant High was relieved by Lieutenant Low for the night tour. I mean, c'mon, who writes this stuff?

See, we thrive on routine. It's armor against the madness. Every inch of that firehouse gleamed testament to our endless, manic scrubbing. Not. But then the universe, bless its twisted little heart, drops a banana peel in your path. You're left sputtering, trying to square that not so military-grade spit shine with the cosmic absurdity of THAT particular shift change.

It became a firefighter's urban legend. Proof that, even with our radios crackling and sirens blaring, life was one big vaudeville act, and we were stuck juggling flaming chainsaws while dodging unicycles.

But the thing is, those weird moments…they became lifelines. Because this job, it gets under your skin, messes with your head. You see the worst, and sometimes it's those missing pot roast days (looking at you, "Mostly"), or the wedding dress in the garbage, which keep you sane. It's the reminder that, yeah, sometimes life really is stranger than any screenplay.

We became connoisseurs of the bizarre. The corner bodega eternally out of those chocolate donuts JUST when the night crew shambles in for their morning fix? A twisted form of torture. Rescuing a tangled-up pit bull instead of the panicked puppy you imagined? Welcome to the Bronx, bud.

See, if you don't learn to laugh, you'll cry. And sometimes, the crying turns to that dry, cracked hysteria only a fellow firefighter understands. So, we'd cling to those oddities, to Lieutenant High handing off to Lieutenant Low, like proof that the world hadn't completely lost its marbles.

This job, it's a full-on assault. One minute you're in hell's kitchen, then some idiot's car gets loose and whacks the rig, and it's a slapstick comedy. The Bronx, she'll break your heart, make you doubt everything, and then…BAM! She'll toss a cosmic joke your way, make you laugh till you hurt.

Because, hey, who else gets to see the entire human tragicomedy unfold in a single shift? Those moments, the ridiculous ones, they ain't frivolous. They're our vaccination against burnout, a twisted reminder that we're alive, even when we smell like death warmed over.

THE SAFETY BATTALION

The Safety Battalion. Those guys were supposed to be the extra set of eyes watching out for us on the big fires. Monitoring the buildings for collapse hazards, making sure we weren't taking unnecessary risks in the chaos. Sounds good in theory, right? But the disconnect sometimes…it was enough to make your blood boil hotter than any blaze.

It all depended on who was running the show. If that safety chief was a veteran, someone who'd walked the walk, who understood the chaos of a major fire firsthand, then those extra eyes could be a godsend. But then there were the other types. You know, the ones from the slower areas, or those more comfortable with a clipboard than a hose line. They'd swoop in, all shiny helmets and stern expressions, and suddenly firefighting became micromanagement hell.

I'll never forget that one fire. We had a whole row of stores going up in flames, a freakin' gasoline tanker adding to the insanity, and our chief was in the thick of it, directing men and machine, strategizing against a beast of a blaze. Then along comes the safety chief, finds our guy, and what's his main concern? Not the precarious wall about to collapse, or the potential for that tanker to explode and take out half the block, but a dude walking around with an untucked shirt.

Our chief went ballistic. In the nicest possible terms, he told that safety guy exactly where he could shove his minor uniform infraction, and if he didn't get the hell out of the way with his nitpicking, there'd be something else getting tucked in some rather uncomfortable places.

It'd be funny if it weren't so infuriating. Those line units, we were the ones knee-deep in the muck, risking our necks to control the madness, and armchair quarterbacks would waltz in, more worried about our collar buttons than the fact we were a breath away from disaster. The disconnect was maddening.

See, firefighting, especially in the Bronx, wasn't about pristine procedures and spit-shined boots. It was about grit, instinct honed through a thousand chaotic battles, and the ability to think ten steps ahead while flames licked at your heels. We respected the risks, lived and breathed the dangers, but sometimes those safety guys got so bogged down in the small stuff they lost sight of the big picture.

That day, midst the roar of the flames and the shouts of firefighters battling an impossible inferno, there was this microcosm of a much bigger issue. It was the clash between those who fought the fires up close, and those who watched from a safe distance. Sure, safety mattered, absolutely. But when a building's about to go, a sloppy shirt-tail is the least of your worries. In those moments, what we truly needed weren't reminders of the rule book, but trust that we knew what the hell we were doing, and the freedom to do it without being second-guessed by someone who didn't have soot on their face, or the weight of a burning city on their shoulders.

R&R

R&R – that hour or half hour of grace firefighters were sometimes granted after a good job…it was a blessing and a curse, dividing the firehouse into two camps. On one side, you had the gung-ho guys, adrenaline junkies who hated the idea of missing even a moment of the action. For them, it wasn't about the rest, but the fear of missing out on the next big one. Then there was the rest of us – grimy, exhausted, longing for a shower and a few moments of peace to decompress before the next alarm inevitably pulled us back into the fray.

The whole thing was left to the chief's discretion. As we pulled away from the wreckage, sweat and soot caked onto our faces, there'd be that tense waiting for his verdict. "Take an hour," he might say, and a wave of relief would wash over half the truck. Other times, it was a curt "take a half," a grudging compromise between necessity and that relentless itch for action. And if he was silent? Well, sometimes, if the call hadn't been a complete gut-wrencher, officers would take matters into their own hands, ordering a detour back to the firehouse for a quick cleanup and a stolen sliver of respite.

Those showers were a lifeline. We'd turn the water scalding hot, trying to blast the filth and lingering anxiety of the fire from our skin. The stink of smoke clung stubbornly, but even a few minutes under the spray could feel like hitting the reset button on a body pushed to its limits.

It was more than just physical, though. That precious hour offered a sliver of mental recovery too. A chance to crack a dumb joke, to chug some half-decent firehouse coffee without the pressure of a ticking clock and that ever-present fear of the voice alarm shattering the fragile peace. We could even pretend, for those few minutes, that we were just regular folks, not the ones called to face the city's worst.

Back at the firehouse, the rest versus rush debate would reignite. The clock ticked down mercilessly, and the tension would build for those who just couldn't stand the wait. Meanwhile, weary bones would find refuge on tattered couches, a few minutes of closed eyes a precious treasure against the inevitable chaos to come.

R&R, it was a concession to the reality that we weren't machines. That even the most hardened firefighter needed a chance to restock, both physically and mentally, before being thrown back into the breach. It was a constant tug-of-war between the need to recharge and the insatiable, relentless rhythm of a city that never truly slept.

Some hated it, saw it as a disruption to the flow of the tour, the ever-present readiness to answer the call. But for most, those snatched moments of rest weren't about shirking duty. They were about survival. Because a refreshed firefighter, a little less ragged around the edges, was a better firefighter. And when the alarm screamed again, ready or not, those precious moments might mean the difference between saving a life and watching helplessly as everything fell apart.

Study and Promotion

Those years studying for promotion…they were a battle waged not in flames, but in stacks of textbooks and the dull ache of a brain pushed to its limits. It wasn't just knowledge we were cramming, but a way of life – firefighting procedures, building codes, electrical codes, housing codes, administrative jargon, everything including the unpredictable chaos of an actual fire. Eight or more hours a day, we'd hunch over those books, the world narrowing to regulations and multiple-choice questions. The smell of burning buildings wasn't replaced by stale coffee and the desperate hum of overworked fluorescent lights but it sure nearly was.

The exams themselves were brutal. Short answers gnawing at details long buried in the books and our minds, essays testing not just your command of the material, but the ability to regurgitate it under pressure. Then the interviews, where the higher-ups peeled back the layers to see if you thought like a leader, not just a doer. Thousands of us across the city were locked in this silent war, our ranks only partially decided by bravery on the fireground, but also mainly by our ability to navigate a labyrinth of rules, regulations, and minutia on the civil service exams.

It took over our lives. Evenings with families were interrupted by studies on obscure building codes, weekends blurred into a haze of practice questions. Marriages strained under the relentless grind, the ever-present textbooks casting a shadow over everything. And for what? The chance to climb the ranks, the promise of a better salary, a bigger pension dangled like a carrot before us. Yet, under the flickering lights of those study sessions, some part of us withered, the adrenaline of the streets augmented by the dry legalese that might decide our future.

The irony of promotion was that it pulled you further from the action. The higher you climbed, the fewer fires you fought from up close and personal. It was a world of paperwork, budgets, and politics, where your success depended on mastering a whole new language of bureaucracy. But something changed in the process. The guy who'd pulled victims from burning buildings, who'd felt the heat on his face and the fear in his gut…he was slowly buried beneath those textbooks, those carefully crafted essays, and the knowledge that a wrong answer could sabotage years of sacrifice.

I'm not saying it wasn't important. Every level demanded more ability, more accountability. But it changed you, that endless studying. Turned you from a firefighter reacting by instinct into a manager calculating risks against regulations. It was a necessary evolution, maybe, but it came at a cost. There was a kind of purity to the fireground, a rawness that got lost to some guys with every promotion exam they aced.

When the results came out, there'd be celebration mixed with bittersweet relief. Then, it was back into the fight, but with a different weight to it. You'd earned it, that new title, but part of you knew that some battles couldn't be won in a classroom. As you climbed the greasy pole of promotion, sometimes you had to wonder if you were moving further away from the heart of why you joined this crazy brotherhood in the first place.

CROSS COUNTRY

In most Bronx firehouses, we prided ourselves on our fitness. Running the NYC Marathon was an annual tradition, and our firehouse sponsored a 5-mile cross-country race through a Bronx park. It was a point of pride. You wouldn't last long in our place if you couldn't keep up. I was a road runner myself, prided myself on my speed and endurance…until my first time running that damn cross-country course.

It looked easy enough on paper. Five miles, sure, I did twice that for training runs. But the park was a beast. The route wasn't just paved paths, but treacherous trails, twisting tree roots, and hidden dips that turned every step into a potential ankle sprain. The other guys, veterans of the course, seemed to glide over the obstacles, while I stumbled like a newborn calf.

I finished with a respectable time; pride battered but intact. The real surprise came the next day when my ankles ballooned into puffy betrayers, every step a symphony of pain. What the hell? I'd pounded the pavement for years without issue, but this backwoods trail had laid me low.

Turns out, city running didn't prepare you for the chaos of the wild. On the road, it was all about rhythm, a steady pace over predictable terrain. But that Bronx park race…it demanded a different kind of strength. Explosive bursts of power to navigate sudden inclines, the flexibility of a mountain goat to avoid hidden hazards. My muscles, conditioned for linear movement, screamed in protest at the constant shifts in balance, the unexpected jolts.

It was a humbling experience. I had the stamina, sure, but not the specific resilience those rough trails demanded. We joked about it afterward – my swollen ankles a badge of my inexperience. But there was a deeper lesson in that pain. Firefighting, like that race, wasn't just about brute force. It was about adaptability, about conquering the unpredictable. My lungs and legs might be strong, but I had to retrain my body to learn the language of the uneven ground beneath my feet.

The next year, you better believe I hit those trails alongside my marathon training. Stumbling less, finding a new rhythm in the unevenness. I never grew to love those root-riddled paths, but I gained a begrudging respect for them. Because they taught me something the city streets never could: to expect the unexpected, to find my footing even when the ground shifted beneath me. And those swollen ankles? They became a reminder that in our line of work, there was always a new challenge to overcome, always another way to prove yourself ready for whatever the unpredictable world threw our way.

DESCENT INTO DECAY

Those tenement basements weren't just a place for the super to hang out, sometimes they were a portal to hell. Or, at least, hell's foul-smelling waiting room. Each step was a surrender to the unseen, a plunge into a world where the air itself felt like a threat.

The smell hits you first. Not smoke, but the greasy funk of old pipes and a hundred years of neglect marinating in darkness. Decay dripped from the walls, a pungent stew of mold, ancient sewage, and God-knows-what festering in the corners. It coated your throat, a rancid reminder that this world below the world had its own ecosystem.

The rats were the landlords down there, fat and brazen. Their beady eyes gleamed in our flashlight beams, a flicker of contempt for the invaders. The cockroaches were their tenants – a seething, skittering tide, an endless wave of black that seemed to make the floor itself move. And the fleas…they were the silent assassins, tiny hitchhikers promising a week of maddening itches as a parting gift. Every scrape of a boot against the slime-covered concrete felt like an invitation for something to crawl, to burrow, to claim a piece of you.

Some basements had supers, their cramped quarters a beacon of human defiance against the rot. But most? They were abandoned to the shadows. Trash piled like grotesque sculptures, animal droppings mixed with the unnameable. Overhead, the pipes moaned, each drip a countdown to some unimaginable horror bursting forth.

Up on the street, fear was a familiar beast – a blaze, a madman, the shriek of metal twisting. Down here it was different, a cold sweat crawling over you, a sense of being outnumbered by the creeping, slithering, disease-bearing things lurking just beyond the beam of your light. You could scrub the filth off, extinguish the flames, but the basement stayed with you. It clung to your uniform, a permanent stain on your soul.

We weren't just firefighters; we were reluctant explorers in a world most pretended didn't exist. Sometimes, the worst battles weren't fought against raging infernos, but in the muck and stench, against the invisible horrors that lingered in your memory long after you climbed back up into the light. Because some fires, the insidious ones, never really go out.

WATER RESCUE

Wards Island…the training center. Those training days were a mix of useful drills and the kind of petty nitpicking that could make your blood boil. It was all about precision, every evolution broken down by those instructors with their clipboards and stern gazes. A hose stretched a fraction too slow, a ladder mishandled slightly, a vent cut without textbook execution, and our unit would get a black mark on some report that might as well have been written in ancient Greek for all the relevance it held during a real fire.

We'd earned a break near the seawall, a moment to catch our breath and swap grim jokes about the instructors' fondness for regulations over real-world experience. That's when the shouts erupted. "Someone's in the water!"

The East River isn't a damn swimming pool. Treacherous currents, a chaotic mix of barges, tugs and pleasure boats, with water so polluted even a fish would think twice. But there, a flash of panicked movement, a figure barely keeping their head above the murky chop.

Louie didn't hesitate. He was one of those guys, a city kid who'd grown up swimming in waters that should have carried a hazard warning. In seconds, his boots were off, shirt abandoned, and he was giving our captain a grim nod that said, "I got this." Then, he was in.

The rest of us were frozen. It wasn't part of the drill, wasn't remotely in the damn book for some stupid training exercise. But Louie, he didn't see regulations then, just a person fighting for their life. Stroke by stroke, he closed in, the treacherous river throwing everything it had against him. He reached the drowning figure, a woman, eyes wide with a terror that eclipsed any fear of the polluted water.

We watched, a collective breath held. He wrapped an arm around her, trod water, but the river kept trying to snatch them apart. Finally, the blessing of a passing pleasure craft, alerted by our shouts. They hauled them both aboard, dripping and gasping, but alive.

Turns out, suicide attempt. One of those desperate acts followed by stark second thoughts the moment it becomes real. On the shore, as medics swarmed, Louie stood shivering, a threadbare towel draped over his shoulders. Some instructor was sputtering about how it was reckless, not procedure, blah, blah, blah. Our captain cut him off with a glare that would've melted steel.

The citation Louie got felt a bit hollow, like an afterthought against the backdrop of that day. The real reward wasn't some piece of paper. It was the look on that woman's face when they hauled her onto that boat, a mix of raw shock and desperate gratitude. It was the quiet way Louie was treated, not with teasing, but a rough respect none of those instructors with their sterile rules could ever earn.

Wards Island, it should have been about controlled burns and ladder raises. Instead, it taught us a raw truth: regulations have their place, but sometimes, the river throws you a curve ball. Sometimes, the biggest test isn't how perfectly you can stretch a hose line, but whether you'll dive in to save a stranger, rules be damned.

The Helmet
Hail Mary

Louie was green back then, still earning his stripes. The fire in that old law tenement was a baptism into the worst the Lower East Side could offer – thick smoke, searing heat, and that maze-like layout that could swallow you whole in seconds. He'd made a gutsy grab on the floor above, found a victim where none should have been. But the way down? Blocked. Heat and smoke billowing up the stairs, turning his intended escape route into a questionable maw. Panic flared in his gut, the rookie terror battling against every bit of training he'd soaked up at the academy.

Old law tenements have their own cruel logic. Roof doors locked tight against junkies and criminals, a necessary evil against the dangers those forgotten rooftops held. But now, that possible padlock loomed like a death sentence. So, he did what desperation demanded – dragged the victim higher. One flight, then another, lungs burning, the roar of the fire a monstrous chorus behind him. Each step was a gamble, a desperate hope that the roof would offer salvation.

It didn't. The bulkhead door was a rusted, unyielding barrier. Nailed shut, a mocking testament to regulations meant for another world. Trapped, the heat rising relentlessly, his world narrowed to the rasping breaths of the unconscious victim and his own mounting terror.

But they'd drilled it into us back in proby school: when everything else fails, helmet out the window. No handie-talkies in those days; the budget wouldn't allow it. A last-ditch effort, a shining beacon of desperation midst the chaos. He hurled it out, felt the sting of the throw reverberate through his exhausted body. It was a primal act, a scream of Mayday carved not in words, but that simple piece of protective gear clattering on the street below.

The shouts came back, muffled through the floors. Footsteps, growing closer, and a sliver of hope slicing through the choking smoke. Someone had seen that helmet, understood. A brother, another fire-fighter pushing past the fear, past the very real danger, to reach those trapped above. The rescue was a blur of motion – a shadowy figure hauling them back, choking coughs as fresh air flooded Louie's lungs, then the frantic stumble down those same smoke-filled stairs that had become an impossible barrier just minutes before.

He survived. The victim did too. But the aftermath lingered. The debriefing was brutal, the flaws in tactics laid bare. We were trained for rescue, not self-preservation. Yet, the limitations of those textbook procedures slammed home in that near-fatal lesson. The need for added training, for a contingency plan when even the standard operating procedures broke down, gnawed at all of us.

Louie learned a different kind of heroism that day. The kind forged in the crucible of a near miss, the kind born out of the realization that even the best training can't predict the brutal chaos of the Lower East Side's back alleys. It was a reminder that sometimes survival isn't just about following the rules, but the desperate ingenuity born of a fight against the inevitable, a testament to the unspoken oath we took to have each other's backs, even when the fire had other plans.

THE PREACHER

My new aide, let's call him John, wasn't quite what I expected when I took over the battalion chief's slot as a short-term replacement. No gruff, old-school NYC fire veteran with a lifetime of street smarts etched on his face. Instead, he was soft-spoken, almost bookish looking, with the hint of a Midwestern twang clinging to his words. This wasn't Plan A for him. Small-town boy, college degree, and theology school. Then some life-altering event brought him to the Bronx and this soot-stained uniform. His wife, also a Midwesterner…she hated New York, the noise, the crowds, the constant tension humming just beneath the surface of this chaotic city.

There was a tension buzzing beneath his calm exterior, too, but not about fireground tactics. He was clearly a bright guy, but the disconnect was jarring. The regular officers, hardened by years in some of the roughest parts of the city, ran this battalion with a grizzled pragmatism. Rules were guidelines, not holy texts. And while John grasped the theory, his face couldn't hide the discomfort with that gap between what the training center taught and what the rules and regulations called for, and the way things actually worked on the streets.

Those first few months, I was a temporary fixture in a world that clearly wasn't his first choice. He did the job, followed orders, but there was a kind of hesitancy in him, like he was holding back a vital piece of himself, but he was good at his job. We spent long hours in the car, rolling from call to call, and the conversations drifted away from fire strategy and into the deeper questions that seemed to haunt him. About faith, family, about the gap between the ideal world and the gritty mess of the one we found ourselves in.

Slowly, something came into focus. Maybe he saw that I wasn't one of the old guard, that there was a shared discomfort in us both, even if our paths diverged wildly. He'd relax a little, a flicker of dry humor emerging as he'd dissect some particularly absurd situation we'd witnessed. The rescue of a disturbed resident on a windowsill ready to jump, or how a rescue could turn into a near-riot, or how a perfectly good meal could be interrupted by a spectacular taxpayer fire. He even confessed to finding a grim amusement in the sheer audacity of the things we saw and did.

When my assignment ended, it felt less like losing a skilled aide and more like watching a man step a little closer to figuring out who he was meant to be. I wouldn't have bet on him sticking it out, not long term, but when I heard he'd gotten hired back in that hometown department of his, I felt a quiet satisfaction. Maybe the right place for a man like him wasn't in the heart of this relentless city but fighting different kinds of battles.

I like to think that somewhere out there he made a damn good fire chief, one who understood the rule book but also the unspoken truths that couldn't be written in any manual. Maybe his detour through the Bronx taught him something about faith – not the kind found in churches, but forged in smoky hallways and the desperate hope echoing in an alarm bell's clang. He might not have been a Bronx lifer like me, but for a while, he fought the good fight right here in this messy beast of a city. And maybe, hopefully he left with a little more than just soot on his boots.

THE CHALKBOARD

The grime-caked chalkboard at the housewatch, a relic from a bygone era, was more than just a place to list assignments. It was a symbol of a department yearning for modernization in a world obsessed with other things. Here, midst the ringing bells and idling engines, a crucial system remained stubbornly analog, a ticking time bomb in a profession where split seconds could mean the difference between life and death.

The officer's ritual – meticulously crafting a riding list every tour, one for himself, one for the rig, and a grand finale of duplication on the chalkboard – was a testament to dedication, not efficiency. It was a system ripe for error. Imagine the chaos when the "crap hit the fan," as some so aptly phrased it. A building collapse, a mayday call – the desperate scramble for a headcount, a frantic search for a misplaced name. Was the list correct? Did someone stay behind on an errand? Was there a last-minute change that never made it to the board?

The irony was almost laughable. A society that could launch rockets and explore distant galaxies couldn't seem to manage a simple digital solution for a firehouse. This outdated system wasn't just inefficient; it was a potential death knell in the face of a real emergency.

The need for modernization was undeniable. A digital roster, synced across devices, accessible in real-time – these weren't luxuries;

they were necessities. Imagine the peace of mind, the knowledge that at a single glance, they could know exactly who was in the fire, who was safe, and who might need rescue.

But budgets, ever tight, seemed to have no room for such advancements. More money for bigger fire trucks, for better equipment – that was understandable. But to streamline a seemingly mundane task? It was often seen as an afterthought, a budgetary black hole.

The firefighters, however, knew better. They understood that progress wasn't just about bigger and flashier. Sometimes, the most significant advancements were the quiet ones, the digital upgrades that saved lives not with brute force, but with the elegance of efficiency. The fight for modernization wasn't about comfort; it was about ensuring that every firefighter went home at the end of their shift, a silent prayer scrawled not on a dusty chalkboard, but etched in the collective consciousness of a department that valued its heroes more than outdated traditions.

Integrity in the Rubble

That civil service promotion list, it wasn't gospel like it should have been. It was supposed to be simple: study your brains out, take the grueling exam, and your score earns you a place on the list, determining your future. But politics had a way of smearing its greasy fingerprints on everything, even the seemingly merit-based system of our department. Old lists "extended" a bureaucratic smoke-screen hiding the hand-picked promotions of those with powerful friends, while those who played by the rules rotted on a new list, their hard-earned spots pushed further out of reach.

I knew a guy – let's call him *Lucky* for his lack of any discernible talent beyond an uncanny ability to be at the right party at the right time and, of course, belonging to the right political party. When the old list was about to expire, his name languishing near the bottom, it, the old civil service list, mysteriously gained new life. Months ticked into more months, and all the while, those of us who had sweated blood to make that new list were forced to play a waiting game, our dreams of promotion put on hold for the sake of some politically connected schmuck.

And then, the idiot gets his promotion. Lands in our division one day, fresh badge, and the swagger of someone who'd never truly earned their stripes. It was a pile of smoldering rubble framed with teetering brick walls, which sealed my disgust. What was once a tene-ment reduced to a mostly collapsed precarious pile of charred wood and twisted steel, with a few wisps of dying embers sending smoke signals into the air. This was after the main blaze, after the all-clear. Nothing at once life-threatening, and no amount of water was gonna turn that wreckage back into a building. Yet, here's Lucky, ordering my guys into harm's way, pointing at those wisps like they were some apocalyptic dragon in need of slaying.

I refused. Point blank. Wasn't risking my guys poking around in that building for a pointless gesture, for some rookie officer's need to play conquering hero on a pile of ash. We could check it, let those embers fizzle out naturally. We had real fires to fight, real lives to save in this city that never slept.

He sputtered, the flush of his unearned authority deepening. It was the clash of two worlds: the firefighter forged in the crucible, and the paper tiger promoted through backroom deals. I didn't mince words. There was no respect in my voice, only the cold disdain for a man more concerned with appearances than the safety of those under his command.

Lucky backed off. He had to – even he was smart enough to recog-nize the line he couldn't cross with a veteran crew that saw through his facade like cheap glass. He left with a mumbled bullshit of some report, but I couldn't have cared less. In that moment, staring at that broken shell of a building, I knew which side I was on, and it wasn't beside some hollow shell of an officer whose greatest talent was kissing the right rings or the right asses.

Later, I'd hear whispers of how Lucky never amounted to much. Another name on the roster, fading into the background as those who earned their way up the chain of command outshone him, their dedica-tion burning far brighter than any politically fueled promotion ever could. He retired a year or so later. There's a satisfaction in that – a vindication of the way things should be. But on that day, with the stink of burned dreams lingering in the air, it was a bitter victory. Because for every Lucky that climbed undeserved, there were good firefighters, the best of us, who got left behind, forced to watch as the system they bled for got twisted out of shape.

No Butts About It

Butt the ladder. It was pounded into our heads from day one of proby school. A simple thing, really – one guy on the rungs, the other with a boot braced solid against the base, a human anchor against catastrophe. It wasn't fancy, wasn't about complex drills, just a testament to the bedrock fact that no one fights alone in this job if it can be helped.

Then there was that day, Jimmy on that folding 10-footer, trying to reach a window. A routine task, barely worth a second thought. But somewhere in the rush, the shouted orders and the urgency that hung in the air, that basic principle was forgotten. No one butted that damn ladder.

I heard the crack before the scream. Not the snap of wood, but the sickening sound of bone meeting unforgiving concrete. Jimmy was down, writhing, and in that one sickening moment, the world fractured. One heartbeat he was climbing, the next, he was a broken heap, a grim testament to how quickly safety unraveled into chaos. He had landed on his feet, and his ankles and the tiny bones in his feet took the brunt of it.

The ambulance drove him away, its siren a futile wail against the weight of our shared guilt. The next day, we visited him at the hospital, awkwardly shuffling into a room heavy with forced optimism and the sharp smell of antiseptic. Each of us carried the invisible image of his fall, the way his face twisted in agony as the ladder kicked out beneath him.

The news was grim. Shattered bones, surgery, a whisper of permanent damage hanging in the sterile air. Jimmy, normally full of rough jokes and an unshakable bravado, seemed shrunken. The fire in his eyes was muted, replaced by a fear that went deeper than the pain radiating through his cast.

He never came back. Not the way we needed him to. We went about our relentless routine – the fires, the rescues, the rhythm of a city that never mourned its losses for long. Yet, the ghost of that fall lingered. It echoed in every ladder we climbed, a silent rebuke that whispered of complacency and cutting corners.

Years later, I saw him on the street at some function. Even with the distance of time between us, I recognized him instantly. The swagger in his stride was gone, replaced by a barely perceptible limp, and there was resignation in his eyes as we exchanged the usual pleasantries. We were both older, lines etched onto our faces not just by age, but by everything we'd seen, everything we'd lost.

I wanted to ask, to find words to express the lingering guilt, the knowledge that we'd failed him that day. But the right sentences never came. Some wounds heal crooked, and some failures never find absolution. We parted ways, him dissolving back into the anonymity of the crowd, a constant reminder of how fragile the line was between hero and victim.

Butt the ladder. It wasn't just a drilled-in tactic anymore. It was a vow, fueled by the lingering pain of Jimmy's fall, a silent promise that for every rung climbed, there would be a brother on the ground, standing resolute against the forces that conspired to pull us under. It was the least we could do to honor the memory of a fallen comrade, and the simple truth that in this unforgiving profession, we were only as safe as the bonds we formed.

THE MARATHON

The animal house, that's what they called our house. It wasn't an insult, but a badge of honor worn with grim satisfaction. Our patch of the Bronx demanded a different breed of firefighter. We weren't just hauling hoses and swinging axes but running a relentless gauntlet of flames and chaos. Being in shape wasn't optional, it was the price of survival.

Jogging became a lifeline. Stolen hours on our days off, pounding the pavement, the rhythm of our footfalls a counterpoint to the erratic beat of the alarms. We weren't built for elegance, those bulky turnout coats hanging off us like lead blankets on a hot summer run. But beneath that weight, muscles hardened, lungs expanded, and a quiet determination bloomed.

The Marathon…that became our annual proving ground. A lot of our guys joined in with the FDNY marathon running team, a motley crew of firefighters from across the city, united by sweat, shared blisters, and a stubborn refusal to quit. It was more than a race; it was a city-wide battle of the badges, with the police team our eternal rivals. That Mayor's Trophy, it wasn't just a hunk of polished metal – it was bragging rights fueled by sweat and sacrifice.

There was a raw honesty to those runs. Titles, ranks, they got stripped away, leaving us all clad in identical shorts, faded FDNY tees, and red baseball caps. The rookie and the grizzled captain slogged it out side by side, grunting through the miles, the shared goal a powerful equalizer. We didn't just get stronger running those routes, but tighter as a unit. When the alarm rang, the trust built on those city streets translated into the instinctive teamwork that meant the difference between life and death on the fireground.

On race day, there were no crowds cheering us from our district. But that didn't matter. Every mile chipped away under our worn sneakers was a mile earned for our guys back in the Bronx. Some guys who weren't running came to greet us when we entered the Bronx part of the race. Gatorade and cookies. We pushed past exhaustion, the sting of cramps, the body's desperate pleas to quit. Because out there, in the anonymity of those 26.2 miles, we ran not for ourselves but for something bigger. Pride. For the unseen battles fought in those burning tenements, for the strength to charge into the inferno when the rest of the world was running away.

Crossing that finish line wasn't always about personal records. Sometimes, it was simply making it back with a time we could face our brothers with. Win or lose against the NYPD, we'd done our part. That trophy, if we were lucky enough to earn it, wasn't just for us – it was a reminder that the fight didn't begin or end with the fire itself. It started in those solitary runs, in the relentless push for better, stronger, faster.

Because when we rolled towards the next blaze, lungs burning and legs trembling with fatigue, we knew we hadn't just run a race. We'd spent those miles forging ourselves into the firefighters the Bronx demanded, one ragged breath at a time.

Air Mail Alley

The alleyways between those old tenements…they weren't just pathways, but festering wounds in the belly of the Bronx. A testament to forgotten corners and desperate pragmatism. It was easier, you see, to airmail your trash out the back or side window than haul it down flights of stairs to the overloaded cans. Bottles, food scraps, old furniture – they all rained down, forming a noxious carpet of decay several feet deep.

Then came the fires. A flash of twisted inspiration ignited by frustration, boredom, or who knows what other demons lurked in those shadowed places. A gallon or two of gasoline, a fed-up resident, a tossed match, and the alley was momentarily transformed into an inferno, burning away the obnoxious trash heap. And guess who got the call? Us, the heroes armed with hoses and not much more, tasked with extinguishing not just flames, but the stench of neglect.

Descending into those blazing depths wasn't like regular firefighting. The air itself became a weapon, thick with acrid fumes, choking us with the essence of rot and decay. The ground underfoot wasn't solid earth, but a touring mass of half-burned garbage that threatened to swallow us whole. No gleaming engines here, just a hydrant and a rig hooked to a snaking line, spewing water into the heart of the filth.

It was a war waged on two fronts. Against the flames themselves, which clung to the trash heaps with stubborn malevolence, and the sheer revulsion the job demanded. The stink permeated everything – our turnout gear, skin, the residue clinging to the back of our throats no matter how hard we scrubbed when the battle was done. We'd emerge, filthy and exhausted, a lingering nausea clinging to us far more fiercely than any smoke.

Those alley fires were a grotesque symptom of the larger disease gnawing at the Bronx. A reminder that some battles we fought weren't just against the elements, but the despair that made this kind of reckless destruction seem like a solution. We could douse the flames, shuffle through the burnt trash that choked those narrow gaps, but the root of it all…that was a much deeper fire, one that would burn long after our engines had rolled away.

In those moments, it was hard to feel heroic. We were more scavengers than saviors, picking through the detritus of lives lived on the ragged edge. The alleyway, with its reeking testament to apathy and desperation, became a grim reflection of the battles we couldn't win with water alone. We did our job, gritting our teeth against the stench and absurdity of it all, but the lingering unease wasn't something easily washed away.

Sometimes, the weight of the city wasn't just the blazing buildings and desperate rescues. It was in those fetid alleyways, where the fire revealed a brokenness far greater than the charred trash heaps themselves. It was a reminder that some of our bravest fights weren't against flames, but the forces that could reduce a human existence to a pile of gasoline-soaked refuse waiting for its spark.

Vacant Lots

V acant lots...they were the scars on the Bronx landscape, where tenements once stood before fire or neglect brought them crashing down. Instead of rubble, these forgotten patches became dumping grounds, a chaotic tapestry of busted furniture, rotting food, broken glass...and worse. The rats loved it, of course. Thrived in it like fat kings ruling a kingdom of decay. We'd get called out for the fires – sometimes a bored kid's mischief, sometimes a homeless person trying to stay warm, sometimes something far more sinister.

Then there were the bodies. Wrapped in dirty carpets like macabre gifts, tossed among the trash with a casual disregard that made your stomach turn. You'd spot within the flames – a flash of exposed skin, an unnatural curve that didn't belong in the landscape of debris. The transformation from 'rubbish fire' to crime scene was swift, the stench of burning garbage replaced by the icy tendrils of dread coiling up your spine.

My boss, a bureaucratic bulldog if there ever was one, had a particular bee in his bonnet about those bodies. It wasn't the human tragedy that got under his skin, but the paperwork it generated. See, if that poor soul had maybe, possibly, died from smoke inhalation while being dumped like some oversize piece of trash, then according to his twisted logic, it became a fire-related death. And fire deaths, those demanded special 30-page reports, a tedious litany of details that did nothing to bring anyone justice.

Never mind that the victim likely met their end long before the flames reached them. Never mind the reek of foul play hanging thicker than any smoke. My boss saw a checklist, not a person. I'd be ordered out there, hours after the detectives and crime techs had gone, to write up some nonsense report about smoke patterns, potential points of origin, names, times, and dispatchers' badge numbers, all for a fire that had likely been started to hide a murder.

Stomach churning, I'd remember that filth, trying to fit my observations to some bureaucratic narrative that held no meaning in the face of the true brutality that often lay at the heart of those lots. The absurdity of it would gnaw at me. The way some lives became mere fuel for a paperwork firestorm, their stories reduced to check marks on a forgotten report.

The rats, they'd watch you with beady eyes, unbothered by the lingering stench of death or the bureaucratic circus that descended upon their decaying kingdom. Their existence mirrored the forgotten nature of those empty lots, both grim reminders that even in a city teeming with life, some losses were swept aside as readily as the trash, forgotten and unseen until a stray spark revealed their presence.

Those reports I wrote never brought closure or justice. They vanished into some dusty file in the bowels of headquarters, as insignificant as the victims themselves to those in their ivory towers. But those vacant lots, the stench of charred trash mixing with the lingering echo of violence, they became seared into my memory. A testament to the cruel underbelly of the city, where lives could end in darkness, swallowed by a landscape of neglect, just another piece of debris in the endless cycle of decay.

DICKY FLOCCO

icky Flocco, the toothless homeless guy who wandered the Borough of Brooklyn, was a living contradiction – kind-hearted, talkative, an easy smile and a hearty laugh disguising the pain and struggle of his existence. He'd rest where he could, grab a meal or coffee when the opportunity arose, and pop up where you least expected him. Sometimes he slept in firehouse basements, bringing the latest rumors as his currency. Once, I even met him unloading boxes at the uniform store at Headquarters!

The very fact that firehouses, these hubs of emergency response, became havens for Dicky highlights a strange kind of symbiosis. He offered gossip and companionship, a break from the relentless intensity of the firefighters' world. In turn, he found a semblance of shelter, a place where he wasn't just an outsider, but held a rough-hewn place within the community.

Dicky's very existence points to the gaps in our social safety net. The fact that a man could make a life, however precarious, flitting between firehouses, reveals how easy it is for people to slip through the cracks. It raises questions about mental health support, affordable housing, and the unseen struggles of those on the fringes of our cities.

One can imagine the firefighters' reactions being a mix of amusement, exasperation, even a glimmer of protective affection. He was likely a disruptive presence, yet he became a part of the offbeat fabric of their lives. This speaks to the inherent humanity of those who dedicate themselves to saving lives – even when the life in need of saving is a scruffy, freewheeling wanderer with a knack for gossip.

Every city has its characters, and Dicky seems to have embodied that role with panache. His acceptance within the firehouses suggests a world where official rules bend to make room for human connection, where unspoken camaraderie can supersede societal expectations. The fact that people still ask about him years later highlights the enduring power of unusual characters, leaving us to wonder what became of him and his unique place in the tapestry of the city.

The tale of Dicky Flocco is a bittersweet one. It's a microcosm of the big city, with its mix of grit, heart, and the ever-present awareness of those who live differently on its edges. His story compels us to think about the unseen support systems that exist, the kindness that can flourish in the least expected places, and the enduring nature of those individuals who defy simple categorization.

Where Tough Love
Saves Lives

A firehouse isn't a democracy, that's for damn sure. You need order, respect for the chain of command, and a clear understanding that screwing up can have consequences far worse than a bad report card. But discipline, real discipline, isn't just about barking orders and doling out punishments. It's about fostering an environment where mistakes get corrected, lessons get learned, and the unit remains a tight-knit machine in the face of chaos.

My way? Yeah, it was old-fashioned. Office cleared out, intercom crackling, and firefighter Smith – or hell, even a seasoned lieutenant – getting the "report to the office" summons. That walk down the hall, it had a certain weight to it. They knew it wasn't gonna be a friendly chat.

But before a word of judgment was passed, they got their say. An explanation, an excuse, maybe even a flash of defiance. I listened hard. Sometimes, there was a good reason buried under a bad attitude. Sometimes, it was pure bull, an attempt to dodge responsibility. But the act of listening, of forcing them to explain themselves, that was the first step.

Then, it was my turn. Laying down the law – why what they did was wrong, how it jeopardized not only themselves, but the crew, the whole damn operation. No yelling, no personal insults. Just cold, hard facts and the promise of repercussions if it happened again.

Was it fair, always? Probably not. But it was consistent. The guys knew where I stood, knew that a screw-up wouldn't be ignored, but also wouldn't result in some arbitrary punishment. It created boundaries, a sense of respect – or at least a healthy dose of fear.

Discipline isn't about breaking someone down. It's about building them up strong enough to function when the heat's on. It's about reminding them that in this job, their actions don't just affect them, they affect everyone who trusts them to have their back when the flames are dancing.

SPARKING A FLAME OF SERVICE

F ire buffs and volunteers...they were always a mixed bag. Some were pure gold – genuinely passionate about the work, eager to learn, a shot of fresh enthusiasm in the middle of a long, grimy shift. But then there were the others, the wide-eyed adrenaline junkies looking for a quick fix, a story to brag about at the bar. The volunteers who came might have a handful of calls in a month back at home – we'd have that before lunch on a Tuesday. Don't get me wrong, if they were in it for the right reasons, they could get a hell of an education.

The worst though, the ones who drove me nuts, were always the camera-happy tourists. A working fire scene is pure, controlled chaos. We're making life-or-death decisions based on experience, on instinct – the last thing I need is some hobbyist buzzing around trying to get that perfect Instagram shot.

And don't even get me started on the special requests. Like that time some bigwig downtown asked me to entertain a group of visiting European buffs. As if I don't have enough on my plate, now I'm their personal guide to the hottest blazes in the city? Sure, they'd pull out some fancy snacks as thanks – who needs lobster when the roof's caving in?

The problem though: it's the liability. One wrong move, one bit of misplaced enthusiasm, and I'm the one with the mountains of paper-work dealing with the fallout. Most times, however, their enthusiasm was really great to watch.

Now, let's be clear – those who came in with the right attitude, willing to get their hands dirty, to learn? No problem. They were always welcome. The thing is, some of those guys saw the heroics, the rush, not the sweat, the burns, the sheer grit it takes to do this job right. They wanted a cool story, not the knowledge that comes from facing down the beast day after day. They had to keep in mind that it's our lives on the line.

Don't get me wrong, most meant well. And hey, maybe a few of them were inspired enough to become real volunteers. But very few of them? They were like tourists in a warzone, snapping away, maybe getting a T-shirt or a shoulder patch, then they'd vanish back into their daily routines. And we were left with the gnawing worry that maybe, just maybe, they were one distraction too many.

I loved their enthusiasm. But firefighting isn't about pretty pictures. It's about the dirt, the exhaustion, the choices no camera can really show. If those guys left with even a sliver of that understanding, great. If not, well... we made some new friends and at least they got a decent story out of it, right?

THE TAXI SERVICE

Our firehouse, tucked under the rumbling tracks of the elevated subway line, wasn't exactly a dream assignment for guys looking to pick up some overtime. Getting someone to voluntarily work on a tour in our patch of the Bronx was like pulling teeth. They either feared the relentless workload or worried their cars would vanish into the night, leaving them stranded in a neighborhood no one dared park in for long.

Limited parking wasn't just an inconvenience for us – it was woven into the fabric of our daily grind. We double-parked on the street, gambling against the possibility of an unfriendly cop. Sideswipes were routine, and waking up to smashed windows was as regular an occurrence as the morning alarm. The sidewalk? That was our made-up lot, minus a sliver for pedestrians, a defiant act against a city that couldn't care less about the firefighters protecting its neglected corners. If you dared venture too far from the firehouse, your car might be a distant memory by the end of your tour.

The result was a logistical nightmare. We weren't just begging guys for extra manpower, we sometimes resorted to offering them an escort service. The chief would spend precious time, both before and during a tour, driving from firehouse to firehouse, picking up reluctant volunteers and then later, ferrying them back. It was an absurd reality – fire-fighters getting chauffeurs not out of luxury, but from grim necessity.

Word spread like wildfire through the department and our firehouse gained a reputation. We weren't just known for the blazes, but for the sheer adventure of getting there. Some saw it as a badge of honor – proof you could survive anything the city threw at you. Others used it as an excuse, turning down the OT we desperately needed with a whispered "nah, I don't want to risk my car in that neighborhood."

We couldn't blame them entirely. There was a kind of madness in how the city seemed to shrug off our plight. Like those beat-up trucks and the soot-streaked walls of our firehouse, the disappearing cars were just another symptom of a place chronically under served and underestimated.

It made the fires burn hotter in a way. Not just the flames we battled, but the frustration kindling inside us. That battle for a parking space, the absurd ritual of the chief's pick-up service, became a testament to our forgotten corner of the Bronx. We were the firefighters nobody wanted to be, in a place everyone tried to avoid, fighting not only the infernos but the constant, ridiculous hurdles placed in our way.

Sometimes, in the back of my mind, I imagine those reluctant OT guys, safely ensconced back at their firehouses with their secure parking spots. Did they ever think about us, double-parked and defiant, a testament to the grit it took to not just fight the flames, but show up to the fight in the first place?

YOUNG STUDS AND OLD CHAUFFEURS

The dynamic between the eager young guys and the seasoned veteran behind the wheel is a classic microcosm of life itself. The impatient youth, fueled by adrenaline and a sense of invincibility, pushing for action. The wizened old-timers, their caution born from hard-won experience and a long tally of close calls.

It's easy to see why the rookies got frustrated. In a world measured in the time it takes a fire to devour an apartment building, the slightest hesitation can feel like an eternity. Every second lost in traffic, battling narrow streets choked with double-parked cars, or gingerly navigating around oblivious pedestrians can feel like a failure before they've even stepped off the truck.

But what those young guys didn't yet grasp was the heavy responsibility those senior drivers carried. They weren't being cautious out of cowardice or complacency, but from the weight of knowing how quickly it could all go wrong. They'd seen the aftermath of reckless driving – wrecked rigs, injured brothers, the devastating consequences written in twisted metal and ruined lives. Their caution was a shield, not against the fire, but the chaos they knew lurked at every inter-section.

I had to have a conversation, finally, after some complaints from the youngsters, with a veteran driver and it likely stirred something in him. Not a direct order to speed up, but a reminder. A reminder of the eager faces behind him, the trust they placed in him to get them to the fire safely, the lives depending on their arrival and what he was probably like as a younger man. The fact that he improved his response times, yet kept it safe, that's the mark of a good firefighter – finding the balance between urgency and calculated action.

That struggle between youthful impatience and seasoned wisdom repeats itself across every profession, every aspect of life. We want results, and we want them now. We chafe against limitations, yearn to charge forward without restraint. But with time, with hard-earned lessons, comes a different kind of understanding. We begin to see those unseen dangers, the potential missteps that only experience can reveal.

The ideal, of course, is a true blend. The unbridled enthusiasm of youth is tempered by the wise hand of experience. The cautious veteran inspired by the urgency of those still learning the ropes. It's a delicate dance, and sometimes it takes an outside nudge, a conversation, to remind both sides what they bring to the fight.

There's something beautiful about that moment when a veteran firefighter, driven by duty and a rekindled sense of purpose, finds that extra gear without sacrificing the hard-won knowledge that keeps his crew alive. It's a testament to the silent bond between firefighters, the understanding that true courage isn't just about charging into the flames, but doing so wisely, so everyone can come back out again ready to fight another day.

THE OLD-DAYS GASOLINE

Back when I started, those engines and trucks were beasts of a different breed. Gas-guzzling engines, manual transmissions that demanded a symphony of double-clutching and steering that was more about muscle power than modern convenience. But the real nightmare wasn't on the streets – it lurked beneath our feet.

Those basement gasoline tanks…they were ticking time bombs. You'd smell the fumes before you saw the source – a creeping stain spreading across the concrete, the sharp tang cutting through the lingering scent of old engine grease. One spark, one careless cigarette, and that basement could erupt into an inferno to rival any blaze we fought.

Refueling days were the worst. The fuel truck pulling up, the rumble of the pump, every drip and gurgle echoing the potential for disaster. We were on edge the entire time, eyes peeled for any sign of a leak, the stink of gasoline hanging heavy in the air. Inspecting that basement became a grim ritual – before, during, and after delivery – holding our breaths in silent prayer that today wasn't the day our firehouse went up in smoke before we even rolled towards the real flames.

There's something uniquely insidious about a danger that's built into your own safe haven. We were trained to battle infernos in crumbling tenements and chaotic streets, but the threat under our own roof was different. It wasn't some unpredictable adversary, but a constant, nagging reminder of a catastrophic failure waiting to happen.

Eventually, we switched to diesel, brought in those automatic transmissions. A relief in so many ways. But that old, visceral fear of gasoline never quite disappeared. It lingered in the back of my mind every time I descended those basement stairs, the echoes of fuel spills and close calls reminding me that some dangers were closer than any burning building.

Firehouses are supposed to be fortresses, the launching point for our battles against the city's chaos. Yet, the specter of those gasoline tanks exposed a hidden vulnerability. It wasn't just the flames and the smoke we had to be wary of, but the potential for disaster nestled beneath our own feet. They were a stark reminder that even firefighters, trained to confront the worst, weren't immune to hazards built into the very foundations of the places they called home.

PASTRAMI AND PICKLES

Those old businesses, the "pickle warehouse" and "pastrami factory," weren't just places we responded to occasionally for calls. They were remnants of a different time, a fading echo of the vibrant Jewish community that once thrived in our patch of the Bronx. We were firefighters, not historians, but even we felt the history of the city beneath our boots.

The pickle warehouse, with its rows of barrels and the sharp, briny tang that clung to the air even after we finished a job close-by, was a testament to an older way of life. You could imagine the horse-drawn carts clattering down those streets, the bustle of deliveries bringing those sour delights to delis and markets across the boroughs. My own great-grandfather was a teamster in the south Bronx in the late eighteen hundreds.

But it was the pastrami factory that really got the taste buds going. That thick, hazy smoke wasn't always welcome when it drifted some folk's way, clinging to your nose long after a slight whiff. But come on…it was worth the minor inconvenience. The owners, faces lined with a lifetime of hard work and tradition, they'd welcome us in, their generosity outstripping even their legendary pastrami. We'd leave with enough to make a dozen or more sandwiches piled high and all for a rock-bottom price, savoring the spice-rubbed meat that was a world away from the usual firehouse fare.

There's something bittersweet about those glimpses into the past, especially in a part of the city as relentless as the Bronx. Even as we fought fires in crumbling tenements, the scent of smoked meat and the sight of those pickle barrels spoke of a different kind of legacy, one built on craftsmanship and community. They were reminders that bustling streets and soot-stained walls held layers of history, flavors and traditions that persisted even in the face of relentless change.

The closing of those businesses felt like more than just shuttered doors. It was another piece of the neighborhood's identity fading away, pushed aside by the forces of neglect and urban decay. We couldn't preserve it all, not with the fires raging around us, but those moments shared over pastrami sandwiches became poignant reminders of the constant evolution of the city.

The Bronx, like part of any city worth its salt, is built on the bones of its past. Businesses rise and fall, populations rise and fall, and even the landscape itself bends to the relentless march of time. Firefighters see these changes in the most visceral way. Our battles aren't just against flame and smoke, but against the forces that reshape the very neighborhoods we protect.

That pickle warehouse might be a vacant lot now, the pastrami factory replaced by some chain store with fluorescent lights and bland uniformity. But for those of us who tasted those flavors, who smelled that old-world smoke, the memory lingers. It's a testament to the enduring spirit of places, and a reminder that even midst the ashes, the echoes of a city's past continue to resonate long after the closing bell rings.

The Changing Neighborhoods

The Bronx…it wasn't a static place, but a living, breathing organism, its neighborhoods shifting and evolving like the restless tide. The changing cast of characters running those small businesses was a constant barometer of who called our patch of the city home. It wasn't always easy, this relentless transformation, but it painted a fascinating mosaic of the urban experience.

The candy stores, those cornerstones of childhood sugar rushes, once run by folks we knew our whole lives, morphed into bustling hubs staffed by recent immigrants from the Middle East. The scent of bubblegum and old newspapers was replaced with unfamiliar spices, the chatter shifting from familiar gossip to accents thick with the promise of a new life built in a foreign land.

The corner grocery, with its worn linoleum and shelves laden with memories as much as merchandise, transformed into a bodega. Bright signs and salsa rhythms spilling onto the street signaled a change of flavor, a reflection of a wave of Hispanic families seeking their own American dream within those same walls.

Pizza joints, their aroma a beacon after a long tour, vanished overnight. In their place sprang up cuchifrito restaurants, the air thick with the sizzling of pork and the clatter of Spanish. The familiar red checkered tables gave way to quick takeout counters, a testament to a different pace of life, a different set of comfort foods sought in the heart of our borough.

Even the Chinese takeout places seemed to retreat behind barricades. No more cozy booths or the comforting clatter of dishes – just a Plexiglas barrier, a narrow slot for transactions, a wary eye peering back at you. We'd have to be extra cautious around those stores – not just the usual hazards, but the knowledge that those storefronts might house more than just pot stickers and lo Mein, that dreams and desperation could turn a humble eatery into makeshift living quarters behind the kitchens.

Yet, the changes weren't all about commerce and cuisine. On Sundays, many of those vacant storefronts, symbols of urban decay, echoed with a new kind of life. The lilting Spanish hymns of Pentecostal churches spilled out open doors, vibrant and full of a spirit that filled the neglected spaces with unexpected beauty. Occasionally, come summer, massive tents sprouted on the abandoned lots, thrumming with gospel choirs from down south and the joyous energy of traveling ministries, a fleeting city within the city.

The Bronx, see, it never belonged to just one group, one tradition. It was a place of reinvention, where the old and the new battled and blended into a symphony of sights, smells, and sounds that was pure, chaotic, and undeniably New York. That constant churn, it could be jarring, could leave you longing for a simpler time. But there was an undeniable energy to it, too.

Each immigrant wave left its mark, adding spice and grit to the melting pot. They brought their dreams and their determination, their culinary traditions, and their unwavering faith. They took over those familiar businesses, imprinted their own stories onto the aging facades, breathing life back into the places where life itself was in constant flux. And we, the firefighters, bore witness to it all, rolling with the changes, adapting as the guardians of a neighborhood forever remaking itself.

Forging Safety in the Flames of Ambition

Fire prevention wasn't all about those classroom visits and handing out coloring books to kids. A huge part of the job was hitting the streets, inspecting the hodgepodge of buildings in our district – some annually, some less often, all with their own unique quirks and potential hazards. We weren't just firefighters, but the first line of defense in preventing a small problem from erupting into a full-blown disaster.

Apartment buildings and private homes, they had rules for a reason. We were sticklers for those public spaces in the tenements, adamant about making sure fire escapes were clear, hallways weren't turned into makeshift storage units. But individual units? Those were trickier. Most times, the only way to get a peek behind closed doors was with a warrant, and that meant red tape and delays. A potential fire trap waiting to happen was a luxury we didn't often have.

The real surprises lay in the commercial buildings where we'd uncover all sorts of hidden industries: a sprawling woodworking shop tucked into the basement of an otherwise innocuous storefront or a factory recycling old mattresses in a packed cellar; a warehouse transformed into a bustling sweater factory with those monstrous knitting machines churning out garments at breakneck speed. And the night-clubs…oh, the nightclubs. Cramming a pulsing, sweaty mass of people into some fire-hazard of a tenement basement or warehouse with dubious exits – that was a recipe for catastrophe.

It felt like a never-ending game of whack-a-mole with these entrepreneurs. Some were oblivious to the dangers they were creating, more focused on profit than the lives at risk. Others were outright defiant, that "you can't tell me what to do, this is America" attitude bristling with every question we asked. And especially with the newer immigrant groups, there were often language barriers and cultural misunderstandings to navigate.

The challenge wasn't just enforcing laws and regulations but making them see why it mattered. Explaining that safety codes weren't arbitrary nuisances designed to stifle business but were forged in the ashes of past tragedies. It wasn't always easy, especially when faced with ingrained distrust of authority or the desperation of those chasing the American dream by any means necessary.

The Bronx embodied that entrepreneurial spirit in its rawest form – the drive to build a business, support a family, carve out your own piece of the promised land. We couldn't fault ambition. But part of our job became about translating those fire codes, those hard-won regulations, into the universal language of survival. Of explaining that the true American dream wasn't just about owning a business, but owning it safely, so everyone – customers, workers, the families living above – had a chance to see those dreams turn into something real, not go up in smoke.

It was a delicate balance. We had to be firm yet unrelenting when it came to safety violations that put lives at risk. Sometimes we had to bring along some firepower in the form of a police officer, but we also had to find common ground, to become interpreters of not just the law, but the shared responsibility that came with being part of a community. One where the ambitious and the safety-minded weren't adversaries, but allies in ensuring that dreams built on hard work had the best chance to flourish, not burn.

Zoo Doo

The Bronx Zoo? Sure, it's got a fancy reputation, maybe even undeservedly as a tourist trap with overpriced hot dogs and sad-looking polar bears. But see, here's the thing folks outside the Bronx don't get – fame comes with a smell. And those zoo critters, well, they don't just roar for the kiddies, they gotta leave their mark, so to speak.

This is how I heard about the weirdest freelance gig ever: "Zoo doo," my driver grins, like he's offering me smuggled caviar. Turns out, those after-hours gates weren't just for the keepers. They'd open up the animal kingdom's finest fertilizer factory…for free! Think less "compost" and more "exotic buffet leftovers." Elephant, zebra, hell, even lion…all top-shelf fertilizer, ready to turbocharge your tomatoes.

Now, I'm a gardener from way back, but imagining my prize peppers plumped up on, say, giraffe droppings…well, it gave a whole new meaning to the term "organic." My stomach did a flip-flop that had nothing to do with a blazing building.

The driver swore by the zoo doo. Said his veggies were the size of alien invaders, the envy of the firehouse. But every time he'd offer those mutant zucchinis, all I could picture was the original source, complete with lingering whiff of antelope butt.

Still…there's something oddly poetic about it all. Even here, surrounded by concrete and chaos, nature's got its rhythm, its outputs. The Bronx finds ways, even if those ways make your nose wrinkle.

It's a bit like firefighting... you've got the familiar flames, the usual risks. Then, there's that call that makes you think twice – a chemical spill, a hoarder's house about to collapse. You could play it safe, or risk it all for the unknown.

Guess it depends on your appetite – for both danger and supernaturally-sized squash. Me? I'll stick to my regular beat. But hey, if that driver ever wins the State Fair with his zoo-doo monstrosities, well... even a veteran firefighter might be tempted, if I've got enough bleach to disinfect those babies before they hit the dinner table.

Helicopter Landings

Helicopters, those whirring beasts of the sky, were mostly an infrequent visitor to the greater part of the city. But when they did descend, it wasn't a casual affair. Whether the urgent thrum of blades for a medical evacuation, the VIP transport buzzing overhead with some self-important official, or a construction site landing, their arrival meant extra vigilance and a whole mess of foam.

First order of business: park the engine strategically for a rapid response if things went south. Then came the foam solution prep. Haul those heavy 5-gallon pails of obnoxious foam concentrate (mostly animal blood), positioned to be ready to mix them into the booster tank, hook up with a specialized nozzle, and potentially 500 gallons of water transformed into a frothy, fire-suppressing concoction. It wasn't the most glamorous part of the job, but the lingering scent of chemicals on our turnout gear was a potent reminder that we were on standby for something unpredictable.

Helicopter operations, they were their own unique breed of risk assessment. You sized up the landing zone – a rooftop, a tight parking lot, maybe a patch of wasteland – with an eye for unseen hazards. You planned escape routes in case of rotor wash, or the sudden whirl of debris that could transform a fender bender into a much more serious accident.

Fleet Week, those were the real spectacles. The Navy choppers swooping in, ferrying those brass hats around with a precision that seemed at odds with the fresh-faced pilots. Those kids, barely old enough for a driver's license, were entrusted with machines of incredible power, executing maneuvers that demanded split-second timing and nerves of steel. The ground personnel, all kids it seemed, scurrying about, flashing hand signals and coded messages all the while engaged in a dramatic ballet of noise and seeming chaos. Watching them work filled me with an unexpected surge of pride.

Firefighting is all about training and grit, but in those moments, it was the military precision that caught my eye. These youngsters, under the unforgiving glare of their superiors, weren't just flying those choppers, but shouldering a responsibility that far outstripped their youthful appearances. It was a reminder that beneath the bravado and easy camaraderie, there was a honed discipline, forged in relentless training and unwavering focus.

Sure, hauling foam buckets might not have been the most thrilling task, and VIP landings had more than a whiff of inflated egos. But those Navy pilots brought a different kind of energy to moments like that. They were a glimpse into the remarkable potential of the American youth, the unseen faces behind our nation's strength. The kind of dedication and skill that made me realize that even midst the grime and chaos of the city, there were young people pushing boundaries, reaching for the sky, and reminding all of us of the unwavering spirit that makes this chaotic, wonderful country tick.

The Gypsy Cab
Passenger

Those moments, they ambush you. One minute, you're a firefighter rolling back from a call, the adrenaline of the run slowly fading, Brooklyn unfolding in its familiar blend of grit and resilience. Then there's a frantic wave from the side of the road, a gypsy cab pulled over haphazardly, and suddenly you're not just witnesses to a city's chaos but thrust into its unpredictable heart.

We pulled over, instincts honed by years on the job demanding caution. The driver, voice trembling, words tumbling out – an unruly inebriated passenger, a threat unseen brewing in the back of his car. Before we could fully react, the passenger appeared, a blur of desperation and what smelled like chemical courage – the unholy mix of booze and crack that fueled so much of the city's senseless violence.

He had a knife. That flash of metal in the dimness was the trigger, shifting us from firefighters to protectors. But the driver was one step ahead in this macabre dance. Out of nowhere, he produced a stick – not some pathetic twig, but a hefty, four-foot length of who-knows-what. One swift, sickening crack echoed in the quiet night, then another.

The fight ended with an abruptness that was almost comical if it wasn't so damn tragic. The knife-wielding assailant slumped; the fight abruptly extinguished by two solid blows to the skull.

We did our part then – first-aid, called for the cops and an ambulance, stood as witnesses to the bizarre tableau. A cabbie defending his livelihood with a caveman's tool, a would-be attacker crumpled, a fresh stain of blood on the unforgiving asphalt. As the flashing lights of the ambulance, with the attacker on board, cut through the night, we slipped away, leaving the aftermath to law enforcement.

Back at the firehouse, the incident didn't just fade into the night. It lingered, a stark vignette of the brutal realities swirling beneath the surface of the city we served. It wasn't the fire that got to you that night, but that desperate scene on a desolate roadside. The realization that the hazards of this city weren't confined to burning buildings and smoke-choked rooms.

The cabbie, a working man just trying to make a living, forced to become his own defender in an unforgiving landscape. The addict, lost to a chemical haze, resorting to desperate, knife-wielding threats. And we, the firefighters, thrust into the role of referees for a street fight with no clear winners.

Each ring of the alarm bell sent us out there, to face the fires and the chaos. But that night, between calls, the true weight of the job settled deeper. It was the echoes of that roadside brawl that lingered, reminding us that even heroes of the everyday, the cab drivers and the bodega owners, sometimes fought their own battles for survival with makeshift weapons in the City's darkest hours. Theirs was a different kind of courage, forged not in the flames of a towering inferno, but in the gritty realities of a world where madness and desperation shared a taxi ride.

FRONT LINE RIVALRY

You would think camaraderie would run deep under those flashing lights, which shared the front line against disaster and would forge unbreakable bonds between cops, firefighters, and EMS. Unfortunately, the reality was a lot messier. Budget battles, internal turf wars, and simmering tension could turn emergency scenes into an entirely different kind of battlefield.

The limited resources were at the heart of it – a shrinking pie that had everyone clamoring for a bigger slice. Police sometimes eyed our budgets with envy, seeing equipment upgrades we got and feeling it came at their expense. Their Emergency Services Unit started encroaching on our domain – carrying hoses on their trucks, angling to take the lead on certain calls. It bred resentment, a feeling that they were more interested in padding their stats for political gains than truly working as a team.

EMS, bless their overworked souls, had their own agenda. Wanting better pay and recognition, they'd sometimes resort to, let's just say, creative report writing at our expense. A car fire misconstrued as a raging blaze, minor first-aid exaggerated into a life-saving intervention. Every interaction held a hidden weight, knowing a misplaced word could end up as ammunition for their cause, painting firefighters as reckless cowboys who made their jobs harder.

This unhealthy competition festered beneath the surface, a constant low-grade infection in the city's emergency response system. Even routine calls held a subtle tension, the weight of unspoken rivalries hanging in the air. And those resentments? In the worst moments, they had a nasty habit of boiling over.

A chaotic scene, smoke and confusion swirling, and suddenly you're not just focused on the task at hand but also watching your back. A snide comment from an emergency services cop questioning your tactics, an EMT tossing blame instead of offering help...those petty squabbles could undermine the whole operation, jeopardizing the lives we were supposed to be saving.

It's a damn shame because in the heat of the moment, those divisions made no sense. When you're pulling a victim from a burning building or facing a crowd turned hostile, your only backup is the guy in the uniform beside you, regardless of the patch he wears. The best members, the ones who truly made a difference, they found a way to rise above politics. Forged camaraderie not in administrative meetings, but in the shared sweat, the unspoken trust that developed in the trenches.

Unfortunately, those backroom battles for resources and recognition poisoned the well too often. It was a disservice to the city we all served, a reminder that even heroes aren't immune to the corrosive power of ego and bureaucracy. The true cost wasn't measured in dollars or stats, but those moments when the focus shifted from the crisis at hand to the petty power struggles playing out between those who were supposed to be on the same side.

SPAETZLE

The bell clangs halfway through my sentence, shattering the stale evening quiet. I'm in charge this night tour, and I'm already sick of the smell of sweat-soaked socks and that lingering hint of burnt popcorn. At least dinner will be a distraction – probably meatloaf again, thick enough to choke a horse. That or some bland slop, courtesy of O'Brien. Kid can't cook, but he insists on playing chef on some tours, just so we don't forget he went to some fancy community college.

Here, mealtimes are a necessary evil. Nobody cares about Michelin stars in this joint. We're a pack of half-crazed masochists who mainline coffee and shove down whatever slop gets dumped on the table. We've got a rapport with the local shop owners. Not the charming kind your mother would approve of, but the kind where they know to duck when we come barreling in, reeking of smoke and probably a little crazed.

But tonight, there's this…this tension in the air. Johnson – yeah, that's the kid's name – is in the kitchen. He's got this manic look in his eyes, like a raccoon that just discovered the sugar bowl. He starts murmuring some foreign-sounding word. Spaetzle? Sounds like one of those diseases they put those quarantine signs up for. Old Man Harrison's eyeing the kid like he's already writing his obituary.

Dinner's the usual pot roast – bless that cow for its sacrifice – but then, blasphemy! Johnson plunks down a bowl of these tiny, slimy pellets beside it. Like albino maggots. You can hear the silence drop as everyone stares. You could practically bounce a quarter off that tension.

Someone – I think it's O'Brien with his usual tact – lets out a choked laugh. Then another. Soon, the whole room's howling. Johnson's trying to sputter out some explanation about his grandma and authentic recipes, but nobody's listening. My sides hurt, and tears are streaming down my face. This beats any comedy club, hands down. The jokes just go on and on.

Alright, maybe those spaetzle-things aren't half bad, once you get past the name and the fact it looks like it belongs in a Petri dish. But there's no way in hell they'll ever replace the holy trinity of meatloaf, potatoes, and burnt coffee in this firehouse. Some traditions are best left undisturbed.

Johnson took the teasing in stride, a sheepish grin eventually splitting his face. This was his initiation, not in fire and smoke, but in the strange, merciless camaraderie of the firehouse kitchen. He'd learned two valuable lessons that night: first, never underestimate the culinary conservatism of a group of veteran firefighters, and second, the quickest way to earn your stripes wasn't just in bravery, but in enduring a night of merciless ribbing with a reluctant smile. From then on, the mention of spaetzle drew knowing smirks, an inside joke that cemented his place among us.

The Bag

Ah, the BAG. Not just a flimsy container, but a looming symbol of the relentless paperwork battles we waged in those pre-digital days. No slick emails, no easily searchable databases – every scrap of information, every mundane report, and every reprimand from on high traveled via that worn leather pouch. It was the lifeblood, and the bane, of the firehouse office.

The nightly arrival of the Division Messenger, a guy on light duty saddled with his rounds, was met with a mix of anticipation and dread. As the Officer on Duty, I was the designated recipient of that cursed bag. Its contents weren't just paper, but hours of my evening swallowed whole.

The first ritual: sorting. Like some bureaucratic triage, the deluge of forms, demands, memos, and incident reports would be laid out across the battered office desk. A fire prevention report requested by headquarters? Drill log updates for the Battalion? Equipment inventories overdue by a week? And those were just the routine items…never mind the curve ball requests, the inquiries sparked by some mishap that found its way onto the desk of an administrative higher-up eager to find someone to blame.

The goal, always, was to leave nothing for the next tour. It was an unspoken code, a firefighter's ethic. Sure, I could dump a half-finished report onto the unsuspecting day tour crew, but that was bad karma. Better to burn the midnight oil, fueled by stale coffee and stubborn determination, than to leave a mess hanging over my brothers' heads.

The hours ticked by in the unnatural quiet of a firehouse between alarms. Responses would still take priority, of course, but between calls, I'd chip away at the paperwork mountain. Some nights, the task seemed insurmountable, the weight of administrative demands a different kind of burden upon our shoulders.

Then there was the morning ritual. The Battalion Chief, out on his unit inspections, would swing by with the fruits of HQ's labor. Individual bags for each company, carrying…who knew what. Maybe it held a much-needed part for our aging rig, perhaps a new training mandate, or worse, disciplinary action trickling down from an incident weeks past. And alongside those deliveries, the daily roll call; the chief wasn't just ensuring our gear was in order, but sizing us up, gauging the unseen weight each of us carried after a grueling tour.

That's the thing no report could quantify – the sheer load we shouldered. The fires fought were obvious, but the battles against bureaucratic red tape were a hidden war. Those bags weren't just carriers of paperwork, but reminders of the endless demands placed on a service that never truly got to rest. It was in those quiet hours, hunched over a form illuminated by a flickering fluorescent bulb, that you felt the full weight of being a fire officer. It wasn't just the flames, but the grind. The physical battles bled into the administrative ones, creating a cycle of duty that only ended when you finally managed to hang up that uniform for good.

When Safety Takes a Backseat

The old chiefs' cars... they were hardly the sleek safety chariots of today. Sedans with worn seats, ashtrays overflowing from an era when smoking was practically a job requirement, and a distinct lack of anything resembling modern safety features. Then came the SUVs, a promise of spaciousness and rugged utility that, sadly, did little to address the glaring dangers posed by their cargo.

Breathing apparatus spare tanks, extinguishers, foam...all essential tools, yet crammed haphazardly into the backs of those SUVs. But the true menace was the spare tanks. Those metal cylinders, heavy and unyielding, rattling around with every bump and turn, could transform into deadly projectiles in case of even a minor fender bender.

Imagine it: a sudden swerve, a collision, and those tanks launch forward with unstoppable force. No seat belt, no airbag, could protect the unsuspecting chief and driver in that front seat. One crushing blow, an unthinkable accident, and all for the lack of some basic restraints.

Every time we rolled out, the grim image lingered in the back of our minds. Those cylinders, nestled among the life-saving gear, were silent reminders of the hazards we faced not just on the fireground, but in our daily operations. It became a perverse ritual – strapping ourselves into that chief's car, knowing that the greatest threat to our well-being might be riding shotgun.

We wrote reports. Voiced our concerns up the chain of command. Yet, the response, if it could even be called that, was a shrug of bureaucratic indifference. Some vague muttering about budgets, some dismissive hand-waving about the statistical unlikeliness of such an accident. Meanwhile, individual crews, frustrated and fearful, took matters into their own hands. Makeshift restraints fashioned from rope and bungee cords – a testament to our ingenuity, and a damning indictment of a system that valued paperwork over our lives.

Each time I climbed into that chief's car, there was a flicker of dark humor mixed with helpless rage. We swore oaths to protect and serve, to charge headlong into danger, yet the absurdity of a preventable threat was almost too much to bear. We were firefighters, damn it! We knew the risk. But being at the mercy of loose spare bottles? That was an insult to the inherent risk of the job.

The blatant disregard, that's what gnawed away at you. Not just the potential for tragedy, but the unspoken message that our safety while on duty was somehow secondary – an afterthought in the grand scheme of administrative procedures. It wasn't the fireground that exposed the true cost of being a firefighter, but those rattling SUVs and the silence from above, highlighting a chilling truth: sometimes, the most dangerous battles we fought weren't against the flames, but against an indifference that could prove far deadlier.

Shoot the Roofman

Roofmen. They weren't just firefighters for that tour, they were a breed apart. Men who looked at a towering inferno and saw, not danger, but a vertical battleground. Their domain was that treacherous expanse between a burning building and the open sky. And getting there? Well, that was an act as dangerous as the fire itself.

The rigs – those ladder trucks were beasts of their own. Tower ladders, with their buckets and limited reach, offered a touch more stability, but it was the rear mounts, those 75 -foot behemoths, which were the true workhorses. Quick to deploy, yes, but offering a precarious perch atop a swaying metal spine. Then there were the tiller trucks, lumbering monsters with their rear-wheel steering. Navigating the tight city streets on those was a feat of skill, but for the tillerman, perched high in his exposed position, every tight turn was a stomach-churning lurch.

The official methods were all about safety…on paper. Position the rig, lower the outriggers; if equipped and carefully raise the ladder. He might use the tip of the ladder to punch through the front windows. If time allows and no victim's showing on the front, he might raise the ladder to the roof. The roofman would climb up, tools in hand, ready to punch those life-saving holes or open a bulkhead door, or find victims at windows to give those trapped souls a sliver of hope midst the smoke and flames. But in the heart of the Bronx, in those relentless tenement fires, time evaporated. Every second was a battle not just against the blaze, but against the relentless possibility of a trapped occupant.

That's where shooting the roofman came in. A dangerous dance, a gamble against regulations and common sense. The roofman, poised on the tip of the nested ladder like a human cannonball, braced on a sliver of rung or the metal frame, hands clenched around the rails as the ladder was ripped from its cradle and swung skyward. He became a living projectile, hurled towards the roof on the tip of the ladder, his fate hinging on the split-second timing of the chauffeur and his own ability to hold on for dear life.

There was an awful beauty to it, and an even greater horror. The arc of that ladder tracing a desperate path against the flames, the roofman a blur of smoke and adrenaline at its tip. A misplaced foot between the layered rungs and his leg became a mangled offering; one slip of those sweat-slick hands and he vanished into the heart of the fire or fell like a rock to the sidewalk below.

That moment of transition, when the ladder met the parapet, was less controlled arrival and more a desperate launch. Throw the tools down to the roof first and listen for them hitting something solid. Then a leap of faith into a smoke-choked void, the hope that solid ground awaited his boots and not a sheer drop into darkness.

The life of a roofman wasn't defined by the fires they fought above, but by the chilling limbo they endured to reach their assignment. Each deployment, a test not just of skill, but of a willingness to look fear square in the eye and take a running leap onto an unforgiving ladder pointed straight at hell. It was a testament to the grit forged in the firehouse, a brotherhood built not just on shared danger but the unshakable trust placed in the man controlling that ladder, and the sheer audacity of the soul who rode it.

DOGS

The Bronx…it was a nightmare of hazards, where danger lurked not just in crumbling walls and billowing smoke, but in the snarl behind the door. Pit bulls, those muscular guardians of the urban jungle, were a constant, unpredictable threat. Every forced entry, every window forced open, was a gamble – were we firefighters about to face flames, or fangs?

Gaining access to a burning apartment was rarely elegant. The blare of sirens was meant to rouse any resting occupants, human or canine. In the chaos, the adrenaline pounding in your veins, you never knew what awaited on the other side of a fire-warped door or a shattered windowpane. A terrified whimper? An empty silence? Or that low, guttural growl that sent a different kind of chill down your spine than any smoke could.

Commercial buildings posed their own challenges. Warehouses, shuttered stores, outdoor enterprises holding precious cargo…those were the domain of guard dogs, trained to protect with relentless, unthinking ferocity. A firefighter's instincts kicked in: search for signs of the animal, any telltale bark or movement. But in the dim interior, shadows shifted, and any glint of light could be teeth or raging eyeballs.

Even fenced-in lots, with their stacks of discarded tires or hulking wrecks, held a hidden menace. The sudden lunge of a dog defending its junkyard territory could derail a fire attack in seconds, turning turnout gear into a flimsy shield against teeth and claws.

There's something uniquely unsettling about facing an animal. Fire, even at its most destructive, is an elemental force. You can predict its path, understand its fury. But the snarl of an enraged, trained-to-kill dog fueled by a mix of fear and territorial instinct is unpredictable, raw, and chillingly personal.

Each encounter was a forced shift in focus. Suddenly, it wasn't just about deploying the hose line or locating the seat of the blaze. It was assessing escape routes should those teeth find their mark, anticipating lines of attack while keeping a wary eye on every darkened hallway. We wore our protective gear like armor, but there's no perfect defense against a dog's desperate lunge.

The best firefighters found ways to adapt, to read the subtle clues that might give away an animal's presence, to employ caution without letting it paralyze. But even the most seasoned among us carried scars not from burns, but the sharp reminder of those moments when the battleground was a confined space, and the enemy wore fur and snapped with fangs.

Those canine encounters were brutal punctuation midst the relentless fight against the flames. A reminder that in the heart of the Bronx, the dangers were as diverse as the city itself. That sometimes, the most primal battle wasn't against the inferno, but against the instinctual fury of a creature defending its territory, unaware that the firefighters breaching its domain were the key to survival for everyone – even the snarling beast itself.

FAMILY

Those trips to the hospital, carried off from a chaotic fire scene in an ambulance or the back of the chief's car, weren't just about physical wounds. They were unseen battles fought by those we left behind – the spouses, parents, kids who waited with a gnawing, unspoken fear.

The worst weren't the major injuries, the ones that came with wailing sirens and a frantic rush. It was the quiet disappearances, a sudden absence from the shouts and the blur of action. A firefighter vanishes into the smoke, then reappears, not at his rig, but being loaded into the back of an ambulance before it peels away, leaving nothing but lingering questions and a knot of dread in your gut.

The Bronx was relentless, and our injuries mirrored its brutal efficiency. Burns, the kind that made your turnout gear feel like it was melting into your skin. Lacerations from unseen debris, a sliver of glass that could slice open an artery faster than any blaze. And always, the smoke – that insidious enemy that seeped into your lungs and left you coughing up soot long after the last embers were extinguished.

In those days, the hospital emergency rooms were hardly havens of comfort. We bypassed the waiting room and headed straight to the place with the medical crew. Bright, sterile spaces, filled with the desperate energy of the city's injured and broken. Junkies muttering in corners, drunks bandaged and belligerent, and me – reeking of smoke and sweat, a firefighter dislodged from the familiar chaos of the fireground into a world of beeping monitors and grim-faced nurses.

They'd patch you up, sometimes hold you for observation, and there was the rub. No phones in those days, no quick text to reassure a waiting spouse. My wife, left alone with the unknown, faced those endless hours stretching through the night. The image of her, tense by the silent phone, fills me with guilt even now.

That first frantic call to the firehouse, met with the vague confirmation that, yes, I'd been taken to the hospital, but they couldn't provide details. The gnawing uncertainty, not knowing the severity, conjuring up a thousand horrific possibilities in the silence.

The aftermath was almost worse; the relief of my return mixed with the unspoken anger, the lingering terror they'd fought to hide while I lay in that emergency room surrounded by strangers. Firefighters faced risk head-on, but our families endured their own kind of battle at home, their bravery waged in those long hours of silence and the unanswered question of when, or if, we'd return.

Those ambulance rides marked not just physical wounds, but the unseen scars they traced on the hearts of those we loved. Each injury was an echo of that unspoken bargain – that the risk we accepted on the fireground sent ripples of fear into the quiet spaces we called home. It was a reminder that the job held its dangers not just on burning rooftops and in smoke-filled rooms, but in every unanswered phone call, and every silent vigil kept by those waiting for our safe return.

The Closed Emergency Room

The stillness of a Brooklyn night at 2 AM is a deceptive thing. Most of the city rests, the usual roar reduced to a low hum, but the darkness holds its own dangers. Returning from a call, the adrenaline still fading, we stumbled upon a scene that shattered the illusion of peace: a man crumpled in the street, blood painting a grotesque pattern in the dim light, the aftermath of a brutal mugging.

First-aid kits were standard, but that gaping head wound…it mocked our meager supplies. The blood flowed relentlessly, each precious second another threat to his fading consciousness. Panic flared in our eyes – where the hell was the closest hospital? Our driver, bless him, always knew the lay of the land, the life-or-death shortcuts carved into his memory.

We piled the victim onto the rig, blood splattering everywhere in our makeshift ambulance. Our siren a desperate wail as we tore through the deserted streets, time slipping away with each crimson drop. The hospital loomed into view, but then the next cruel twist: doors locked, lights dim, a fortress against suffering in those darkest hours. *CLOSED,* the sign read.

Do you believe it? A goddamn hospital, closed for the night. The absurdity of it all – a city that never rests denied the care it desperately needed – fueled a righteous fury. We weren't just firefighters anymore, but warriors against a system that left the weak to bleed out in the dark.

Banging on that door, voices raw with urgency, it was a scene straight from some surreal nightmare. Finally, a disheveled figure appeared, annoyance flickering in their eyes. "We're closed," they repeated, like they couldn't see the desperate tableau of blood-stained firefighters carrying a blood-stained victim laid out before them. The bureaucracy, the rules…they were razor wire against our frantic pleas.

We pushed inside, carrying our bleeding cargo into the sterile purgatory within. Our shouts turned to threats, our focus now a battle to save one man against the apathy of an institution. The victim grew delirious, thrashing against the help we so desperately wanted to give. It took all of us, firefighters trained for far different battles, to hold him steady on the operating table while they stitched the wound, while the sedative finally took hold.

As we finally left, the sky began to lighten, there was only a bone-deep weariness. We were firefighters, goddamn it, not social workers. But that night, in those flickering fluorescent lights, we'd waged a battle not just against a street mugging, but against the callous heart of a city that could close its doors to the dying.

The aftermath hung heavy as we pulled back into the firehouse. It wasn't just the call itself that lingered, but a chilling sense that some-how, even in the midst of the grit and tenacity of Brooklyn, we were fighting forces far greater than any fire. Tonight, we'd glimpsed a dark-ness that stretched far deeper than any blaze – the indifference of a system that allowed a man to nearly bleed to death on a doorstep built for healing.

SCHOOLS

The schools of the Bronx…. They weren't just places of learning, but a stark reflection of the city's harsh inequalities. Those fire safety visits, meant to be about extinguisher demos and evacuation drills, often turned into a gut-wrenching confrontation with a reality we could never fully extinguish.

Picture it: a school shoehorned into a converted movie theater, the lingering scent of stale popcorn echoing beneath the rumbling roar of the elevated train. No sprawling playgrounds here. Gym class consisted of jumping jacks on the sidewalk, a symphony of shouts swallowed by the screech of metal on metal as the train rattled overhead on the elevated subway line.

Security guards, their presence sometimes rivaling the number of students, a grim reminder that even the pursuit of knowledge wasn't immune to the dangers lurking just beyond the schoolyard gates. My mind would flash to my own kids, to their suburban schools with the green fields, the shiny new science labs, the Olympic-sized pools shimmering in the sunlit extension. The disparity hit you like a punch to the gut.

And beneath it all, the kids. Those eager eyes peering out from behind the institutional drabness. You knew it, right down to your boots – the smart ones, those with something burning bright inside, they'd claw their way out of this, transcend the limitations and the noise, and build a future somewhere far from the roar of the trains. The others, most of them, they'd become good folks, find their own ways to contribute, carve out decent lives against the odds, because that's what generations of immigrants and tough city kids had done before them.

The teachers, though, were a different breed. To choose to work in those schools wasn't just a job, it was a mission. You saw it in every weary line etched on their faces, an unwavering dedication and a kind of desperate hope battling against the relentless realities they faced each day.

There's this hopeful voice that'd chime in, a whisper of reassurance. "Our parents, our grandparents," it would remind me, "they faced tough times too, worked their way out of worse, and look at us!" The Bronx tested that optimism with every school visit, every glimpse into classrooms barely holding back the chaos of a city that never stopped to catch its breath.

And yet, there was always that nagging feeling, the kind that lingered long after we'd pack up the fire hoses and escape back into the sanctuary of our fire trucks. A sense of injustice, of potential stifled, of a system stacked against those bright-eyed kids with too few resources and too many obstacles. It wasn't sadness exactly, or pity, but a kind of profound unease that burrowed into your soul and never quite left.

The Bronx wasn't built for surrender, and neither were its kids. You held those two truths in uneasy balance. The knowledge that many would rise above, just like those generations before them, and the painful awareness of the unseen battles they'd have to fight to win that chance. It was in those schools, under the rumbling subway line, that the heart of the Bronx revealed itself; raw, resilient, and painfully uneven. You couldn't truly save a city without saving the souls within it, and that was a kind of fire we were ill-equipped to fight.

THE RAPES

3 AM. That hour when the Bronx holds its breath, the tireless energy of the city ebbing momentarily before dawn. We were rolling back from a call, weary, hoping for a few snatches of rest before the inevitable clang of the next alarm. Then came the screams.

Two women, disheveled and distraught, stumbling into the street, their sobs shattering the stillness. Returning from a night out in Manhattan, their world irrevocably shattered just steps from the subway station. Attacked. Raped. The words hung in the air, heavy and brutal, the gun used now vanished into the city's shadowy embrace.

The world tilted on its axis. We weren't just firefighters anymore, but protectors, guardians against an unseen horror that lurked even in the familiar streets. Call the cops, of course, but that seemed a pathetically weak response against the enormity of the moment. Stay with them, give them the sanctuary of the rig, offer what meager comfort we could, until the cavalry arrived.

Never forget. That became our silent pledge as they choked out their story, as the distant wail of a siren offered a sliver of hope, a promise of justice that felt frustratingly hollow. Two lives ruined…no, shattered beyond mere ruin. The echoes of those screams wouldn't fade with the sunrise.

But the echoes went deeper. Six men on that truck, each with a wife, daughters, sisters, resting safely in suburban homes miles away. That unspoken realization hung like a specter over the scene. What if it wasn't here, but our own towns? What if that unimaginable violation happened in the quiet streets meant to be a haven? The distance between the Bronx and our sheltered lives suddenly blurred, replaced with a chilling understanding of the vulnerability we took for granted.

The aftermath, it rippled out in ways we couldn't fully comprehend. Back at the firehouse, rest became a fitful thing, each rustle of wind a potential threat, each call carrying the unseen weight of those women's shattered innocence. Anger flared – at the perpetrators, at a system that did not protect them, at the helplessness we felt even with our strength.

And there was guilt. The guilt that we got to go home to safety, while those women would never truly return to the world they knew. The guilt that lingered in hushed conversations, in the shared glances that said more than words ever could.

The fires, the rescues, those became a desperate counterbalance. We threw ourselves into our work with renewed ferocity, as if saving a stranger from a burning building could somehow make amends for the evil we couldn't undo. Our turnout gear became a shield not just from the flames, but from the vulnerability we'd witnessed in those tear-streaked faces on the dark street.

It's a story that never fully leaves you. Those screams, they linger in the quietest hours. A reminder that the true fires sometimes burn unseen, that heroism isn't always about a raging inferno, but the strength it takes to bear witness to the darkness, and to keep fighting for the light. It shaped us, hardened us, reminded us that even in the heart of a tough city, true evil could lurk, and sometimes the greatest battles were fought in the shadows, for the safety we never truly appreciated until we saw it stolen in the blink of an eye.

THE SUBTERRANEAN BBQ

The shrill scream of the alarm tore through the firehouse like a banshee wail. Sirens wailed in concert as we roared down the street, red lights flashing a frantic rhythm. Smoke in a six-story tenement – not good.

We arrived to find a big H-type building choked with a curious haze. The source, according to a frantic tenant, was split between the first and sixth floors. Split flames? Unlikely. Split stupidity? Now that was a distinct possibility.

Splitting our team, some headed up the stairs, smoke thinning with each floor they climbed. On the sixth floor, all was clear – a quick call down to the boss over the handie-talkie.

Meanwhile, in the basement, we discovered the true culprit – a makeshift barbecue pit glowing ominously in the building's belly. Smoke billowed from the basement like a grumpy genie refusing to return to its lamp.

There, in a scene ripped from a bad survivalist show gone wrong, stood the super, Miguel, and two equally bewildered-looking friends, tongs in hand. A trussed-up goat, looking decidedly less enthusiastic than before, on a spit over a makeshift grill fashioned from cinder blocks and a rusty grate.

"What. The. Hell?" I said, smoke curling around my words like quotation marks.

Miguel, a portly man with a handlebar mustache that would make a biker jealous, looked sheepish. "Uh, what's the problem?" he offered, gesturing vaguely with the tongs.

The rest of us exchanged exasperated glances. This wasn't a comedy show, it was a recipe for disaster. A wood fire, in a confined basement, of a multi-story building – the violations echoed louder than the sizzling goat fat.

"Problem?" I scoffed, stepping closer. "You call roasting a goat in the basement normal?"

Miguel's friends mumbled something about "tradition" and "ancestral cooking methods," but their words were drowned out by the increasingly insistent crackle of the fire.

The argument was legendary. We may have saved the building from Miguel's unique culinary adventure, but not before a full-blown lecture on fire safety, and the sheer insanity of using a basement as a smoker.

In the end, the goat ended up outside (much to the dismay of Miguel's friends who kept insisting it was "perfectly good idea"), and Miguel faced a hefty fine. As for us, we emerged from the smoky basement, smelling faintly of charred meat and the singed dreams of a delicious barbecue.

That night, back at the firehouse, the story became instant legend. Miguel's "Subterranean Barbecue" joined the ranks of our most bizarre calls, a reminder that sometimes, the biggest threats come not from raging infernos, but from misplaced cultural traditions and a questionable sense of culinary adventure.

THE GARDEN

The Bronx sun beat down on my helmet, sweat stinging my eyes. I squinted across the street at the skeletal remains of what used to be Mrs. Rodriguez's bakery. The fire, a week ago, had been brutal, leaving a hollow shell of blackened brick and vacant stares where windows once displayed golden baked bread and flaky donuts.

A pang of nostalgia hit me. I remembered Mrs. Rodriguez, a tiny woman with a smile as warm as her ovens, always slipping me a free cookie when I was a kid. Now, the only warmth emanating from the building came from the sun reflecting off the crudely nailed tin sheets that covered the empty window frames.

I shifted my weight, the familiar ache in my back a constant reminder of the job. Across from me, a group of kids, no older than ten, peeked through a gap in the boards fencing off a vacant lot next door.

"Hey!" one yelled, waving a scraggly hand. "You gonna let us in, mister fireman?"

I chuckled. This lot wasn't condemned, just waiting for an uncertain future. But enterprising folks had other plans. Mismatched boards and salvaged scraps of metal created a makeshift fence, enclosing a hidden world.

"Not my call, kid," I replied, raising my voice slightly. "But it doesn't look too friendly in there."

A skinny girl with bright eyes popped her head through the gap. "It's not! It's our garden! We got tomatoes and peppers and stuff."

Intrigued, I approached the fence, peering over the makeshift barrier. Inside, a surprising oasis bloomed. Sunflowers, their faces tilted towards the sky, competed for space with vibrant tomato plants heavy with red fruit. A carefully tended herb patch sent a fragrant message on the warm breeze.

A woman, her face weathered but her eyes sparkling with life, appeared from behind a makeshift trellis. She wore mismatched gardening gloves and a smile as broad as the sunflowers.

"Well, hello there," she said, her voice surprisingly strong. "Didn't know we had visitors."

"Uh, hi," I stammered, surprised by this hidden haven in the heart of a burned-out block. "Sorry to bother you, just curious."

The woman gestured at the garden. "Curious about the green in the rubble, eh? We call ourselves the 'Phoenix Posse'. This lot, it may look like nothing, but life finds a way, doesn't it?"

I nodded, a newfound respect welling up. Squatters, maybe, but they were creating something beautiful amongst the ashes.

"It's…impressive," I managed. "What are you growing?"

She launched into a passionate explanation, detailing the different vegetables, the challenges of urban gardening, and their plans for a small compost pit. I listened, captivated.

As I turned to leave, the woman called after me. "Hey, fireman!"

I stopped.

"Thanks for keeping the flames away from our little patch of paradise," she said, her voice warm. "We appreciate it."

I smiled, a genuine one this time. "My pleasure, ma'am. And hey," I added, looking through the gap in the fence. "Maybe next time, a slice of tomato on a homemade roll?"

The woman's laughter echoed down the street, a sound that mingled with the chirping of birds and the distant hum of the city. I walked away, the weight on my back a little lighter, carrying with me

the unexpected beauty I found hidden in the shadows of a burnt-out
dream.

Hanging by a Thread - The Oil Truck

The call crackled over the radio, a garbled mess that sent a jolt of adrenaline through me. Overturned oil truck, Major Deegan Highway – the words painted a picture of potential disaster. We raced to the scene, sirens wailing a symphony of urgency.

The sight that greeted me was a trucker's nightmare. A behemoth of a vehicle, an oil tanker laden with 6,000 gallons of #2 heating oil, lay on its side, precariously balanced at the edge of the highway. Below, a dizzying drop to the opposing lanes, fifty feet down. We quickly stabilized it until a plan could be hatched.

The tanker had been flirting with fate. The driver long gone in a familiar disappearing act. Desperately, the fool had fled the scene, leaving behind a potential environmental catastrophe.

The tension was thick enough to choke on. Police swarmed the area, blocking off a domino effect of traffic chaos. Hazmat and rescue units arrived, their specialized vehicles a grim testament to the situation.

I surveyed the scene. The tanker teetered on the brink, a grotesque metal sculpture defying gravity. Luckily all the hatches had been tightly closed preventing any spill. One wrong move, and the oil could escape, coating the highway, choking the area in foul smelling oil, and potentially causing a fiery inferno.

My boss was a ghost. Calls went unanswered, leaving a vacuum of leadership. But in that absence, a different kind of strength appeared. Cooperation at its finest. I took charge of getting the truck upright and the police handled the traffic nightmare.

A plan was hatched, a desperate gamble. Numerous tow trucks arrived, their hulking forms the instruments of a precarious ballet. The idea: use the tow truck cables like marionette strings to coax the tanker back upright while using safety cables to hold it back from going too far in the other direction. A simple solution, yet fraught with peril.

With each agonizing inch the tanker rose, hearts pounded in unison. Sweat trickled down my face, a mixture of heat and nervous anticipation. The precarious angle mocked their efforts.

"Slow and steady," I barked, my voice tight with controlled anxiety.

They were in the final stretch, victory tantalizingly close. Then, a sickening lurch. The tanker groaned, threatening to topple over the edge. A collective gasp escaped our lips. Thank God for the safety cables we had rigged earlier.

But then, a miracle. The groaning stopped. Silence descended, thick and heavy. The tanker, as if exhausted from its defiance, settled back onto its tires, upright and seemingly unharmed.

A cheer erupted, ragged but heartfelt. High fives were exchanged, a brief moment of camaraderie forged in the crucible of tension. The oil tanker, a testament to their combined efforts, stood tall once more.

The rest was a blur. Hook up the tanker to a big tow truck and haul it away with the sun peeking over the horizon, painting the sky with streaks of pink and orange.

Exhausted but exhilarated, I watched the tow truck haul the tanker away. Not a single drop of oil had spilled. The city, blissfully unaware of the averted disaster, would wake up to another ordinary day.

But for me and my guys, the memory of that night would linger – a stark reminder of the fine line between catastrophe and a job well done, a testament to the courage they found not in themselves individually, but in each other.

Night Tour – The Absurd and the Mundane

Night tours in a Bronx firehouse were like staring into a kaleidoscope of the absurd, the mundane, and the sometimes terrifying. Through the small window set in the apparatus door, you watched the city transform as decent folk tucked themselves into bed, leaving the streets to the denizens of the night.

There was the woman in her underwear, a blur of vulnerability and defiance striding past as if the sidewalk were a runway. I'd watched her vanish into the shadows, wondering about her story, about the battle she carried with her into the uncaring night.

Then, there was the man who shot at streetlights, a drunken cowboy waging war against urban illumination. The crack of gunfire and the tinkle of glass obliterated the predawn calm, leaving behind a trail of darkness and pointless destruction. I would sound the alarm, but part of me pitied the man stumbling aimlessly into the consequences of his liquor-fueled rage as the cops closed in.

But it wasn't all tragedy and bizarreness. Sometimes, the unexpected took a far more peculiar turn. That night at 3 AM, sitting alone at the housewatch desk with the apparatus doors open, I noticed a flicker of movement from the corner of my eye. I turned, and there it was – an opossum, lured by the dim lights and promise of silence.

The creature was a grotesque curiosity, its beady eyes reflecting the night, its claws scratching an eerie rhythm on the concrete floor. It made a leisurely circuit around the trucks, sniffed curiously at a forgotten boot, and then – as if it had checked this item off its odd bucket list – it turned and ambled back out into the night.

These moments, they were the punctuation marks between the adrenaline-fueled chaos of the alarms. Reminders that in the Bronx, the expected was never a guarantee, especially when darkness fell. There was violence, yes, and flashes of human fragility that sometimes made the fires seem less daunting.

But there was also the strange, occasionally comical tenacity of life. The opossum ambling through the firehouse was a stark reminder that even surrounded by steel and soot, the wild heart of the city beat on. It was a city that mirrored the firefighter's life: danger and duty punctuated with the absurd, the mundane, and those moments where you simply scratched your head and said, "you couldn't make this stuff up." That window was a portal into a world never dull, never predictable, and endlessly, relentlessly fascinating.

Narrow Misses

The empty buildings, I thought, were like hollow shells, their vacancies holding a thousand secrets – stories of neglect, desperation, and sometimes, a sinister intent. These were the calls that sent a shiver down even the most seasoned firefighter's spine. Here, the rules of the game changed.

Why were they vacant? Often, the answer reeked of something far more nefarious than a simple eviction. Greedy landlords, tired of paying for repairs, might force tenants out through neglect or harassment. Even worse, some might play a deadly game of arson insurance roulette – setting the building ablaze to collect a hefty payout.

Some vacant buildings wore a scarlet letter – a bold, ominous X painted on their facade. This was our grim warning, a message that screamed *Stay Out! Structurally unsound!* But the problem with these Xs was as chilling as the warning itself. Who painted them? When? Was the information current, or was it a relic from a long ago inspection, a ghost marking a forgotten tomb?

The stairs were another treacherous battleground. Missing marble treads left only the skeletal metal framework; a precarious tightrope walk for firefighters burdened with bulky equipment. Each step was a prayer, a silent plea that the rusted metal wouldn't crumble beneath their weight. Fire escapes, once symbols of safety, became potential deathtraps. Rusted and neglected, they could betray you in a heartbeat.

One night, seared into my memory, we arrived at a six-story tenement and possible inferno. Flames roared from upper windows, painting the night sky an angry orange. With a hose team, we charged up, the hose line snaking behind us like a wounded serpent. We reached the fifth floor, the heat a physical presence, scorching our lungs.

The officer, a grizzled veteran with eyes that had seen too much, paused at the burning apartment door. "Hold on," he rasped, a tremor in his voice. "Something's not right."

His words hung heavy in the air. Just then, a sickening groan echoed from within and the floor lurched beneath our feet. Before anyone could react, the entire wing – the section they were about to enter – gave way, collapsing in a fiery avalanche.

Silence descended, heavy and thick with the dust of oblivion. Then, the crackle of the radio, evacuate, the officer's voice then, rough with emotion saying, "thank God, I listened to my gut."

That night, we used up a collective lifetime's worth of luck. Five lives saved, a testament to the silent language shared among firefighters, a language where instincts spoke louder than words.

Vacant buildings were a gamble, each call a roll of the dice. You went in with nine lives, they liked to say – some used them all up, retiring with a tremor in their hands and a lifetime of close calls etched on their faces. Others, like those who would have perished in that collapsed wing, never came back.

In the face of these silent predators, these vacant buildings with their secrets and hidden dangers, firefighters became a cautious kind of brave. They were the warriors walking a tightrope, the ones who stared into the abyss and refused to blink. They knew the rules of the game here were different, written in the whispers of the wind and the creaks of the decaying structures. And they knew, with a chilling certainty, that sometimes, even the best instincts could only buy you a borrowed moment.

HYDRANTS

Most, they watched a firefighter battle a blaze, and saw only the drama, the fury of the flames, the sweat-streaked faces. What they didn't see was that behind every firefighter was a lifeline: the mighty hydrant. Those black and silver-painted sentinels were the unsung heroes, the source from which the engines drew their power.

But the city, especially the Bronx, wasn't built with firefighters in mind. When an alarm rang out, it wasn't just a fire they were racing towards, but a battle against indifference, against the unyielding obstacles thrown in their path by everyday life.

Double-parked cars were a nightmare. Drivers left their vehicles straddling those precious hydrants, heedless of the chaos they could cause in an emergency. There's an image burned into my mind: a woman screaming from a smoke-filled window, and firefighters scrambling to weave a hose line around a hulking SUV parked squarely on the hydrant that meant life or death for those trapped inside.

When bureaucracy failed, frustration took over. Some firefighters took matters into their own hands. Busting out car windows with the heavy head of an ax, threading the suction hose through the gaping hole – it was a brutal tactic born of desperation. Others, their anger simmering after a fire was finally extinguished, took a different kind of revenge. The sharp point of their halligan tool, a firefighter's multi-purpose weapon, puncturing tires with a satisfying hiss. It was a petty act, perhaps, but fueled by the knowledge they were fighting not just the fires, but the indifference that could cost a life.

Tickets? The cops wrote them, stacks of them, but they were useless scraps of paper to a driver who didn't value a human life more than their own convenience. There were nights I came back to the firehouse, hands still blistered, and felt the futility of it all. The fires, those they could fight. But the ignorance, the carelessness that could snuff out lives before they even had a chance…sometimes, that seemed like the biggest inferno of all.

And the worst thing? The irony of it. On those streets, a firefighter was at the bottom of the food chain. They'd risk their necks to save a complete stranger, pull out a child from a smoke-filled apartment, and then walk out and find their rig blocked in by some yahoo heading for the bodega to get a pack of smokes.

Those guys on the engine, they depended on the chauffeur to get them water. No water, no chance. It was a race against time, every time, and the obstacles they faced were not just the flames, but the indifference of a city that turned a blind eye to the lifelines their survival depended on.

The Reporter and a Gutsy Proposition

The firehouse was a living organism – the rumble of idling trucks, the clanging of tools during routine checks, the low murmur of shared stories, all forming a heartbeat beneath grime-streaked walls. Then, the invasive buzz of a TV crew cut through the routine like a hot blade through butter. They came with permission from headquarters to film for a day.

The reporter, a whirlwind of energy wrapped in designer jeans and carefully tousled hair, was a force to be reckoned with. Camera guy, sound guy, and a harassed-looking producer danced in her wake, their gear an intrusion on the firehouse's worn-in orderliness.

They trailed firefighters for hours – a routine drill cut short by a genuine call-out, a chaotic fire scene, then the weary return to the firehouse, faces smeared with soot. The footage piled up, a reel of life beyond the nightly news snippets.

At the day's end, the crew gathered in the heart of the firehouse: the kitchen. Its battered table bore witness to both late-night poker games and heartfelt confessions. The reporter, perched on a bench, crossed her legs with calculated casualness and turned her megawatt smile on the room.

"Alright," she declared, voice sharp and cutting over the simmering stew, "so, which one of you is coming home with me tonight?"

The silence wasn't disbelief, but a collective amusement tinged with exhaustion. These guys had seen it all – flames, floods, the full spectrum of human folly and desperation. A brazen proposition from a media darling was just another Tuesday in the Bronx.

A grizzled firefighter, leaning against the scuffed refrigerator, finally broke the silence. "Sweetheart, we just crawled out of a four-alarm inferno. A good shower and eight hours of rest sounds a lot better than whatever you've got in mind." A rumble of laughter echoed through the room.

The reporter flushed, but rallied, a flicker in her eyes that hinted at admiration. She'd met her match, a roomful of men who understood grime and grit far better than glamour. The city, it was theirs – the fire-fighters, the cops, the paramedics, the sanitation workers, the ER nurses holding vigil in the wee hours. They sweated, cursed, and saved lives in the shadows, unseen by most until the flames licked too close to home or the sirens pierced the night.

As the crew packed up, the feeling in the room wasn't defiance, but a quiet understanding. Some stories were told in flickering television montages, others were etched on soot-stained souls. The reporter left with her footage; a sliver of the real city tucked away on a hard drive. The firefighters returned to their stew, their weary camaraderie a bond no camera could fully capture.

The city, a beast of steel and ambition, roared on. But within its underbelly, the unseen heroes kept watch, carrying on with a gritty resilience that defied any spotlight. They were the ones on the front lines, the guardians of the night, and they understood, deep down, that some stories were meant to linger in the quiet glow of an un-extin-guished ember, or the unspoken answer to a bold proposition.

COMPACTORS

The high-rise public housing projects of New York were concrete giants, and back in the day, each had its own personal digestive system – incinerators with hungry shafts gulping down mountains of trash. But then, the environment became a cause, and incinerators were cast out, replaced by compactors, a roach's dream come true. A cleaner solution, or so they thought.

For firefighters like us, it was a recipe for chaos. See, people, bless their hearts, couldn't seem to grasp the concept of "don't put things down the chute that shouldn't go down the chute." Mattresses, old furniture, maybe even bodies – you name it, someone tried to shove it down that metal gullet. The result? Clogged chutes, overflowing trash rooms, and a symphony of frustrated sighs from the firehouse down the street.

Then came the "solutions." Some bright spark, facing a mountain of garbage blocking their chute freedom, would decide fire was the answer. A quick blaze, they figured, would melt the plastic bags and whatnot, and everything would magically flow again. Then there were the others who thought they would call every possible city agency for some relief. We'd get the call – "compactor" – and there we'd be, hauling up cobblestones like knights on a garbage quest. Up we'd go, one man on the top floor, carrying a few cobblestones, ready to unleash the rocky wrath down the metal abyss. A satisfying "thunk" would echo through the building, and with a bit of luck, the clog would break, sending a cascade of trash raining down the chute to the compactor room below.

But that wasn't the worst of it. Sometimes, even without a rogue fire, the compactor room would turn into a festering nightmare, and not just from the hordes of roaches. Maintenance, it seemed, wasn't high on their priority list. Trash would pile up, a monument to human consumption, and all it took was a single, misplaced cigarette butt to turn it into a full-blown inferno.

Then came the real fun part – hauling that smoldering, putrid mountain of garbage out of the compactor by hand. Tons of it, reeking to high heaven, a biohazard obstacle course that would make a maggot gag. It was a job that tested more than just their firefighting skills; it tested their humanity, their ability to soldier through the idiocy of some and the negligence of others.

These were the moments that made us truly appreciate fire. Fire, the thing they battled every day, was a force of nature, at least some-what predictable. But the fire of human carelessness, the stubborn refusal to follow the most basic rules – that, my friend, was a blaze far more frustrating to extinguish. The high-rise chutes were a microcosm of life, it seemed – a constant reminder that some folks just couldn't seem to grasp the simple concept of not making a mess for everyone else. And the firefighters, well, they were the ones left to clean it up.

INTERCHANGE

The word *Interchange* hung over the busiest firehouses in the Bronx like a dubious promise: a night or two of respite, a temporary reprieve from the relentless barrage of alarms. On paper, it made sense – swap a beat-up, smoke-stained engine from a chaotic area with a shiny rig from out in the slower area, give the exhausted crews a chance to recharge, and ensure fire coverage stayed consistent.

But reality was a messy beast, and Interchange was no exception. For us, it was a mixed bag of frustration and quiet defiance. Most of us thrived on the action, the adrenaline rush of a crackling roofline and the quiet satisfaction of a life saved. Trading our battleground for a few nights of boredom in a slow neighborhood felt like being benched in the middle of a championship game.

The crews from the slower units were wary, too. They'd heard the horror stories, maybe even had done their time in hell, remembered the whispers of firestorms that erupted within minutes. Plunging into that unpredictable chaos wasn't on anyone's wish list. Then there was the pride factor – no one wanted to be seen as the "B squad" called in to cover for the big boys.

Interchange nights were a flurry of phone calls and muttered curses. The officer in charge of the busy unit would dial up their designated slow counterpart, a tense negotiation often followed by an unwritten agreement. Interchange canceled, status quo maintained, and no one upstairs the wiser.

Even when an Interchange went through, doubts lingered. If there was a ladder company attached to the busy house, they were often left behind and not interchanged. They didn't trust the slower engine to be there in a pinch, to have the experience and grit needed for those moments when the routine erupted into chaos. Teamwork wasn't something conjured from a memo; it was forged in the fires they faced together.

Headquarters might have seen the Interchange program as efficiency; as a way to spread the burden a little wider. But on the front lines, in the middle of battered trucks and exhausted faces, it was bureaucracy butting heads with brotherhood. The men on the ground knew their territory, the unique dangers, the rhythms and rituals of their district. They also knew the unspoken pact – sometimes, bending the rules was the way to keep the city safe, and each other alive.

The official policy might be written in thick manuals, but the real rules were etched on the soot-streaked faces of those who lived and breathed the Bronx. Interchange, like so much else, was a challenge to be met, an obstacle to be finessed. And like always, the firefighters would find their own way, a quiet middle finger to the system, a testament to the grit, instinct, and unwavering camaraderie that couldn't be managed from above.

SCHOOLKIDS ON TOUR

School kid tours. Ugh. The firehouse door would open, and instead of someone reporting a blazing inferno, you'd get a swarm of thirty first graders in matching neon T-shirts, buzzing like a hive of hormonal mosquitos. Don't get me wrong, a little break from washing the rig and the endless rounds of daily chores was sometimes welcome. But these kids were a recipe for disaster.

See, tours had their own rhythm, a way of minimizing the chaos. We'd make them schedule in advance, pretend like we were doing the community a massive favor. Doesn't always work, of course. Some days you're elbow-deep in a plate of questionable nachos and suddenly there's Mrs. Whatever-her-name with her human tornado looking for penguins after getting sidetracked from the Bronx Zoo or something.

It's the guys that drive you nuts. Old Man Sal would grunt a few safety tips, then vanish to the kitchen faster than a cat spotting a bath. Then you have rookies like Ricky – bless his enthusiastic, misguided soul – who turn every tour into a one-man circus. Helmets on kids, that cheesy *Stop, Drop, and Roll* routine, maybe even some interpretive dance about the dangers of leaving the oven unattended, all in some weird, desperate attempt to charm the chaperoning teacher or mom. Sometimes, well, sometimes it's just not about the show.

This one tour, though…something shifts. Middle of the usual spiel, right as my eyes start to glaze over, this tiny girl raises her hand. Not one of those "can I go to the bathroom" deals, but a real question. About different sirens, about those creepy masks we wear, and hey, do you really fight kitchen fires with baking soda? Even old Sal starts to perk up.

Suddenly, everyone's talking. Stories about everything firefighting, anecdotes I haven't thought of in years. We're drawing smoke monsters on the walls, turning the whole truck floor into a fire-fighting fairytale. And those kids, even the ones who came in picking their noses, are hanging on to our every word.

As they file out, the little girl with the questions lingers behind. "Thanks," she says, quiet-like, and suddenly there's this lump in my throat. All the bravado and jokes fade away. It hits you then: yeah, we wear the silly hats and clean the rigs, but for these kids, we're practically superheroes. Sometimes, it's not about Ricky and his flirting attempts or the boredom of the daily grind. Sometimes, it's about those wide, trusting eyes, seeing the job through a whole new lens. And for a few hours, this dusty old firehouse isn't just a workplace, it's a place where magic happens.

RELOCATION

In the heart of the city, where the sirens sang their urgent song, there existed a system known as *Relocation* – a desperate attempt to keep the firefighting ballet from turning into a chaotic mosh pit. The idea was simple: when a firehouse was emptied by crews battling a stubborn blaze, units from quieter areas would be dispatched to fill the gap, ensuring no neighborhood was left vulnerable.

On paper, it looked elegant. Relocation was a game of musical chairs played on a burning inferno. Dispatchers, juggling incoming calls and depleted resources, became orchestra conductors of a fire symphony gone rogue.

The busiest houses, like ours in Manhattan, were the epicenters of this chaos. A prolonged fire would send us scrambling, leaving our firehouse a ghost town. Then, the cavalry would arrive – relocated units, shiny trucks brimming with unfamiliar faces. The problem? These newcomers, plucked from their not so busy firehouses, were like fish out of water. They didn't know the streets, the hydrant locations were alien symbols, and the rhythm of the lower east side, a city within a city that pulsed with a fire of its own, was a foreign language.

The result? A domino effect of relocations. The freshly arrived unit, no sooner than settling in, would catch their own fire, leaving a fresh hole in the coverage map. More units would be scrambled, more trucks clogging the already cramped firehouse. Soon, boots and gear would be strewn everywhere, a testament to the transient nature of their presence.

The chaos wasn't just logistical. Trust, the cornerstone of any successful firefighting team, was a fragile thing. These relocated crews, working alongside strangers in unfamiliar territory, lacked the unspoken language of experience, the shorthand built on shared battles and near misses. It was like trying to perform open-heart surgery with a team of talented strangers – technically skilled, perhaps, but lacking the seamless coordination honed by countless emergencies.

The worst nights were a symphony of clanging metal and shouted orders, the frustration palpable. Five relocated units crammed into a single block around the firehouse, a mechanical ballet teetering on the edge of disaster, was not an unusual occurrence. Returning rigs would find themselves blocked by a maze of unfamiliar trucks, precious seconds ticking by as they wrestled for position.

Relocation, a well-intentioned plan, exposed the cracks in the system. It highlighted the need for a deeper understanding of the city's diverse firegrounds, and the crucial role familiarity played in effective firefighting. These firefighters weren't just interchangeable cogs in a machine; they were warriors who thrived on knowing their ground, their comrades, and the city's unique heartbeat. The dance of relocation might keep the flames at bay, but for a truly flawless performance, they needed a permanent stage, not a revolving one.

A City's Cold Embrace

Winter, in the concrete canyons of New York, wasn't a season of cozy nights by the fireplace. For firefighters like us, it was a relentless enemy, chilling our bones and testing our resolve. 2 AM. The piercing wail of the siren ripped through the frigid air. Just another call, they thought, but outside, a 5-degree nightmare awaited. A biting wind whipped around them, a knife twisting in exposed flesh. Their bodies, still sluggish from rest, were thrown into a battle against not just fire, but the very elements themselves. Ice was the enemy. Frozen hydrants, hastily drained fire hose. Frozen bodies are too brittle to work fluently.

Uncontrollable shivers wracked your frame. Teeth chattered, lips turning a pale blue despite the woolen balaclava struggling to hold the escape of your breath. Every movement felt like wading through molasses, muscles stiff from the cold. Here, the fire hose wasn't just a weapon; it was a potential executioner. Water, their ally, became an icy serpent, freezing to their gear, turning them into human icicles.

Standing high above in the ladder bucket, directing the stream from the stang nozzle onto a blaze in a vacant building, was an ordeal by ice. Exposed to the windchill, you felt your core temperature plummet. Your hands, encased in thick gloves, were numb, your fingers mere clumsy sausages struggling to control the nozzle. Yet, you persevered, a warrior clad not in shining armor, but in layers of fire-resistant gear that offered little comfort against the winter's bite.

Then, in the middle of the frozen chaos, a beacon of warmth appeared. The Salvation Army or Red Cross disaster truck, a lifeline in a snowstorm of misery. Hot coffee, steaming and fragrant, cupped in calloused hands – a simple act that rekindled hope. A donut, a sugary burst of warmth, a momentary escape from the icy grip of the night.

These unsung heroes, the people of the Red Cross and Salvation Army, were warriors in their own right. They didn't charge into burning buildings, but they stood resolute against the cold, offering a haven of warmth for the city's shivering defenders. A cup of coffee, a donut, a kind word – these seemingly insignificant gestures were life-lines thrown to those battling a different kind of inferno.

As the city slumbered beneath a blanket of snow, oblivious to the silent war being waged, these unlikely heroes, firefighters and volunteers alike, stood shoulder-to-shoulder. One fought fire, the other fought frost, both testaments to the unwavering spirit of a city that refused to be cowed by flames or the icy grip of winter. Theirs was a battle fought not for glory, but for the safety and well-being of their fellow citizens, a silent symphony of courage played out against the backdrop of a frozen city.

THREADS BETWEEN LIFE AND DEATH

The 1960s and 70s – a time of flower power and bell bottoms – wasn't exactly synonymous with cutting-edge firefighter safety gear. For me, a boss in a busy New York City firehouse, the uniform situation was less "fashion statement" and more "walking into a fire in your pajamas."

Your outer shell came in two dubious choices – a rubber coat or a canvas one. Neither offered even a shred of fire retardancy, a terrifying thought when facing a raging inferno. On your feet, you sported clunky rubber boots more suited for wading through a swamp than scaling a burning building. The pants? A flimsy cotton blend offering about as much protection as a paper towel against a blowtorch.

The dress code, as it was, felt like a cruel joke. Regulations stipulated blue shirts but enforcing that in a firehouse full of strong personalities was an uphill battle. Some guys just craved individuality, a splash of red or white midst the blue sea. Was it vanity? Maybe. But sometimes, I wondered if it was a desperate attempt to stand out, to be set apart from the chaos, a subconscious prayer for recognition if the worst came to pass.

The boots were another source of discord, especially for the ladder company. Ascending a 100-foot ladder in those clunky boots felt like wearing lead weights. Shoes, some argued, offered better dexterity, the ability to feel the rungs, to navigate the precarious climb with a nimbler step. Sure, they might not have steel toes, but the risk of a twisted ankle or a crushed toe paled in comparison to plummeting from a towering inferno. It was a gamble, a life-or-death trade-off that gnawed at us. Pushing for regulations meant potentially endangering my men, but ignoring the dangers felt like a betrayal of their trust.

The frustration ran deep. We were warriors on the front lines, facing a relentless enemy, yet our protection was a patchwork quilt of outdated equipment and flimsy regulations. It wasn't until the 80s that the tide began to turn, that advancements in technology finally trickled down to the firehouses. But those years in between, those were the years of holding your breath, of praying that a frayed rubber coat and a misplaced sense of individuality wouldn't be the difference between life and death for you or your men.

Ours wasn't a fashion show – it was a constant negotiation with fate, a desperate scramble for any edge in the face of the flames. Every call was a gamble, and the stakes couldn't be higher. We were firefighters, yes, but we were also men caught in a system that hadn't quite caught up to the reality of the inferno we battled every day. We fought for the city, we fought for each other, and we fought for the day when our uniform wouldn't just be a symbol of courage, but a true shield against the flames.

SUMMER BURN

I f winter in New York City tested our resilience, summer turned the city into an open furnace. All of us, beneath the weight of our gear, weren't just fighting fires; we were fighting the relentless oppression of a 90-degree scorcher.

Each step felt like wading through molten lead. Every breath of super-heated air seared your lungs. The tank of oxygen strapped to your back wasn't a lifeline, it was an irritating weight, sinking you further into the sweltering misery. Racing up ladders, clambering across fire escapes, battling flames that turned the air to shimmering waves of agony – it was a brutal dance against the relentless sun.

Sweat poured from you in endless rivulets. It mixed with soot and grime, turning your gear into a suffocating second skin. Inside your boots, your feet began to poach. Every movement was a test of endurance, a silent battle not just against the flames, but the crushing weight of heat that threatened to sap your strength.

But the battle wasn't over. The fire extinguished and smoke cleared, then came the aftermath. Overhaul meant tearing into charred walls, ripping ceilings down, searching for hidden pockets of fire. Hose lines, heavy and water-laden, had to be drained and then dragged back to the engine, every twist of the metal couplings an angry bite against blistered hands.

There was no respite. No time for a shower, no chance to strip off the sweat-soaked gear. The next alarm could come at any moment, and they needed to be ready. The stench of their own bodies, a mix of sweat, smoke, and city grit, became a constant companion.

Dehydration was a constant threat, but even gulping down precious water was an exercise in futility. Within minutes, it would evaporate in the merciless heat. Sometimes, the mirage of an ice-cold beer after work was the only thing keeping them going, a promise whispered through cracked lips, a reward for surviving another brutal tour in the city's unforgiving crucible.

The firefighters of New York City weren't just firefighters, they were warriors of the sun. They battled not only flames, but the insidious assault of a relentless heat that looked to break them both physically and mentally. Each summer call was a descent into a fiery inferno, a test of will against a season that held as much danger as any structural fire. They emerged from those merciless months, eyes etched with exhaustion and skin stained with sweat, the invisible scars of those scorched days testament to the silent war they waged against an indifferent season.

SOPHIE'S CHOICE

The air masks. A firefighter's lifeline, or an unwelcome burden? For some, it was a love-hate relationship as complex as the infernos you battled. Back in the day, these masks were treated like relics, locked away in black wooden cases on the rigs. Reaching for one on a critical first arrival was like trying to unlock a treasure chest during a bank robbery – precious time wasted in the face of hungry flames.

Then came NASA, a knight in shining armor (or perhaps a heat-resistant space suit) to the firefighting world. Their intervention yielded a new generation of masks – lighter, more comfortable, a small victory in a world of discomfort. The department finally loosened its grip, allowing them to be readily available, within arm's reach. No more frantic fumbling with ancient locks. Just grab and go, or better yet, don it while charging towards the inferno.

But even these marvels had their limitations. Ten minutes of air, a precious commodity measured in desperate breaths. The old masks forced you to fight for every lungful, a constant struggle against resistance. The new ones, however, offered a reprieve – a newer breathe-on-demand system, a small taste of freedom within the confines of a burning building.

There was still the problem of vision, though. The plastic face plate, a necessary shield against smoke, super-heated air, and an eye puncturing obstacle, was a constant battleground for clarity. Scratches accumulated, turning the world into a blurry nightmare. Some firefighters, risking reprimands and worse, took to crafting their own solutions – makeshift mouthpieces cobbled together in home workshops, and attached secretly to the masks by replacing the facepiece, a redneck rebellion against limited visibility. We called them "cheaters," these jury-rigged contraptions, and they were a testament to a firefighter's desperate need to see the enemy they were fighting.

The choice was stark: breathe a little easier, fight the suffocation, but be trapped in a world of blurred vision, or risk smoke inhalation and worse for a clearer view of the flames. A firefighter's Sophie's Choice, a decision made in the blink of an eye under the suffocating grip of smoke and fear.

These masks were a double-edged sword, a symbol of progress tainted by the ever-present reality of limitations. They offered a chance, a fighting opportunity, but they couldn't erase the inherent dangers of the job. Firefighters, ever the resourceful bunch, adapted, improvised, and even gambled with their own safety, all in pursuit of a single goal – survival, theirs and the civilians they swore to protect. Theirs was a world of blurred lines, where clear vision sometimes came at a heavy price, and every breath, a gift to be cherished.

ELEVATOR: A NOT-SO-MERRY RIDE DOWN

Claustrophobic. Confined. A metal box hurtling down a vertical shaft – elevators, for most, were a mundane part of daily life. But for firefighters like me, they were a potential death trap, especially when dealing with a particular fire hazard: mattresses and overstuffed furniture.

These seemingly benign household items harbored a deceptive secret. Their fluffy insides, a labyrinth of fabric and foam, were tinderboxes waiting for a spark. Imagine a slumber party gone wrong, a rogue cigarette igniting a corner of a stuffed chair. Within minutes, the filling could transform into a raging inferno, spewing thick, suffocating smoke. A quick extinguishment with a few pots of water by a harried apartment dweller.

The real nightmare begins when panic sets in. Instinct screams: escape. Put the chair fire out with a pot of water and then drag it to the elevator; readily available, seems like a natural choice. But for a mattress or overstuffed chair on fire, the elevator shaft became a trap, the descent a terrifying journey into an inferno. The embers hidden inside turn into flames, fueled by the confined space and available oxygen; they would lick upwards, turning the elevator into a metal oven.

There was nowhere to run, nowhere to hide. The descent, designed for a sense of ease, became an agonizing race against time. Smoke inhalation, the ever-present threat for firefighters, became a guaranteed death sentence in this metal tomb.

The key, we drilled into the men repeatedly, was prevention, not reaction. If a mattress or overstuffed piece of furniture caught fire, a pot of water wasn't enough. It had to be soaked, drenched to the core, until no ember, no spark, could ignite the hidden inferno within.

Education became their weapon; their message clear: treat mattresses and overstuffed furniture with the respect they deserved. These weren't just places to rest your head or sprawl out with a good book; they were potential fire hazards, and elevators were not escape routes for a fire already burning within.

The alternative wasn't pleasant. Dragging a soaking wet stuffed chair down multiple flights of stairs wasn't exactly a walk in the park and throwing it out the window was sometimes just not feasible. But compared to the fiery descent of an elevator, it was a walk you'd gladly take. The goal: to ensure every elevator ride remained a routine part of daily life, not a terrifying journey into the heart of a hidden inferno. Because for firefighters like us, vigilance wasn't just about responding to emergencies; it was about preventing them before they even started.

BEHIND THE WHEEL

The chauffeur gripped the steering wheel, a lifeline for the men behind him. He wasn't just driving a truck, he was piloting a chariot of bravery, a metal warhorse carrying the city's last line of defense. Sirens screamed as he navigated a sea of panic, dodging cars, civilians darting across roads with the frantic energy of fleeing insects. He was the ferryman, delivering his brothers to the fiery shores of their battlefield.

The engine roared its arrival at the scene, and the real work began. He slammed the brakes and men leapt from the rig like a swarm unleashed. Hose lines unfurled in a blur, tools clattered on asphalt. His transformation took place behind the wheel. He wasn't just a chauffeur; he was the heart of their fire-pumping beast.

The search for a hydrant started – a frantic chase among double-parked cars, panicked drivers, and a maze of other emergency vehicles. Spotting the telltale dome was a victory, a beacon in the chaos. He wrestled a heavy wrench, the hydrant his defiant prey. Muscles screamed as he fought the unyielding metal, sweat stinging his eyes. But water was life, the blood that would flow through their hoses.

A radio crackles – "start water!" He was their lifeline. No time to hesitate. With the opening of a valve for the booster tank, he unleashed the precious water stored within the tank, a temporary sacrifice to feed the lines. His hand hovered over the pressure controls, calculating, anticipating. The fire's location, the length of the hose, the pressure needed at the nozzle– all variables in a deadly equation.

Then, victory – the hydrant wrenched into compliance, a gush of water signaling success. His work wasn't over. He balanced pressures, a delicate dance of throttle and valves. Too much, and the hose could burst, leaving firefighters stranded, defenseless against the flames. Too little, and their weapons would be useless streams, unable to reach the heart of the inferno. Open the hydrant valve slowly and close the booster valve while lowering the rpms to account for the differences in pressure. A delicate but important balance playing out midst the craziness at the scene.

Above, the aerial ladder of the truck unit rose, a metal giant extending towards the fire. Victims trapped on higher floors would depend on the deft control of the ladder chauffeur. His world was balance and angles, every movement potentially the difference between rescue and tragedy. He was acrobat and engineer, maneuvering his metal steed while carrying the weight of life on its massive shoulders.

The title of "chauffeur" felt inadequate. They were the unsung heroes, the ones behind the wheel and at the controls, who made the valor of those charging into the flames possible. No, they didn't get extra pay, nor did they expect it from an uncaring city. The silent nod of acknowledgment from the men returning, soot-streaked and exhausted, was their reward.

They were the foundation, the unseen force that kept the battle against the flames alive. The chauffeur, hunched over the pump controls, his ears ringing with a symphony of shouts, water surges, and crackling fire, knew the truth – without him, without those like him, the firefighters were simply men, vulnerable and alone. With him, they were an unstoppable force, a testament to the silent courage of the ones behind the wheel, fighting their own war for the survival of their brothers in arms.

Annual Inspection

The Annual Inspection. For some, those words conjured a sense of dread that rivaled the wail of a midnight alarm call. It wasn't the prospect of scrutiny they feared. Firefighters thrived on order, meticulous routine the foundation upon which life-or-death decisions were made. No, it was the theater, the absurdity of a system that seemed designed to create more chaos than it remedied, that sent a shiver down your spine.

Weeks, sometimes months, were spent transforming a firehouse – grimy testament to countless fires fought – into a gleaming display of spit and polish. Floors scrubbed and polished by borrowed machines until they could rival a surgeon's operating room. Apparatus polished and buffed until it blinded like a rogue disco ball. Every nook and cranny underwent a surgical cleansing, revealing layers of accumulated soot and grit unseen since the last inspection.

The men themselves faced their own transformation. Dress uniforms, long ignored in lockers, appeared wrinkled and smelling faintly of mothballs. Frantic tailors were called, measurements reassessed after years of hard-earned calories. Badges shined; shoes polished to a reflective gleam. It felt like playing dress-up in a life where comfort and function took precedence.

Then came the day itself. The inspecting boss, all starched grandeur and stern expressions, descended upon the firehouse. It could be a quick once-over, a testament to the unit's reputation and the boss's indifference to formality. But sometimes, a truly meticulous officer transformed into a whirlwind of obsessive scrutiny.

It was this kind of inspection some dreaded. Each firefighter lined up as if awaiting sentencing. Uniform inspections were followed by gear checks – the dates meticulously noted – as if a bunker coat had a mystical end date known only to those in the ivory tower of headquarters.

The pièce de résistance: the ID numbers. Every firefighter had a unique stamp which was supposed to be emblazoned on their gear. Some bosses, maybe a man with the eyesight of a hawk and the enthusiasm of a tax auditor, would meticulously cross-reference the numbers on the gear against a weathered ledger. Gear swaps, lost gloves, faded numbers – every discrepancy was a potential demerit, a black mark on the unit's otherwise spotless (for one day, at least) record.

There was an unspoken code in the chaos. Uniforms were borrowed from anyone slightly resembling the right size. Steamers were rented, friendships exploited, all in a desperate bid to create the illusion of unerring perfection.

Afterward, in the dusty office of the firehouse, the inspecting boss would likely partake in a "quick snort," a euphemism as transparent as the charade that preceded it. In those moments, the farce of it all sank in. Weary from weeks of forced meticulousness, we could only chuckle under our breath. Come morning, the firehouse would return to its rightful chaos, and the next fire wouldn't give a damn about a shiny badge or a properly stamped helmet.

The Language of Smoke

Smoke wasn't just a choking haze for us; it was a language, a dialect spoken by the flames themselves. Each fire had its own unique vocabulary, a vocabulary deciphered through years of experience and a healthy dose of fear.

Mattress fires, those lazy, smoldering infernos, were notorious for their treachery. The smoke, thick and acrid, clung to everything it touched – clothes, hair, lungs. It was an insidious enemy, seeping into every crevice, choking the senses before the flames ever made their full appearance. Top floor fires were similar – slow-burning beasts that lingered in the hidden spaces, filling the air with a suffocating, pre-explosion tension. You never quite knew when the smolder would erupt into a full-blown inferno, the smoke morphing from a sluggish gray to a terrifying, hungry orange.

Then there were the oil burner fires. Black. Thick. Ugly. Imagine the nastiest oil spill you'd ever seen, set alight, and then translated into an airborne assault. This smoke wasn't content with just filling your lungs; it coated everything it touched with a greasy, gooey film. Viscous and unforgiving, it transformed firefighters into grotesque, oil-slicked marionettes, their movements sluggish, their vision blurred. These fires were killers, silent assassins disguised in a cloak of sooty despair. It took days afterwards to clean the black gook from your nostrils.

Car fires, though brutal, spoke a more straightforward language. Black and gray, swirling plumes that danced with the heat, they signaled a battle of steel and rubber. But some smoke held a deeper terror, a color that sent shivers down the spine of even the most seasoned firefighter. A deep, purplish gray, an unnatural bruise blooming across the horizon of the flames. Backdraft smoke. The harbinger of a violent explosion, a silent scream trapped within the building, waiting to be unleashed. The air grew heavy, the hairs on the back of your neck stood on end. This wasn't a battle; it was a stand-off, a tense negotiation with an invisible enemy, the stakes impossibly high.

Each inhalation was a gamble, a dance with death disguised as a breath of air. The acrid tang of burning plastic, the metallic bite of superheated metal, the sickly, sweet cloying of overheated electronics – every scent a story, a clue to the fire's origin, its intent, its next move. These were the smells that filled your nightmares, the olfactory ghosts of battles past.

We trained for the heat, the physical exertion, the constant barrage of adrenaline. But the language of smoke, that was a different beast altogether. It was an ever-evolving dialect, a secret code whispered by the flames. Learning to understand it wasn't about memorization; it was about a primal instinct, an unspoken bond forged in the crucible of fire. For us firefighters, smoke wasn't just an annoyance; it was a vital clue, a whispered warning, a life-or-death conversation carried on the wind.

Holiday Haunting

The holidays were a time of joy, of twinkling lights and festive cheer. But for me, a seasoned firefighter, the festive spirit came laced with a grim undercurrent – the ever-present threat of a Christmas tree fire. Live trees, those symbols of seasonal merriment, could turn into deadly infernos in the blink of an eye.

One story, etched in my memory with the starkness of a nightmare, served as a glaring reminder. A high-rise apartment building, the promise of a joyous holiday season hanging heavy in the air. Then, a flicker of orange, a plume of smoke, and the high-pitched wail of sirens shattering the festive peace.

The cause: a Christmas tree, its desiccated branches the perfect kindling for a carelessly used cigarette lighter. What began as a childish prank in an elevator quickly spiraled into an inferno. The elevator, an enclosed, nowhere to hide box, acted as a crematorium, enhancing the flames and their effects. By the time we arrived, the damage was done. The cheerful holiday decoration, once a symbol of family celebration, had become a fiery tomb.

The aftermath was a scene of unimaginable horror. The elevator door, forced open with desperate urgency, revealed not a scene of escape, but a chilling tableau. Silhouettes, skeletal remains against the backdrop of the charred remnants of the once-festive tree. A stark reminder of the innocence lost, the holiday cheer extinguished in a moment of carelessness.

News of the tragedy spread like wildfire (a grimly ironic turn of phrase); a chilling cautionary tale whispered by the families as they decorated their own homes. I, along with my fellow firefighters, redoubled our efforts in public education campaigns. The message was simple: live trees were beautiful, but they could also be deadly. Proper care, ample watering, and responsible disposal were paramount.

The holidays were a time for family, for togetherness, for celebrating life. And for me and my guys, it was a time for vigilance, a constant reminder of the potential danger lurking beneath the boughs of a seemingly harmless Christmas tree. Our goal: to ensure that every twinkling light represented joy, not a flickering harbinger of tragedy. Ours was a battle fought not just against flames, but ignorance, a fight to ensure that the holiday season remained a time of celebration, not a haunting memory.

THE HEART ATTACK

The urgency pulsed through the cramped bedroom like a silent alarm. A man lay crumpled against the faded blanket and plush pillows, his face a mask of agony, gasping for air that wouldn't come. Every ragged breath was accompanied by a primal scream, a raw, animalistic sound that sliced through the tense silence.

Sweat dripped onto the worn carpet as we worked, our movements a desperate ballet against time. Oxygen, and the practiced rhythm of life-saving measures – but they felt like futile gestures in the face of his overwhelming pain. The EMTs arrived, a storm of focused professionalism, but the man was slipping away, each agonizing scream a nail pounded into our collective conscience.

And then, the woman. His wife. She hovered on the edge of the chaos, not with the wide-eyed panic of someone seeing a crisis, but a terrifying, steely resolve. Her words, delivered in a brittle staccato, stopped time itself: "no." Not that hospital. She demanded he be taken to the one on the other side of the borough.

Arguments spiraled. Reason collided with desperation. The EMTs, seasoned veterans with a thousand emergencies under their belts, pleaded with her to see sense. The closest hospital was minutes away, a lifeline within reach. Each second of delay felt like a hammer blow, the man's screams a relentless soundtrack to our rising helplessness.

Her reasons were lost in a jumble of broken words: a past experience, a distrust born of some unknown trauma, a fear so entrenched that it outweighed the terrifying reality unfolding before her very eyes. We could feel the man weakening, the minutes bleeding away along with his fading cries. Calls were made, protocols strained, precious time ticking off against the stubborn set of her jaw. The apartment became a prison, the city lights outside a mocking reminder of all that was being lost.

Somehow, she won. The ambulance, its siren a mournful dirge, turned away from the nearby lifeline towards a destination shrouded in darkness and uncertainty. We stood outside, feeling the weight of the cool night air mingled with a suffocating helplessness. This wasn't a fire we could battle head-on, no flames to beat back. It was a different kind of inferno, a battle of wills and fear raging within the walls of a tidy apartment, leaving us as shell-shocked witnesses.

The aftermath felt like a bitter stain. We went through the motions, debriefings, a forced return to normalcy. But the echoes lingered. The man's screams, the woman's haunted eyes, the chilling awareness that sometimes, even armed with the best training and intentions, the forces that break a person are beyond our reach.

Did the man survive? Did that agonizing detour cost him everything? We never got the answers, the follow-ups lost in the bureaucratic jumble that so often swallowed the victims we swore to save. All that remained was a lingering unease, a reminder that on the front lines of human existence, not every battle is meant to be won, and sometimes, all we are left with is the terrible weight of bearing witness.

TRAPPED BETWEEN FLOORS

The wail of the siren wasn't always a harbinger of flames. Sometimes, it was a call for a different kind of rescue, one that sent shivers down a different kind of spine – elevator emergency. These weren't battles against roaring infernos, but silent struggles against confinement and panic.

Our arsenal? A set of specialized keys – lifelines forged from tempered steel. These keys weren't your average household variety. They boasted a unique hinge, allowing them to flex and navigate the narrow confines of the elevator door's access hole. Inserting this key was a delicate dance, a single wrong turn potentially delaying the rescue of those trapped within the steel box.

Communication was paramount. A calm voice, a reassuring presence – you needed to project both through the metal barrier, to quell the rising tide of panic within the elevator. One firefighter would make his way to the roof of the building, the highest point of access to the elevator shaft. His job: to cut the power, preventing any accidental movement of the car that could send it plummeting, transforming a rescue mission into a tragedy.

But the real tension began when the door to the shaft was opened. A gamble. The car could be anywhere – at the landing, a quick fix, or precariously perched between floors, a life hanging in the balance.

Every peek into the shaft was a moment of suspended breath, a silent prayer that the trapped individuals wouldn't be dangling precariously close to a deadly drop.

Sometimes, the solution was relatively straightforward – accessing the roof hatch within the car itself, creating a temporary escape route. But other times, the situation turned grim. A call for someone who fell out of a car stuck between floors. That victim was now at the bottom of the shaft, dead or alive, and it meant working beneath a suspended car, a constant, unnerving reminder of the potential cost of a misstep. The air grew thick with the metallic tang of fear, the weight of the dangling elevator a physical presence in the cramped space.

These elevator rescues were a test of nerves, of ingenuity, and of unwavering focus. It was a firefighter's duty to become a locksmith, a negotiator, and a calm figure in the storm of panic. For the trapped individuals, the elevator wasn't just a means of transportation; it became a temporary prison, a symbol of vulnerability.

And for us, these rescues were a stark reminder that danger lurked not just in the flames, but in the seemingly mundane aspects of daily life. We were the guardians not just against fiery infernos, but the silent entrapment that could strike anywhere, anytime.

Bypass the Bureaucratic Maze

The bane of a fire officer's existence wasn't just the flames – it was the paperwork. For us, "tour swapping", or "mutuals", a simple, practical solution for scheduling flexibility, became a bureaucratic nightmare. Swapping tours, a seemingly straightforward act, transformed into a multi-legged beast demanding triplicate forms, signatures from a chain of command, and the patience of a saint.

The official system was a paperwork monstrosity. Filling out a form in triplicate was just the first hurdle. Then came the odyssey of approvals – a signature dance with the company officer, a waltz with the Battalion for their blessing, and finally, a long wait for the paperwork's triumphant return. By then, the desire to swap tours often lay buried beneath a mountain of frustration.

The captain, a man who craved efficiency as much as he did a well-cooked steak, decided to take a stand. He approached the Battalion Commander with a proposition, a deal struck in the smoky, dimly lit chief's office of the firehouse, away from the prying eyes of excessive bureaucracy. His offer was simple: he would guarantee four or five firefighters and a chauffeur on every tour, and in turn, the chief would accept a streamlined system – the paperwork graveyard would be abandoned.

The Battalion Commander, a man who understood the value of a good firefighter and a strong cup of coffee, saw the logic. A handshake sealed the deal. Paperwork? Gone. In its place, a humble hardcover calendar book took center stage on the company office desk. And then came the pièce de résistance – a custom-made rubber stamp.

This wasn't your average office supply store stamp. Oh no, this was a firefighter's ingenuity manifest. It displayed the pre-scheduled groups for each tour, a bureaucratic relic of the past. But next to it, a blank column awaited its true purpose – the realm of practicality. Here's where the magic happened.

When a "mutual," as the firefighters called it, took place, the swapping process became a ballet of black ink and camaraderie. The firefighter requesting the change simply crossed out their name on the list for that tour and, in the adjacent column, inked in the name of their comrade willing to cover the tour. A quick approval from the company officer, a silent nod of acknowledgment, and the deal was done.

This new system was a thing of beauty. No more wasted hours filling out forms, no more waiting for approvals to trickle down the bureaucratic chain. It was a testament to the firefighter's spirit, a way to navigate the labyrinthine bureaucracy with a rubber stamp and a shared sense of purpose.

It wasn't perfect, of course. It existed in a gray area, a secret pact between the companies and the Battalion. But for us, it was a small victory, a way to reclaim a sliver of our time and sanity. We had bypassed the bureaucratic maze, not by defying the system, but by finding a creative loophole, a firefighter's way of getting the job done, paperwork be damned.

The Unsung Hero Behind the Chief

There he sat, behind the wheel of the unassuming chief's car – not just a driver, but a cornerstone of the firefighting operation. He was the chief's aide, a man who wore many hats, and whose importance often went unseen during the fiery chaos.

His role transcended mere driving. He was the chief's eyes and ears, a sensory extension in the heart of the inferno. While the chief strategized, barking orders into the radio, the aide functioned as a human antenna, relaying messages between the fireground, dispatch, and other responding units.

But his job wasn't just about communication. He was a scout, venturing into the inferno's fringes, assessing the situation with a keen eye. Buildings neighboring the fire, the dreaded "exposures," became his focus. Were they in danger of succumbing to the flames? His observations, relayed back to the chief, informed critical decisions, potentially saving lives and preventing the blaze from spreading.

Yet, the aide's duties extended far beyond the fireground. Back at the firehouse, he transformed into a paperwork titan, battling mountains of forms and reports. He was the staffing maestro, ensuring every tour was adequately manned, a logistical chess player anticipating future needs.

And then there was the unseen world – the backroom. Here, the aide shed his official role and donned the cloak of a seasoned fire-fighter. He was a typist, crafting reports with the practiced ease of a veteran. He was a negotiator, his calm demeanor a balm in times of high tension. And, most importantly, he was a link, a bridge between the chief's command center and the rank-and-file firefighters. Rumors, information, and unspoken camaraderie flowed freely in this smoky sanctuary.

One glance at the aide often revealed a story etched in his eyes. These were men who had "spent their time in hell," seasoned fire-fighters who, for whatever reason, sought a different role, a different kind of heat. They weren't stepping away from the action; they were evolving. The aide wasn't a lesser role; it was a strategic shift, a way to continue serving the brotherhood from a different vantage point.

They were the silent partners in the dance of firefighting, the shadows of command. They were the chief's aides, the men behind the wheel, and the unsung heroes who ensured the symphony of rescue played flawlessly, even midst the cacophony of the fireground.

The Duality of a Fire Officer

The firehouse was a crucible, a place where brotherhood and hierarchy forged an uneasy alliance. At the helm stood the officer, a leader perched on a tightrope stretched between authority and camaraderie. In a well-oiled machine, this balance was a thing of beauty; in its absence, chaos reigned.

A well-run unit was a symphony of respect. The officers, radiating an air of quiet confidence, didn't need to scream for order. The firefighters, the "men," as they were called, understood their place. It wasn't about blind obedience; it was about a shared trust, a recognition that in the face of flames, discipline could mean the difference between life and death.

But this tightrope walk wasn't for the faint of heart. A weak officer, one craving approval from their men, was a recipe for disaster. The firefighters, a rough-and-tumble bunch, were quick to sense weakness. An inch of slack could easily turn into a mile of disobedience, a descent into a dangerous free-for-all. The inmates cannot run the asylum.

The key was a delicate dance – keeping authority without stifling camaraderie. Firefighters weren't just colleagues; they were family, a bond forged in shared meals, late-night poker games, and the gut-wrenching stories whispered in the smoky backroom. Officers knew their men's wives and kids by name, had shared beers at barbecues, and saw their vulnerabilities. This closeness bred a unique kind of respect, a loyalty that transcended mere rank.

However, this familial bond couldn't cloud judgment. Coming into the office to use the phone without a quick heads-up, a sloppy hello instead of a proper "Lieutenant," or shirking maintenance duties – these were the termites eating away at the foundation of authority. These seemingly trivial infractions, left unchecked, could snowball into a disregard for safety, a potentially lethal consequence in a world where split-second decisions meant everything. No one should be allowed to eat your lunch.

Being a fire officer meant walking a tightrope. You were a leader, but not a tyrant. You were a confidante, but not a pushover. You were a brother, but you were also the one responsible for bringing everyone back from the flames. It was a tough balancing act, but for those who mastered it, the rewards were immeasurable. They fostered not just a well-run unit, but a place where respect, camaraderie, and discipline existed in perfect harmony, a firehouse where even the toughest fires could be faced with a united front.

FIRE PATROL

From the chaotic streets of New York City emerged a unique breed of fire protection – the men of the Fire Patrol. A private organization, funded by concerned insurance companies, they were the guardians of warehouses and commercial spaces, tasked with mitigating damage and preserving whatever could be salvaged from the jaws of a commercial building fire or emergency.

They were, in many ways, firefighters in waiting. Aspirants fueled by an unwavering determination to join the ranks of the FDNY. Some were held back by the grueling physical tests, others by the maze of written exams. But what none of them lacked was heart.

Armed with canvas, tarps, and a hodgepodge of tools, they raced into inferno-engulfed buildings alongside city firefighters. While we focused on extinguishing the blaze, they worked frantically to limit water damage, spread tarps over valuable merchandise, and salvage whatever they could. These men weren't just handymen; they were firefighters in training, absorbing knowledge with every crackling beam and smoke-filled room.

The Fire Patrol was their proving grounds; each fire a baptism in sweat and grit. They saw the inner workings of a blaze, the strategies employed by seasoned firefighters, the brutal realities of a job that was as much about brains as brawn. Those of us who worked alongside them noticed. They weren't just laborers; they were future brothers-in-arms.

Their dedication was infectious. Many of these men, fueled by their experiences, became some of the finest firefighters and chiefs the FDNY ever had. The desire that drove them to cover precious goods in smoky warehouses eventually led them to command in the FDNY. They were men shaped by their experiences, forever marked by the smell of canvas and the weight of responsibility.

Some, their dreams delayed or detoured, found firefighting homes in other cities and departments. But they carried the spirit of the Fire Patrol – the tenacious drive, the hands-on experience, and the unwavering passion that made them forces to be reckoned with.

The Fire Patrol was more than just a job; it was a brotherhood forged in flame. They were the underdogs, the ones determined to overcome every obstacle until they could proudly wear the FDNY badge. And from their ranks rose some of the department's finest – men who never forgot their humble beginnings and who understood that true firefighting wasn't just about extinguishing flames, but about preserving, protecting, and rising from the ashes.

THE FIGHT FOR FITNESS

The city's budget, it seemed, didn't extend to the well-being of its firefighters. No gleaming fitness centers, no ultramodern exercise equipment graced our firehouses. But the city ablaze demanded peak physical performance, and those of us who took the job seriously weren't about to let bureaucracy hold us back.

So, we turned firehouses into makeshift gyms. Backrooms with dusty floors transformed into weightlifting arenas. Cement slabs out back, overlooked by tangled laundry lines, morphed into handball or racquetball courts. Ingenuity became our greatest asset, and scrappy determination our strongest muscle.

Bosses looked the other way, a silent acknowledgment of our initiative. They knew, as well as we did, that this DIY fitness wasn't about vanity; it was about survival. We funded these makeshift gyms with our own money, sweat equity our greatest investment in ourselves, and in the communities we served.

Some setups were laughably simple. A metal bar wedged across a doorway became a pull-up challenge. Each run, each alarm, meant adding another rep. By the end of a 25-run tour, that last 25th pull-up felt like raising a skyscraper, your arms screaming in protest. Crazy things, born from sheer necessity and a steely determination to stay one step ahead of the physical demands of our job.

Weight sets cobbled together from scrap metal and concrete; handball courts outlined with faded chalk, some courts had the overhead covered with chain link fencing to keep out unwanted air mail from neighboring buildings – these weren't just places; they were symbols of our commitment. A testament to our relentless pursuit of excellence, born from a harsh reality. The city might not have cared about our fitness, but we sure as hell did.

In these rough-hewn firehouse gyms, a peculiar camaraderie thrived. We groaned, grunted, and cheered each other on, forged by a shared purpose that extended far beyond the blazes we fought. Those backyard handball courts weren't just entertainment; they were grueling training grounds where we honed our reflexes and our stamina.

The city, oblivious to our struggles, slept soundly at night. They didn't see the sweat poured into those makeshift gyms, the aching muscles that fueled every heroic rescue, the discipline that transformed firefighters into athletes. But we knew. And when the alarm bell shattered the night, it was that self-made strength, born in those backroom gyms and backyard courts, that carried us into the inferno, ready to face whatever the city threw our way.

When Hope Wears a Uniform – Big Enough

The Bronx is no playground but a concrete jungle with its own damn heartbeat, and that beat isn't always friendly. Saw this rookie cop once, fresh out of the academy and barely five feet tall, walking her tour like she owned the block. Uniform crisp, eyes wide – too green for the stuff these streets dish out.

Me, I was in the rig, sweat dripping down my neck, the summer heat making the asphalt shimmer like a mirage. Traffic snarled, everyone honking and cursing, same old symphony of the city. I rolled down the window, not to be friendly but to get a breath of air, and yelled out at her, "how big is that gun you're carrying?"

She didn't flinch. Just turned, those eyes going hard, and snapped back, "big enough." Then kept walking, head high.

Some folks might've laughed, called her cocky, some dumb broad too naive to be scared. Me? I saw something different. The gun on her hip, yeah, that was firepower, but the real weapon was in her voice. No hesitation, no doubt. She was carrying a whole lotta guts under that uniform, a stubborn kind of defiance that said, "I belong here, and I ain't backing down."

The thing is, the Bronx – the world, really – chews up that kind of spirit, spits it out if you let it. Seen too many good guys get the light in their eyes snuffed out. But sometimes, just sometimes, that stubborn streak, that "big enough" attitude, it's the only thing that keeps you standing when everything else wants to knock you down. Don't know what happened to that rookie, but I hope she kept that fire burning. Hope it was enough.

THE GAS STATION

You got to respect the guy's audacity, even if he's a few bricks short of a load. Robbing a gas station? Seen it a few dozen times. But trying to get the loot using the cash drawer full of gasoline? That's some next-level desperate, or next-level stupid, depending on how you look at it. Let's break this down:

First, the image. Dude, with the pump hose stretched tight, fumbling with that nozzle where it doesn't belong, screaming threats while gasoline fills the cash drawer, and he holds the lit cigarette lighter. It's like a scene out of some low-budget action movie, but with a whole lot less planning and a lot more flammable consequence.

The worker, bless her heart, she gets the "locked in the booth" part right. That's the move, create that barrier when some lunatic's at the pump. But then, BAM, she levels the playing field. Shoves that drawer out, sending a wave of high-octane payback right back at the idiot. The whoosh of ignition, the screams…man, you couldn't script that kind of instant karma.

Now, the aftermath. The aftermath isn't pretty. Burns like that, they leave a mark even if you survive. A whole life wrecked for a few hundred bucks in a register, if he was even lucky enough to get that. And that worker? Yeah, she stopped the robbery, but that kind of thing sticks with you. Night shift at a gas station takes on a whole different meaning after watching a guy burst into flames right in front of you.

Bet that hospital emergency room was one tense place. Cops keeping an eye out for a bandaged-up moron looking to get patched up quickly. Doubt anyone was cracking jokes, even the kind a situation like this calls for. When things go sideways that fast, when life and death are balanced on the edge of a gas pump, the dark humor gets choked off for a while.

Makes you think, doesn't it? The desperation in that robber's move, the split-second decision that saved the worker, the sheer absurdity of it all. Reminds you that any night, behind any brightly lit gas station, under the hum of the security camera, there's the potential for the world to get real damn weird, real damn fast. Maybe it ends in handcuffs, maybe in the emergency room, maybe in something even worse.

The night tour, man…it isn't for the faint of heart.

COMMAND DECISIONS-
PRIVATE TALKS

Being a fire officer wasn't just about barking orders and fighting fires. It was about navigating a labyrinth of human emotions, fragile egos, and the ever-present pressure to make the right call, sometimes with lives hanging in the balance.

Take the case of the speed demon driver. One minute he was a reckless fireball, endangering the entire crew with his disregard for red lights and stop signs. A stern warning, you'd think, would be enough. Instead, he devolved into a snail's pace, a deliberate act of defiance disguised as excessive caution. An infant's response, you thought. But there lay the challenge.

Discipline wasn't about crushing spirits; it was about ensuring safety. The reprimand, the threat to take him out of the driver's seat, wasn't a punishment; it was a calculated risk, a way to protect the crew and the public. It was a tough call, but sometimes leadership demanded tough love.

Then there was the accident-prone driver. Three mishaps in a month spoke volumes. Was it carelessness? A lack of skill? Or something deeper? The quiet conversation in the office wasn't about assigning blame; it was about understanding. A gentle nudge, a question – "Do you really want to drive?" – opened a door to a hidden truth. Maybe driving wasn't his calling. Maybe the stress, the split-second decisions, were taking a toll. His decision to step down, while difficult, was ultimately a victory. It was the officer recognizing a potential disaster and guiding the situation towards a safe resolution.

These were just two examples; a microcosm of the tightrope walks fire officers undertook daily. They were leaders, yes, but also counselors, confidantes, and sometimes reluctant disciplinarians. The weight of command wasn't a badge of honor; it was a constant reminder of the responsibility they shouldered – the well-being of their crew, the safety of the public, and the delicate balance between discipline and camaraderie.

There were no easy answers. Every situation demanded nuance; an understanding of the human element intertwined with the technical expertise. It was a thankless job, often misunderstood. But for those who thrived in this complex ecosystem, the rewards were profound – a crew that functioned like a well-oiled machine, a brotherhood forged in trust, and the quiet satisfaction of knowing they had kept everyone safe, another day, another fire.

Propane Nightmares

Propane tanks. Those damn tanks. They were like ticking time bombs hidden everywhere you looked, especially during a scorcher of a July. One minute you're at the firehouse pouring yourself a cup of coffee, the next the alarm's shrieking about an "odor of gas" call. Roll up to a full parking lot, heat shimmering off the asphalt, and there it is – a car baking in the sun, two twenty-pound propane tanks stewing in the back seat like a recipe for disaster. No sign of the owner, of course. Just the unmistakable hiss of the safety release valve venting off pressure, building a bomb inside a tin can.

We scrambled. MacGyver-ed a shield from whatever we could find, knowing one wrong move could turn this into a fireball. Then the heart-stopping part – shattering the car window, the rush of gas, the hope that our makeshift protection would hold. Disarming that silent threat, the pressure sighing out, leaving behind the metallic tang of fear in the air. Just another day at the FDNY, right?

Wrong. Because that was just Tuesday. Last Wednesday, it was a homemade RV with a pair of big propane tanks, T-boned by another vehicle and erupting in flames. And, of course, it wasn't sitting neatly on a quiet street. No, it had to become wedged under the freaking El train, spewing fire towards the tracks. Cool the tanks, put out the fire, stop traffic – yeah, easy as pie. Except throw in the heart-pounding urgency of stopping the trains too, because if a tank blows it becomes a missile headed straight for the El platform.

Those were the calls that made the adrenaline surge, the ones where danger wasn't a flickering flame in the distance, but a snarling beast right in your face. You never knew what you were rolling into. A basement flooded with who-knows-what, a tangled mess of car wreckage, a roof parapet on the verge of collapse. But propane tanks? They held a special kind of terror. Silent, unassuming, and always one wrong move away from turning your world into an inferno. Just another reason why rest was a luxury firefighters rarely indulged in. Because the next call, the next nightmare, could be right around the corner.

THE STRIKE

Contract negotiations – they were always a circus, a tug-of-war with the city suits who held the purse strings. We all knew the drill: we asked for a raise, they laughed like they'd heard a new joke, and then came the bargaining. We'd trade overtime for better equipment, safety measures for a few extra bucks on the paycheck. "A raise," they'd call it, but it felt more like robbing Peter to pay Paul.

But this time, something shifted. The talks soured, turned ugly faster than a tenement fire. The city wasn't just squeezing pennies, they wanted to rip out whole chunks of our contract. The whispers grew louder in the firehouse: they wanted to gut our health benefits, take away the hard-earned vacation time that kept us sane. A low, simmering anger spread, the kind that comes from being backed into a corner.

The unions didn't back down. They rattled their sabers, talked of a strike. A gamble, a high-stakes poker game with the lives of millions hanging in the balance. The city scoffed, called their bluff. They didn't think we'd do it. Leave our posts, turn our backs on the people we swore to protect? Damn right, we would.

The strike hit like a gut punch. It wasn't like we wanted to be out there, picketing on the sidewalk instead of pulling folks from burning buildings. But every firefighter knew the hard truth: if we didn't fight for ourselves, no one else would. And if we let them chip away at us now, what would be left when the next contract rolled around?

Those few hours, they were a strange kind of limbo. We stood shoulder to shoulder with our brothers, fueled by a mix of righteous anger and a gnawing unease. The camaraderie was as strong as ever, but the silence of the firehouse bell was louder than any picket line chant.

We all had folks back home, families relying on us, bills to pay. We'd hear snippets of news – the chaos, the rising tension as the city scrambled to fill the gaps we left. And somewhere, deep down, the worry gnawed: what if something big happened, what if we weren't there?

Then, just as suddenly as it started, it was over. Some backroom deal, a compromise that wasn't a victory, but wasn't a complete surrender either. We went back to the job, a bitter taste in our mouths. We'd held the line, maybe even moved it back an inch or two. But the city knew, and we knew, this wasn't the last fight. Just one round in a battle that never seemed to end.

It left a mark, that strike did. Shook our faith in the system, reminded us that the men in fancy suits saw us as expendable pawns, not the ones putting their lives on the line day after day. But it also forged something stronger – a unity, a stubborn determination to keep fighting. Because in this city, the fire never truly goes out, and neither does the will of those who answer the call.

THE LAYOFFS

The word "layoffs" hung in the air like smoke, thick and suffocating. We'd seen departments get squeezed dry, scrimping on supplies until paperclips became precious commodities. But closing companies? Laying off firefighters? It was the kind of nightmare scenario tossed around during crazy late-night tours, not a possible reality.

Then came the meeting. The higher-ups with their grim faces, delivered the news like it was some natural disaster, not a human-caused one born out of their own incompetence. Budget cuts, they called it, a fancy way to disguise the fact that the morons in City Hall had screwed up royally, splurging on God knows what, and now the guys risking their necks daily were the ones paying the price.

The list of companies, the numbers, they blurred together. Not just statistics but faces. Young guys with families, the ones still carrying that bright-eyed rookie hope. Old-timers who'd seen more tragedy than most people ever imagined, were now facing possible retirement. It wasn't just about salaries, but the whole structure crumbling – fewer companies meant longer response times, more risk in a job where seconds made the difference between life and death.

The aftermath was a toxic mix of anger, fear, and a bitter kind of betrayal. Guys with spotless records, years of service, suddenly handed pink slips and told to hit the unemployment line. Families plunged into uncertainty, the shame of it cutting deeper than any fire ever could.

Nights were the worst. Lying awake, staring at the cracked ceiling, hearing the muffled sobs, knowing your wife was crunching the numbers, terror gnawing at her too. Pride wasn't worth much when you couldn't pay the mortgage, when you watched your kid's eyes fill with that unspoken worry.

Unemployment checks? A slap in the face after you've built your life around serving this unforgiving city. You'd go on interviews for security guard gigs or truck driving jobs, swallowing your pride with each rejection, feeling like a discarded tool instead of the lifesaver you were.

Some guys fell apart. Too many drinks chased away the demons, but only for a while. Others clung tighter to the brotherhood, patching together side hustles, taking any work to stay afloat. The firehouse, even with the gaping holes left by the empty spots, became a refuge. It was in the knowing nods, the forced jokes, the silent determination to survive this, that we found some kind of solace. Those still working formed a makeshift arrangement to help those laid off, contributing to a firehouse fund to be distributed among those brothers in need.

The city moved on, the scars of the layoffs papered over, forgotten by the suits with their fancy budgets. But for us, for those families, the wound festered. A reminder that even after everything you give, after all the sacrifices and unseen battles, you're still just a number on a spreadsheet, easily erased when the numbers don't add up.

Lazy Chief's Aide

The air hung heavy as the chief slammed the report folder on the table. "Missing reports? Dozens of them!" His voice boomed through the room, shattering the usual pre-shift banter. We exchanged worried glances. Missing reports were a nightmare – a bureaucratic sinkhole that could swallow hours of precious time.

It turned out the culprit was the relief chief's aide. A nice guy, sure, but enthusiasm wasn't exactly his strong suit. We all knew he cut corners, but missing reports this extensive? That was a whole new level of laziness.

Anger bubbled in my gut. We risked our lives out there, battling infernos and pulling people from wreckage, and this guy couldn't even fill out some damn paperwork? It was a slap in the face to everything we stood for.

The conversation wasn't loud, but the fury radiating from the office was palpable. The man in question had been promoted the previous week to Fire Marshall and had mumbled a quick goodbye, gone to a new unit before we had realized his sorry scheme.

We spent the next few weeks digging ourselves out of the mess he created. Old incident reports were dredged up from the back of our minds, interviews conducted, and countless phone calls made to verify details. It was tedious, frustrating work, taking away from training and preparation for the next inevitable emergency.

The good news was he wouldn't be darkening our doorway again. Word from downtown was clear: a permanent blemish on his record, a one-way ticket to a different unit. He might have been gone, but the consequences of his laziness lingered.

It was a harsh lesson, a reminder that a single bad apple can spoil the whole bunch. But it also solidified the bond within our guys. We had each other's backs, not just in the fires, but in the administrative trenches as well. And that, in the end, was worth more than any perfectly filled-out report. Because a firehouse functioned not just on skill and courage, but on a shared responsibility, a commitment that ensured even the most mundane tasks didn't become life-threatening delays. And that guy, with his brand of laziness, had no place in that equation.

SAXOPHONE SPACEMEN

This whole cultural shindig had "disaster" written all over it. You see, I'm not one for fancy concerts and that cathedral-sounding stuff; give me a ballgame and some overpriced beer any day. But, with my shiny Chief's uniform and all, I get sent to supervise this saxophone show in a famous Manhattan Cathedral, sponsored by some country I've never cared about, promising pyrotechnics and…wait for it…saxophones? Yeah, thrilling.

The thing is, this cathedral, they're fixing it up, which means blocked exits – a firefighter's worst nightmare. The boss calls, says to keep the crowds down, yada yada. Like that's gonna happen when you dangle free tickets in front of a New Yorker. Soon, it's a mob scene out there. Forget protocol – I fling those cathedral doors open, praying to every saint I can remember. This crowd's gonna stampede if those saxophone guys don't start their show soon.

No cops, no backup, just me and my poor aide sweating bullets while this mob shuffles in. I'm about to lose it when the show starts. And then…hell, I don't even know what happens next. My aide and I just burst out laughing. Like, doubled-over, tears-streaming laughing.

Why? Well, imagine this: a beautiful old cathedral, and what do you see dangling there from the ceiling, from the pillars and on the walls? A bunch of dudes in silver jumpsuits, faces covered – astronauts, aliens, who the hell knows – clutching saxophones for dear life. And the sounds coming out…let's just say it ain't exactly what you play at a wedding. More like a bunch of alley cats fighting over a tuna can. All we could do was laugh, laugh, and laugh some more at the craziness we almost lost the crowd for.

See, maybe I'm just a lowbrow kind of guy. But here we are, minutes from chaos, possibly dozens of crushed victims and what saves the day? Space suits and saxophones. Who'd have thought? Makes you appreciate the insanity of this city – one minute, you're facing a human tsunami, the next, you're cracking up at some avant-garde jazz performed by aliens.

Turns out, those foreign dignitaries were proud as peacocks about this show and mad as hell that we limited the crowd over the exit mess. Me? I learned a thing or two. Sometimes, you need a dose of the ridiculous to keep from going crazy. And hey, cultural exchange can be a hell of a lot funnier than you'd expect, especially when it involves saxophones and defying gravity in the name of experimental art.

THE DYNAMITE
BROTHERS

Look, I've seen the underbelly of this city – the junkies huddled in doorways, the domestic disputes that make you consider switching careers, the aftermath of horrors no one should have to witness. But there's a special kind of cold that chills your bones when it's not just some random tragedy – there's intent behind it. A calculated kind of crazy in their eyes.

That's what I saw in the "Dynamite Brothers" – that pack of posturing kids in their sagging pants and misplaced rage. We had a tussle with them at a job where they tried to keep us out of a building and we had whacked a few of them with the halligan tool during the fight. Sure, a whack on the head with a halligan tool stings, but that wound heals. It was something else that stuck around, the call from the NYPD Intelligence unit about credible death threats. Then the echo in the back of my mind every damn time the alarm sounded. "Gonna kill a fireman." Words aren't just words, not anymore. They had tried once before to get us when they set fire to a vacant building at the end of a dead-end street. After we rolled in, they blocked the way out with a few stolen cars, trapping us inside. We survived that one but now this.

Suddenly, every response to a tenement fire, every routine medical call was tinged with something new – paranoia. The guys got quieter, the jokes didn't flow as easily, and we rolled to calls with a friggin' police escort. Me, a firefighter, needing cops for protection just for doing my job.

The threat passed, they say. But that tension…some part of that tension gets stitched into your soul when you realize there are people, bored kids maybe, out there who view you as a target instead of someone who one day might pull their sorry asses out of a burning building. It isn't about bravery anymore, it's about basic survival, and that changes how a city looks. Changes how you look at the faces in the crowd. Makes you wonder, is it the kid with the oversized hoodie or the grandma at the window who's going to be the problem today?

Bailouts

Fires aren't polite. They don't give a damn about your training, your bravado, or your reputation. Sometimes, they crack something open inside a guy, something you never see coming. A look in their eyes, gone hollow like the gutted building we're in, and you just know.

Seen it happen more than once. Good firefighters, damn good, for a moment just swallowed whole by the chaos. Maybe it's a flashback to something else, a flicker of something they can't outrun in the heat. Or maybe the animal fear we all hide down deep claws its way to the surface.

Ain't no shame in it. Hell, I've had days where that thin line between pushing forward and bailing felt razor-sharp under my boots. So, when someone bailed on me mid-blaze, hose going limp in his hands? No words needed. Didn't even look back. Someone else just slid in, took the nozzle, and we kept driving the beast back. We sorted it out after, over coffee if he was willing, silence if he wasn't.

Thing is, in this job, limits aren't a weakness you can hide forever. They surface one way or another, either in a controlled break, or in a way that gets someone hurt. Better an honest bail in the heat of the moment than a frozen hesitation when a life's on the line. Some tours break you down bit by bit, and all you can do is pick up the pieces and decide if you'll fight another day.

CALL AN AMBULANCE

Junkies. They became part of the landscape, as common as busted hydrants and stray cats. Some days, you'd swear half the city was nodding off in alleyways, their eyes rolled back in their heads, needles sticking out like grotesque trophies.

Every alarm brought the same routine. The concerned citizen, hands wringing, voice edged with either disgust or pity. The limp body, the shallow breaths, the frantic check for a pulse. Sometimes there was the rush of clarity, a jolt back to the land of the living. Most days, it was just hauling another wasted piece of humanity into the ambulance, and the crew rolling their eyes.

It isn't that we were heartless, not at first. But you get burned out on saving the same guy a few times in a week, only to find him back on the same corner three days later. The frustration bubbles up like hot tar. Makes you want to scream at the world, "fix your own damn problems!"

That's what Mike was doing the day the woman stormed in, frantic about the junkie on the sidewalk. "Is he on fire?" Mike asked, not even looking up from his crossword. The woman stammered, horrified, "no." He replied, "then call an ambulance." We weren't there to solve the addiction crisis. We were there for the flames, the crashes, the imminent disasters.

Yeah, we responded quickly to the overdose, like always. But that edge, that cynicism…it was growing thicker with every call. It was becoming a shield to keep us sane in a city that was slowly drowning in its own despair.

Walls Built in a Moment

The tension simmered between us and the crowd like the heat radiating off a burning building. The sirens, the flashing lights, the coils of hose – they transformed a normal street into a warzone. And the civilians caught in the crossfire? Their frustration crackled in the air, ripe for a spark.

Most folks understood. Muttered curses, maybe, but they got that fires didn't give a damn about their rush hour commute or grocery run. But some days, some guys, they reached their limit. The sense of entitlement, the screaming matches over a parking spot, the sheer obliviousness to the chaos we were trying to contain…it'd make anyone snap.

That's when it happened. The lieutenant, usually unflappable, face locked in a glare as some dude ranted about his car being blocked in by the engine. And out of his mouth came the line, "you don't like it? Go back where you came from." Not yelled, not even with a threat. Just flat, dismissive, laced with the exhaustion of a thousand similar battles.

I hated that phrase. Hated the poison it dripped into the air, the way it painted us versus them, made us no better than the flames we fought. It was a shortcut, a way to vent frustration, but it did nothing good. Not for us, not for the community we were meant to serve.

See, the thing about a fire is, once it's out, those folks are still our neighbors. We're the ones buying coffee at their bodegas, waving at their kids on the street. That line wasn't about keeping the streets clear, it was about creating a chasm. And anyone who's battled a blaze knows building walls isn't nearly as hard as tearing them down once the smoke settles.

WHERE INK RUNS AND SANITY WITHERS

The upstairs office? Call it Purgatory, 'cause that's what it damn well feels like. Supposedly some haven, a quiet spot tucked away from the apparatus floor. Yeah, right. On a summer day, with that glorious New York soundtrack cranked up to eleven, it's Vietnam in here.

Every damn train squealing by feels like they're taking a rusty nail to your eardrums. And don't get me started on the traffic. Symphony, my ass. More like a death metal concert featuring car horns and screaming gypsy cab drivers. Blast some bad salsa beats from those passing boomboxes, toss in a fight outside the corner bar, and you got yourself a soundtrack beamed straight from the ninth circle of hell. You couldn't even hear the screams from the guy getting stabbed on the El train platform outside.

They ain't kidding calling this joint *The Animal House*. Lieutenants are bent over paperwork, growling like bears with toothache, phones ringing themselves hoarse. That poor dispatcher – barely hear him over the static, spitting out addresses like he's got a mouthful of broken glass.

Add the goddamn heat on top of that. Turns this sweat box into a sauna. The window AC blasts out its own desperate howl trying to keep up with the unbearable heat. Ink runs, tempers boil over, and trying to find a lost pen turns into a UFC cage match. The only escape? When the voice alarm sounds, and we scramble out into the blessed, simple chaos of a fire. Hell, I'd take a five-alarm inferno over this any day.

Some guys try to play deaf. Rookies with those headphones attached to their ears like it'll save 'em. Don't work. Old-timers hunched in the corner, looking like they're about to start channeling Buddha or maybe Manson, depends on the day.

But that noise…it sneaks in. Finds the cracks in your skull. That one car alarm that sounds like your ex screaming your name, the kid blasting his skateboard into a garbage can…snap. Eyes go crazy, hands start shaking, and the next thing you know, some poor bastard's taking off down the stairs, praying for the sweet release of fire, of anything but this goddamn symphony of madness.

This isn't just about fighting blazes anymore. This is war. Us against the symphony of the city, and trust me, most days, the city's winning.

HOUSE TAX

ouse tax. A necessary evil, a reminder that even in a firehouse, bills had to be paid. Coffee didn't brew itself or magically appear in the firehouse kitchen, and that leaky shower wasn't going to fix itself. And damn sure the city wasn't going to foot the bill for milk in the fridge or a new roll of paper towels.

Most guys understood it. The paycheck hit, they grumbled, but they coughed up their share. It was a way to keep the place running, to keep that semblance of a home away from home. But some tours, some guys...they were stretched thinner than overcooked spaghetti. Families to feed, mouths that seemed to multiply, and a paycheck that felt like it vanished into the wind.

Seeing them sweat over house tax, it dug into you. These weren't fools blowing their money on fancy toys. These were guys working two jobs, sending money home, patching holes in their boots instead of getting new ones. I knew that struggle, had lived it early in my career. But I also knew that letting things slide was a slippery slope.

The brotherhood, see, it was built on fairness; the knowledge that everyone pulled their weight, everyone contributed. So, when someone fell behind, it wasn't just about twenty bucks but the unspoken resentment that could fester, the cracks it could form in the foundation.

First, it was a quiet reminder. A gentle nudge that they hadn't forgotten. Most times, that was enough. Pride's a funny thing, and they'd scrape together the cash, even if it meant cutting back somewhere else. But sometimes, it went beyond pride. Sometimes the well was dry.

That's when the talking started. Not some high and mighty lecture, but sitting down over a cup of burnt coffee, understanding their situation. Maybe we could work out a temporary payment plan, spread the burden. Maybe, if it was bad, we'd dip into the discretionary fund we kept just for emergencies.

Hated to suspend privileges – no mutuals or whatever – that was a last resort. It was humiliating for them, and resentment could linger. But there had to be a line, a sense that the rules mattered for everyone. It was a balance, a tightrope walk between compassion and keeping order. We were brothers, sure, but we were also a unit, and that unit had to function even when the world outside squeezes a man dry.

Bad Apples

Every brotherhood has its share of bad apples. Guys who walk in with the shine of heroism in their eyes and quickly tarnish it all. We had a few gems in our ranks over the years: the chronic complainer, the credit card Casanova, even a ketchup kleptomaniac (seriously, who hoards ketchup?).

Now, in the good old days, a swift "whack-a-mole" session in the basement might've solved the problem permanently. But unions and pesky things like "legal consequences" got in the way. So, we were stuck with a different kind of fire – the internal kind that threatened to burn down the whole brotherhood.

The counseling unit became our purgatory. A forced vacation, a chance for them to, you know, "work on themselves." But let's be honest, it was just a way to shove the problem under the rug for a few weeks. Transferring them? Damn near impossible. Paperwork, bureaucracy and unions, a tangled mess that made getting a hose untangled look like child's play.

So, the bad apple remained, festering in the locker room, a constant reminder that the system wasn't perfect, and neither were we. Their presence cast a shadow over the camaraderie, the trust that was the lifeblood of this job. They made you question every newcomer, every handshake.

Dealing with it…well, that was the real nightmare. You couldn't scream, couldn't threaten them physically – not anymore. You had to document, report, and play this tedious dance with downtown. It was frustrating, deflating.

But here's the thing – the brotherhood. It wasn't just about beers and bad jokes. It was about a shared purpose, a reliance on the guy next to you when the flames licked at your back. So, we found other ways. A few phone calls downtown by a connected member, or to a friend at the union. More importantly, we redoubled down on our own integrity, making it clear that this kind of behavior wasn't tolerated.

It wasn't perfect, this new way of dealing with things. But it was all we had, and somehow, we managed to keep the bad apples from spoiling the whole damn bunch. The brotherhood, you see, even with a few blemishes, was still the fire shield that kept us safe. Even if, sometimes, the flames came from within.

Beyond the Smoke and Flame

Smoke inhalation on TV? A dramatic cough, a bit of squinting. Reality? You can't see a damn thing. You feel your way through. Crawling. It's a fist squeezing your lungs, a metallic tang that scrapes your throat raw. Some guys walk in with Hollywood in their eyes – visions of heroics, the dramatic rescue through billowing smoke. Then they get a taste of the real thing, and let me tell you, the dream curdles faster than sour milk.

We called them *smoke-busters* – guys who choked at the first whiff of a smoldering cigarette, let alone a full-blown inferno. The department at first did its best to accommodate them. Transfers to slower units, maybe a cushy gig on the fireboat – anything to keep them from becoming a liability in a real fire. But sometimes, the solution was a one-way ticket out.

There was Tommy "Two-Strikes" – that was his nickname, not mine. First fire, he went down like a cheap suit, hacking and wheezing. Disability retirement became his holy grail – a ranch upstate, a life free from smoke inhalation. Every fire after was a performance – a full-body reenactment of a man on the verge of pulmonary collapse. We knew, he knew, but proving it? Different story.

Then there was Mark, decent guy, good firefighter…until his wife filed for divorce. Custody battle, family drama – suddenly, every fire alarm was a crisis that demanded a trip to the ER for "chest pains." He ended up requesting a disability retirement, a fresh start out west with his kids. Made sense to him, but it didn't pan out, a reminder that sometimes, life throws a bigger wrench than any personnel issue.

And let's not forget Billy. Great firefighter, but his kid was a walking disaster zone – drugs, stolen cars, the whole nine yards. Every other week, it seemed, Billy was "needed" at home, dealing with the fallout of his son's latest escapade. We covered for him, sure, but the tension simmered. A team's only as strong as its weakest link, and Billy's personal life was threatening to snap the chain.

Personnel problems weren't an everyday occurrence, thank God. But they were a monkey wrench, alright, a disruption in the rhythm of the firehouse. They forced us to confront the fact that heroism wasn't just about bravado; it was about facing your demons, whatever form they took, smoke-filled or not. And sometimes, the hardest battles weren't fought with hoses and axes, but with understanding, tough love, and the hope that despite the occasional wrench thrown, the brotherhood would hold.

WHERE NECESSITY
TRUMPS THE RULEBOOK

The apparatus floor was sacred ground. Gleaming engines, the polished curves of the rigs, all lined up with military precision. This was the heart of the firehouse, where the beasts that roared into the night were meticulously cared for. The written rule was simple: only the rigs belonged here.

Well, mostly.

Firefighting wasn't just about flames and smoke. It was about making the system work; however you damn well could. There was this dance between order and chaos, and sometimes a little bending of the rules was the only way to keep things running.

There was the chief, for instance. Most times, his ghetto car sat in a spot out front where everyone else parked. But if there was some room inside, even a chief had a touch of the practical in him. You'd hear the garage doors rumble open, and in he'd back, squeezing between the ladder truck and the engine with a skill born of desperation, not bravado. It wasn't about privilege; it was about making room outside for one of the men.

Now, sometimes a man would have a problem with his car on the commute in and needed to fix the damn thing so he could get back home. Then the chief would keep his car outside and let that poor guy push his car inside so the guys could try fix it. So, on those cursed tours, the unspoken rule got quietly adjusted.

Out would come the battered toolbox, the muttered swears, and something resembling a car repair would start right on the apparatus floor. The smell of grease mixed with the lingering scent of diesel, and there'd be a kind of unspoken camaraderie in it. Guys passing by, tossing a wrench, offering advice, or better yet, a cup of the awful firehouse coffee. It wasn't a long-term solution, but it was about seeing a brother through until those wheels could hit the road again.

Now, some might call it bending the rules. But out there, when lives were on the line, you learned that sometimes the best kind of order was born out of a bit of necessary chaos. The apparatus floor was the symbol of our readiness, and damn it, being ready sometimes meant getting your hands dirty, squeezing a chief's car between two behemoth rigs, or turning into a makeshift mechanic shop when the situation demanded it.

THE PROFESSOR

The address screamed trouble: a tenement building a stone's throw from the bustling college campus. These calls were a toss-up – absent-minded professors with overflowing ashtrays or students neck-deep in ramen noodles gone horribly wrong. This one, though, was a different kind of tragedy entirely.

After the occupant would not unlock the door, we forced it open, the usual splintering wood a dull counterpoint to the dread knotting in my stomach. Inside, the acrid tang of smoke hung heavy, a sickly, sweet perfume masking the underlying char. And then we saw him.

A man stood swaying in the middle of the smoke-filled room, a horrifying caricature of a human being. Half his clothes clung to him in smoldering tatters, revealing burnt flesh oozing a sickly yellow. His arms, the most prominent feature, were a canvas of melted, raw flesh, the agony etched on his face a silent scream.

It looked like a scene straight from hell – a man who'd fallen asleep, oblivious in his apparent alcohol-induced stupor, until the flames became his unwelcome wake-up call. It was ten in the morning, a time most folks were just starting their day, a detail that hammered home the senselessness of it all.

He mumbled something incoherent, a denial of the pain twisting his features. He insisted that he was fine and did not need help. The EMTs swarmed him, their practiced movements a stark contrast to the man's flailing resistance. He was a man adrift, apparently lost in a haze of alcohol and the aftershock of scorching heat.

Reasoning failed. His pleas of being "fine" were heartbreaking mockeries of the truth. We eventually had to resort to the straight jacket, a cruel necessity to get him the medical attention he so desperately needed. As they strapped him onto the gurney, his eyes locked mine for a fleeting moment. A flicker of something – fear, maybe, or a sliver of recognition – passed through them before they glazed over again.

We left him to the sterile lights of the ER, another victim of a fire that didn't discriminate. Professors hunched over dusty tomes or homeless folks huddled in doorways – the muse of tragedy, it seemed, wasn't swayed by social status. This call, like so many others, served as a stark reminder: sometimes the fires we battle aren't confined to buildings, but rage within the hearts and minds of the people trapped inside them. And on those days, the weight of that knowledge settled heavy on our shoulders, a burden carried alongside the soot and the smoke.

Lost in Translation: Fire Reports Edition

Every fire call, every medical emergency, every blaring siren was accompanied by its silent shadow – paperwork. Mountains of reports documented our actions, but these forms held a hidden frustration: the struggle to obtain names from the people we were trying to help.

Imagine responding to a gas leak in a bustling apartment building. The air is thick with the pungent odor, a ticking time bomb waiting to explode. You find the source, secure the area, and then comes the question – "name?" often, met with silence or nervous mumbling.

For many immigrants, this simple question becomes a minefield. Fear, a language barrier, or a cultural aversion to getting involved creates a wall of resistance. They might be undocumented, worried about repercussions, or simply uncomfortable with the official nature of the situation.

The result? A helpless shrug, a mumbled excuse, and a blank space on the report form. Exasperated, the officer resorts to a familiar name – Rodriguez, perhaps, or Garcia. It's a small act of frustration, a placeholder to keep the paperwork moving.

But this seemingly harmless solution snowballs into a bigger problem. Imagine a computer churning through data, a fire report analysis system blinking red flags. "Apartment 3B, gas leak – reported by

Miguel Rodriguez. Apartment 3B, smoke odor – reported by Miguel Rodriguez again. Is this the same Miguel Rodriguez starting all these incidents?"

The system, designed for efficiency, becomes a caricature of prejudice. A single name, used as a placeholder countless times, paints a false picture, potentially jeopardizing innocent people. Suddenly, cultural misunderstanding translates into a data nightmare.

This frustration highlights a deeper issue – the need for better communication, for bridges built not just of brick and mortar, but of empathy and understanding. Imagine if firefighters could explain the importance of cooperation. Imagine if cultural sensitivity training became standard practice, fostering trust and dismantling the walls of fear.

The solution isn't about browbeating people into giving their names. It's about creating an environment where they feel safe, where they understand that our presence is to help, not punish. It's about recognizing that a nameless report is more than just a bureaucratic inconvenience; it's a missed opportunity to build trust, a testament to a system that hasn't quite figured out how to translate the language of fear.

GHOSTS AND EMBERS

The boots are the first to go. I kick them into the corner with a satisfying thunk. The smell of smoke and ash, sweat and fear – it clings to everything. I swear those boots have seen more than my own eyes should. The gear gets peeled off next, layer by layer, like shedding the weight of the world.

The shower runs hot enough to scald, but cold would be a lie. It's a half-assed attempt to wash away the ghosts – the faces you couldn't save, the ones that flash in the silence before rest. Some nights, the silence howls louder than any siren.

They tell you it's about the wins – dragging the kid out of a burning apartment, reviving someone at the brink. Sure, the wins are there, little victories midst the wreckage. But those victories don't erase the rest. They don't fill the holes burned into your memory.

Some guys find solace in the camaraderie, the backslapping, and the gallows humor at the firehouse. I just want to forget. To find a patch of quiet where the ringing in my ears isn't the echo of desperate screams. Maybe it's at the bottom of a glass, maybe in a hundred miles of open road…haven't found it yet.

Why do I stay? Sometimes I ask myself that, staring at the ceiling while the darkness closes in. It isn't about bravery, sure as hell isn't about the paycheck. Maybe it's the stubborn flicker that sometimes ignites when the world feels like nothing but cinder and ash. Or maybe I'm just as damned crazy as everyone says.

Tomorrow the boots go back on, though. Tomorrow, there will be another alarm, another burst of adrenaline, another dance with the devil in the flames. And, somewhere deep down, I'll swear to myself that, this time, it'll be different. Even if I know I'm lying.

AM I DONE

The alarm shrieks like the banshees from my worst hangover sent to deliver a personal kick to the head. It's either another four-story building fire or the old lady on Maple who burnt the microwave trying to poach an egg at 3 AM. God only knows. Either way, you can stick a fork in me, I'm done.

My boots find their way onto my feet by what I like to call "muscle memory fueled by pure rage." The rest of the guys are already a blur – turnout gear, helmets, curses, and diesel fumes. I fumbled my way into the rig, praying somebody remembered to fill the damn thing with diesel.

It's not the flames that get you, most days. It's the waiting. Waiting for the heart attack in a smoke-clogged kitchen. Waiting for the dumbass kids to get out of the apartment so you can douse whatever flaming disaster they cooked up this time. Waiting for the adrenaline to wear off, the sweat to dry, the ringing in your ears to stop.

The old timers, they'd tell me this was an honorable calling. A sacred brotherhood. Honestly, it's mostly bad coffee, worse food, and the kind of exhaustion that makes you question your own sanity. They didn't mention that in the recruitment poster. And don't get me started on the pay.

But hey, when you pull a kid out of a burning bedroom, or you get

Mrs. Maple's flooded basement sorted out because, yes, those things happen way more than they should, there's a flicker. A flicker of something that isn't cynicism. Not quite hope, maybe…purpose. Something.

Enough to get me back on that thundering red rig tomorrow. Or at least until I can convince someone that being something else is way less likely to get me killed.

THE DOUBTS

I leaned against the chipped, soot-blackened concrete of the firehouse, a single curl of cigar smoke twisting up to join the hazy smog that choked the Bronx sky. Sweat mingled with ash on my brow, an uncomfortable grit that never truly washed away. It was an August scorcher, the kind that melted tar and warped tempers. Even at this late hour, the oppressive heat refused to loosen its grip, a furnace blast with every opened door, every passing truck groaning down Jerome Avenue.

The clang of the alarm was a merciful release, a galvanizing shock that snapped me from my sullen reverie. Routine took over, muscles tensed with familiar adrenaline – shoes yanked on, gear buckled, the scramble into the rig. Sirens pierced the oppressive heat, chasing away the languid thoughts gnawing at my conscience.

It wasn't the flames that got to you, not anymore. Rookie year, yeah, I hadn't slept for a week after pulling those kids from that blaze. Still saw their wide, panicked eyes in my nightmares. No, it was the aftermath that twisted in my gut like a rusty knife. The charred husks of tenements, belongings reduced to stinking piles on the sidewalk. Families left staring at nothing. I could fight the fires, save a life here and there, but the real inferno raged on backstreets and corner shops, in dingy walk-ups and whispered deals. That was a blaze beyond our hose's reach.

This call wasn't one of those towering tenement pyres. A back alley behind a row of stores, already deserted for the night. Flames weren't leaping high, just a sullen orange licking oily puddles of gasoline. Even through the thick smoke, the reek of gasoline overpowered everything else. Still, duty was duty. We moved through the motions, water cutting through the darkness with a hiss and sending up stinging tendrils of steam.

I didn't know, and to be honest, didn't give a damn about what started the fire. Wasn't my turf war to play. Call the Fire Marshals. They'll investigate. But when the fire was doused, when the thick stench cut through with the tang of copper, one thing clicked into place in my mind: the charred wooden crates. Not burned in the blaze, they were the source. Arsonists, maybe? Or something bigger, a different kind of poison being moved through the veins of the city?

As the cops rolled in, lights strobing through the lingering smoke, I made a silent vow. The siren's call would still wake me, I'd still drag on those boots. But now there was a different kind of fire kindling under my ribs, a different fight calling. It was a dangerous flicker, one that could get a guy burned even worse than those flames… and I couldn't shake a strange thrill at the prospect.

SECOND THOUGHTS

The silence of the firehouse at 3 AM was a heavy blanket, but rest for me was a distant dream. Memories, like embers fanned by an unseen wind, flickered to life behind my closed eyelids.

The glow of the two-story house, the frantic shouts of neighbors, the mother's anguished cry – "My babies! They're trapped!" I saw myself, younger, stronger, charging up the ladder, the heat a physical blow. But the flames had claimed victory that night, the second-floor window a vacant stare mocking my efforts.

These were the ghosts that haunted every firefighter – the ones who slipped through their grasp, the lives lost in the relentless dance with fire. The homeless man, huddled for warmth in a vacant warehouse, his makeshift shelter becoming his pyre. The young woman, a victim of violence, her apartment transformed into a horrifying inferno. The old lady, raped and left for dead, her cries lost in the roar of the flames, her final moments shrouded in smoke.

Each face, a searing portrait etched into my memory. They came to me in the quiet moments, in the dead of night, whispering doubts that gnawed at my soul. "Did I try hard enough?" "Was there another way?" "Did we make a mistake?"

The firehouse's camaraderie offered a fragile shield. Shared experiences, unspoken words, a knowing glance across the smoky aftermath – these were the threads that bound them together, a brotherhood forged in the crucible of loss. But even among brothers, the burden remained.

Sometimes, a late-night alarm would trigger it all – a voice on the radio, a description that echoed a past tragedy. The "almost had him" stories, whispered over stale coffee, were a grim reminder of the razor-thin line between victory and defeat.

There were coping mechanisms – black humor, stoic silence, throwing yourself into the next call with reckless abandon. But the ghosts never truly left. They were the silent witnesses to a firefighter's bravery and despair, a constant reminder of the price paid in the line of duty.

I knew there would be more nights like this, more faces that would forever haunt my dreams. But I also knew that dawn would come, and with it, the strength to answer the next call, to face the inferno once more, forever carrying the weight of the ones who didn't make it, a burden that fueled my determination to never let another flame steal a life on my watch.

STENTS

The fluorescent lights buzzed overhead, a relentless hum that seemed to vibrate through my whole skeleton. Flat on my back, staring up at the sterile white tiles, I felt like a rotisserie chicken about to be cranked up a notch. Two nurses, faces a blur of nervous smiles and latex gloves, poked and prodded, prepping me for the inevitable. The cardiologist, a young buck with eyes too bright for this fluorescent purgatory, laid down the verdict – two clogged arteries, stents on the menu.

"Surprised to be here, Doc," I rasped, throat scratchy from the pre-surgery cocktail. "Used to pound the pavement like a champ, marathons and all."

He flashed a quick smile. "Marathoner, huh? Me too. Love a good long run to clear the head."

Yeah, well, some heads needed a lot more clearing than a jog could manage. This one, for example, was filled with twenty-seven years of FDNY memories, a montage of the good, the bad, and the enough-to-scar-your-soul ugly. Fire. It called to a certain kind of guy, adrenaline junkies with a morbid fascination with chaos. Didn't take long for that fascination to turn into a kind of weary acceptance.

Those rookie years, though…man, I was invincible. Didn't know fear from a busted water main. I remember the first time we pulled a kid from a blaze, a soot-covered whimper of a thing clutching a melted teddy bear. That high, the elation of saving a life, chased away the smoke and the fear for a while. Didn't last.

The bad? Plenty of that. People cooked alive in their own kitchens; families left with nothing but the charred ruins of their dreams. The sights, the smells, they stick with you, burrow into the corners of your mind like whispers in the dark.

And the ugly? The stuff you shove down deep, pretend it doesn't exist. The corruption, the bureaucratic bullshit that choked life out of urgency, the way some folks in suits seemed to view us as disposable meat shields.

That's the carousel spinning in my head now, under the buzz of fluorescent lights and the sterile scent of disinfectant. Maybe it's the meds, or maybe it's the irony of a runner getting sidelined by a bad ticker, but this feels like the real fire bell ringing. Time to face the smoke, the real inferno burning inside. Let's see what this procedure throws at me. Doc says he's a runner. Good. Let's get it over with. Some say that before you go, your life flashes in front of you. I hope I don't find out anytime soon.

GOODBYE

The coffee shop's warmth, a stark contrast to the chill of memory, seeped into my bones. I traced the rim of the chipped mug, feeling the rough texture ground me in the present. Maybe this pilgrimage, unplanned and instinctual, wasn't about erasing the past or finding some neat resolution. Maybe it was about facing it head-on, acknowledging the weight of it all.

I glanced again at the faded photos lining the wall. Young firefighters, eyes gleaming with a mix of duty and trepidation – just like I once was. Heroes who gave themselves over to the relentless pulse of this city, to its unforgiving rhythm of crisis and salvation. A tremor shook me, but this time, it wasn't fear. It was the weight of understanding, hard-earned and bittersweet.

The ghosts of my firehouse days wouldn't be silenced, not entirely. The victories, the crushing losses, the faces of the saved and the forever gone – they were etched into the fabric of who I had become. But somewhere in the act of facing them, there was a sliver of peace to be found. An acknowledgment that even within the chaos, there had been moments of grace.

I drained the last of my coffee, the bitterness a counterpoint to the sweetness of memory. Time to rejoin the present, to navigate the bustling streets toward the gleaming lights of the theater district. My wife would be there, worrying giving way to her familiar, exasperated smile the moment I appeared. She didn't understand this pull towards my past life, but she understood me. That was the anchor that had held me steady through the turbulent years.

I stepped out into the relentless hum of the city. Buses roared past, their destinations a blur against the fading evening light. The crowds jostled, a sea of faces, each with their own stories hidden beneath the surface. I was one of them, my story marked by smoke and sirens, but also by an unwavering love that waited for me with a ticket in hand and a question in her eyes.

As I slowly ascended the stairs, back to the elevated platform and the ride back towards the heart of Manhattan, a strange lightness settled in my heart. It wasn't forgetting the past, or the delusion of a burden lifted. It was the quiet knowledge that for all the gritty chaos, for all the pain and heroism my career had held, I'd walked through the flames and emerged on the other side. Scars and all, I was still standing. And in its own way, that was a victory hard-won, and one to be cherished.